Higher Education
in Partnership
with Industry

David R. Powers
Mary F. Powers
Frederick Betz
Carol B. Aslanian

Higher Education in Partnership with Industry

Opportunities and Strategies for Training, Research, and Economic Development

 Jossey-Bass Publishers

San Francisco　•　London　•　1988

HIGHER EDUCATION IN PARTNERSHIP WITH INDUSTRY
Opportunities and Strategies for Training, Research, and Economic Development
by David R. Powers, Mary F. Powers, Frederick Betz, Carol B. Aslanian

This page continues on page 367.

Library of Congress Cataloging-in-Publication Data

Higher education in partnership with industry.

(The Jossey-Bass higher education series)
Bibliographies: pp.
Includes index.
1. Industry and education—United States.
2. Education, Higher—Economic aspects—United States.
I. Powers, David R. II. Series.
LC1085.2.H54 1988   378'.103   87-46348
ISBN 1-55542-071-0 (alk. paper)

Manufactured in the United States of America

The paper in this book meets the guidelines for
permanence and durability of the Committee on
Production Guidelines for Book Longevity of the
Council on Library Resources.

JACKET DESIGN BY WILLI BAUM

FIRST EDITION

Code 8759

The Jossey-Bass
Higher Education Series

Contents

Tables and Figures

Preface

Some changes in higher education are unremarkable, merely characteristic of a healthy system that is adapting successfully to evolving conditions. Other changes in the system command attention because they seem to hold the potential of causing still more widespread or fundamental changes.

When educators and the public identify an agent that seems capable of producing significant changes in higher education, certain primary questions arise. Educators want to know how the changes will affect the traditions of their profession and the economic well-being, missions, and policies of their particular institutions. The general public is concerned with the effects of the changes on the quality of education they are providing their children—a factor that may be determined for the strictly practical by whether their children are employable following graduation. Educators and the general public alike want to know whether the changes will conflict with expectations for education that remain so widespread as to be characteristic of our culture: for example, our beliefs that education should be available to all those who want to learn, that education is a path to a life that is intellectually richer and financially more secure, and that the quality of the education system of the United States is crucial to its remaining a world power.

Such primary questions are currently being asked about the effects of university-industry partnerships, in which colleges and universities offer training, research, and various consulting

services to businesses to help improve their products, management, manufacturing procedures, service delivery systems, or
other factors that influence their productivity. Essentially, educators and individuals throughout the public and private sectors
who have reason to be attentive to the proliferation of cooperative
relationships are performing crude cost-benefit analyses, trying to read the future to determine whether the benefits of such
relationships are likely to outweigh the drawbacks over the long
term. This book discusses many of the main issues commonly
addressed in such analyses.

As a result, a theme that recurs through this book—sometimes explicitly, more often implicitly—is how, over the short
and long term, business–higher education partnerships may affect the traditions of higher education, institutional policies and
practices, and public expectations regarding higher education.

The second theme that recurs in the book is the relationship between higher education and business productivity and
competitiveness. The third theme is the opportunities for leadership that business-higher education partnerships present.

Higher Education, Business Productivity, and Competitiveness.
Numerous immediate and long-term goals and potential benefits
(described in Chapter One) underlie the enthusiasm with which
so many institutions of higher education have embraced cooperative relationships with business, the generally positive—if sometimes guarded—receptiveness to such relationships that has been
displayed by the business community, and the significant investments that have been made by state governments and federal
agencies in university-industry partnerships. As Chapter One
makes clear, the most important reason colleges and universities
have entered into partnerships is to improve their financial situations. Likewise, the most important reason industries have
responded positively is to improve their productivity and competitiveness. Improving the well-being of the American business community is also one of the most important reasons state
governments and federal agencies have supported cooperative
projects.

Productivity and competitiveness became familiar—almost
banal—concerns in the the mid 1980s as the United States con-

tinued to relinquish to Japan and West Germany its role as the world's leader in creating and devising applications of new technologies. A balance of trade unfavorable to the United States, high labor costs, education that for many workers was inadequate to meet the demands of the workplace, and computerization of manufacturing, service, and information industries were some of the factors that affected the nation's economy in the mid 1980s.

In a 1986 report, Eric Bloch, director of the National Science Foundation, stressed the need to increase national productivity. Bloch pointed out that a major goal of research supported by the federal government is to increase the competitiveness of the nation's economy. He stated: "To be economically competitive, we must have high productivity. But in recent years, productivity has averaged a scant 0.3 percent annually. Our competitors have done ten to fifteen times as well" (p. 2).

What can be done about this problem? Bloch argued that to be successful in international markets requires advanced products and competitive pricing. Competitive pricing depends on production efficiency, which, in turn, depends on developing automated production systems. Thus, research is a key to competitiveness because it is through basic and applied research that both advanced products and efficient production methods are developed. For years, National Science Foundation programs have not only supported basic and applied research but have also promoted technology transfer to the private sector to help industries develop the advanced products and production processes they need to remain competitive. Colleges and universities promote economic development not only by undertaking research and engaging in technology transfer activities, but by offering training, retraining, professional development opportunities, and technical and management assistance programs to businesses. These activities are described at some length in Chapter One and elsewhere in the book.

Opportunities for Leadership. In exploring one of the questions—"Why cooperate?"—that are asked early in the book, discussion focuses on concerns of employers when entering university-industry partnerships, rather than on professional motivations of the employees who are charged with implementing their employers' decisions. Yet the answers that such employees find to the question "Why cooperate?" are also important, because they are crucial to the success of cooperative efforts. Initiatives are far less likely to be successful if they lack champions—on the shop floor and in the research laboratory as well as in the boardroom—who are willing to fight for them.

Many college and university presidents, other administrators, and faculty members have become interested in developing business–higher education partnerships because opportunities exist in this arena for exerting leadership. Many of these opportunities occur because partnerships can be a forceful agent for change in institutional policies and practices, in mission, and in institutional program funding and faculty income. By their nature, partnerships provide opportunities for leadership not only at the top but throughout an institution, from trustees and presidents, through vice-presidents, deans, department chairpersons, and faculty members. Some of the most fruitful partnerships have been initiated at the departmental level and have been managed by the faculty members involved. At the same time, presidential interest and commitment by the vice-presidents for academic affairs, research, and finance are crucial for an institutional climate to develop in which such efforts can thrive.

Striking out in a new direction is usually fraught with problems, but it also can be fun. Great satisfaction can come from building, from knowing that what one is doing could positively affect the future of one's institution. In higher education, during the growth decades of the late 1940s through the late 1960s, building facilities and faculties defined the arena wherein lay prime leadership opportunities. During subsequent years, when growth halted at most institutions and shrinkage occurred in many, leadership took on a different cast. Exerting leadership in institutions with declining enrollments and budgets is far more difficult than guiding expansion, in no small part because the pain/pleasure ratio for the leaders can increase so significantly.

Business–higher education partnerships are not new. In particular, land-grant institutions have been engaged in partnerships with businesses and industries—many of them agricul-

tural—since the Morrill Act defined their service mission in
1862. Despite this long history, not until the late 1970s and early
1980s did the growth curve of business–higher education partnerships begin to increase markedly, not only in types and numbers of relationships but across the spectrum of institutions, large
and small, public and private.

Future partnerships may be increasingly innovative. For
example, groups of educational institutions may band together
with area businesses and state and local government to invest
in computer-integrated flexible manufacturing equipment that
can be used for training and research and by the businesses on
a time-sharing basis for small-batch production. The Emilia-
Romagna (Italy) model involving sophisticated networks and
support systems among small, high-tech businesses also holds
much promise.

The continued rise in numbers of cooperative relationships is probably a fairly reliable indicator that to some extent
they are meeting expectations of all partners in the enterprises.
It remains to be seen whether, over the long term, positive outcomes for universities will outweigh negative effects, results for
companies will justify expenditures, and economic gains will
be commensurate with state and federal investments in cooperative programs. The balance in all three arenas may be affected
significantly by how well college and university personnel, from
trustees to faculty members, understand the implications of the
rewards and stresses of engaging in partnerships with businesses
and industries, and how responsibly they react to them.

Who Should Read This Book?

Because business–higher education partnerships have
become common and play a significant role in the nation's economy, all members of the university community should be familiar with the subject. Presidents, vice-presidents, deans, department chairpersons and faculty team leaders, trustees, foundation
officials, government leaders, and consultants may be interested
in the scope of business–higher education partnerships. At some
institutions, readers may gather some ideas on new partnerships

they wish to develop, or learn how to make new or existing partnerships more successful. They may be stimulated to ponder the effects that current partnerships may be having on the missions and well-being of their institutions.

Businesspeople also will find information of interest in this book. To be sure, it does not attempt to examine business-higher education partnerships in detail from the point of view of the business community. Even so, businesses that have entered partnerships or intend to do so can benefit from learning about how their college or university partners view such endeavors. Partners that understand one another's needs, goals, cultural goals, and cultural assumptions may work better together and often are more productive over the long term.

Subjects Examined. Economic development is such a broad and complex topic that it cannot be examined in depth in this book. Instead, the book reviews the role that higher education can play in efforts to improve regional conditions. This emphasis is not intended to imply, however, that higher education is a predominant variable in all successful economic development efforts. So many complex variables are involved in economic development that such an inference could not be warranted.

The book explores a number of issues central to the subject of business–higher education partnerships that may be of interest to leaders in such relationships. Chapter One outlines reasons higher education and business find cooperative relationships worthwhile and describes how such cooperation is perceived to affect economic development. Chapter Two sketches the range of business–higher education partnerships, which has become broad and internally diverse. Chapter Three describes examples of innovative cooperative programs, and Chapter Four discusses factors conducive to the success of business–higher education partnerships. In Chapter Five, common ways of resolving and avoiding problems that may occur are explored. Chapter Six provides advice on writing sound contracts and on project oversight. Chapter Seven contains general comments and conclusions. Chapters One through Seven were written by David R. and Mary F. Powers.

Chapters Eight and Nine, written by Carol B. Aslanian,

relate basic principles of securing and fulfilling training contracts. Chapters Ten and Eleven, written by Frederick Betz,
discuss major centers and projects funded by the National Science Foundation and industry to promote technology transfer
to the marketplace from university-based laboratories engaged
largely in basic research.

The Resource at the end of the book, whose principal
author is David R. Powers, provides an example of state-level
guidelines or regulations that may be useful when university-
industry partnerships are being set up.

Acknowledgments

The authors wish to thank those who helped with the
manuscript. Sharon Martin, Susan Fout, and Jennifer Byrd
typed drafts for David R. Powers and Mary F. Powers. Sue
Forrest relentlessly pursued library material through interuniversity loans. Susan Seferian served as research assistant for
Carol B. Aslanian, and Deborah Carey assisted with her manuscript.

Special thanks are extended to Kathryn Mannes of American University for writing the sample training agreements that
are included in Chapter Nine.

Mary F. Powers was editor of the project.

Throughout the book, when the singular masculine pro-
noun is used to denote an individual member of the human race,
sexism is neither implied nor intended.

Charleston, West Virginia   David R. Powers
February 1988   Mary F. Powers

Reference

Bloch, E. Basic Research: *The Key to Economic Success.* Washington, D.C.: National Science Foundation, 1986.

The Authors

David R. Powers, senior vice-chancellor for academic affairs of the West Virginia Board of Regents, which governs the state's system of sixteen colleges and universities, received his B.A. (1963), M.A. (1965), and Ph.D. (1971) degrees in political science from the University of Pittsburgh. In the mid 1970s, while vice-provost at the University of Pittsburgh, Powers led in the establishment of an Office of Research, a forerunner of multiple structures that later developed at that institution to promote university-industry partnerships.

In 1979, as newly appointed vice-president for academic affairs at George Mason University in Fairfax, Virginia, Powers conceived the idea of that institution's developing a mature new mission by designing certain of its key programs to meet the educational and research needs of emerging "beltway industries" surrounding Washington, D.C. Powers played a key role in convincing the State Council of Higher Education of Virginia to approve new master's and doctoral programs related to high-technology areas in which federal research funds were available and in creating the George Mason Institute (D. R. Powers, 1980, 1981) to promote university-industry partnerships.

In 1980, Powers led faculty members and administrators in developing a strategic planning document (George Mason University, 1981), which emphasized partnerships with the business community. The U.S. Chamber of Commerce has called that and subsequent related efforts "a model for other universities making the business community connection" (Simmons, Kelleher, and Duckworth, 1987, p. 44).

In the early 1980s, as academic vice-chancellor of the West Virgnia state system of higher education, Powers created the Regents' Center for Education and Research with Industry (CERI), a statewide network for identifying business needs and mobilizing corresponding faculty expertise. In 1986, Powers contributed to key sections of West Virginia's Economic Development Act of 1986, parts of which called for establishment of research and development centers at three graduate institutions in the system to encourage university-industry partnerships and promote economic development. The act also created a program that could provide matching funds for research, technical assistance, and training projects undertaken by the centers. He is coauthor of *Making Participatory Management Work: Leadership of Consultive Decision Making in Academic Administration* (with M. F. Powers, 1983).

Mary F. Powers, coordinator of the Science and Technology Center of Southern West Virginia, Inc., holds a B.S. (1961) degree in bacteriology from Pennsylvania State University and an M.A. (1984) degree in experimental psychology from George Mason University. She served as instructor in microbiology for Pennsylvania State University until 1969, when she became a writer, editor, and consultant specializing in matters related to higher education, particularly educational administration.

The Science and Technology Center of Southern West Virginia, which Powers currently heads, is a nonprofit corporation created to promote higher education–business partnerships. Initial funding came from a grant from the West Virginia College of Graduate Studies Foundation. Still in its infancy, the center is serving as a mechanism for interinstitutional cooperation among the College of Graduate Studies, the West Virginia Institute of Technology, and West Virginia State College, as well as other public and private institutions in southern West Virginia. The goal of this consortium is to further the economic development efforts of higher education in the southern sixteen counties of West Virginia, an area of the country hardest hit by the recession of the early 1980s. Programs organized by the center involve training and research in fields such as chemical manufacturing systems, materials handling, distribution, and transportation, and computer-assisted design and manufacturing (CAD/CAM). Other programs offer opportunities to employees for professional development to utilize the satellite uplink completed in 1987 on the West Virginia State College campus.

Mary F. Powers is coauthor of *Making Participatory Management Work: Leadership of Consultive Decision Making in Academic Administration* (with D. R. Powers, 1983).

Frederick Betz is program officer of the Division of Cross-Disciplinary Research of the National Science Foundation (NSF). He received his B.S. degree (1958) in physics from the University of Chicago and his Ph.D. degree (1964) in physics from the University of California at Berkeley. From 1965 to 1967, Betz was a postdoctoral fellow with the Social Sciences Group of the Space Sciences Laboratory at the University of California at Berkeley. He has held faculty appointments at the California State University at Hayward, the State University of New York at Buffalo, and the Wharton School of the University of Pennsylvania. He joined the National Science Foundation in 1975 as senior planning analyst in the Office of Resources and Personnel Management.

In 1978, Betz became program manager of NSF's Industry-University Cooperative Research Program, described in Chapters Ten and Eleven. The program sponsored fundamental scientific and engineering research performed jointly by industrial and university researchers. Cooperative research projects were sponsored in physics; chemistry; materials research; biology; and chemical, electrical, mechanical, and civil engineering. The projects were intended to advance the fundamental knowledge base for new technologies and were conducted by major U.S. universities and high-technology industrial firms.

In his current position, assumed in 1986, Betz assists in managing the programs that support the National Science Foundation's engineering research centers and industry-university cooperative research centers. He is the author of *Managing Technology* (Prentice-Hall, 1986).

Carol B. Aslanian is director of adult learning services at the College Board. She received her B.S. degree (1963) in psychology from Cornell University and her M.Ed. degree (1964) from Harvard University. She has long been interested in adult learning, not only in her current position with the College Board but also during an earlier appointment as director for education and in her work with a New York–based services firm, Policy Studies in Education.

Aslanian joined the College Board in 1977 as associate director of the program called Future Directions for a Learning Society, funded by the Exxon Education Foundation. From 1977 to 1980, the program published more than thirty studies and reports, including two coauthored by Aslanian: *Americans in Transition: Life Changes and Reasons for Adult Learning* (recipient of the Imogene E. Okes Award for Research) and *Adult Access to Education and New Careers: A Handbook for Action,* a guide to development of adult career counseling centers.

Aslanian was appointed director of the Office of Adult Learning Services of the College Board in 1980. She directs the Community Assessment Program (CAP), a market analysis service that assists colleges and universities in assessing the learning requirements of adult learners in their communities. Aslanian has overseen needs assessments for more than 20 colleges and 400 companies throughout the United States. The Community Assessment Program is described in more detail in Chapters Eight and Nine. In 1986, Aslanian was honored for her contributions to adult learning by the National Council on Community Services and Continuing Education.

References

Powers, D. R. "Proposal: Northern Virginia Institute of Science and Technology." Planning document. George Mason University, 1980.
Powers, D. R. "The George Mason Institute: A Partnership with Science and Technology." Organizational document. George Mason University, 1981.

Powers, D. R. "Regents' Center for Education and Research with Industry."
Organizational paper. West Virginia Board of Regents, 1984.

Powers, D. R., and Committee for Research of the Mission Statement. "A
Framework for Planning: Mission of the University and Plans for the 1980s."
Planning document. George Mason University, 1981.

Powers, M. F. "Science and Technology Center of Southern West Virginia, Inc.:
Mission, Organization, and Action Plan." Organizational paper. Charleston,
W. Va.: Science and Technology Center of Southern West Virginia, 1986.

Simmons, J. M., Kelleher, W. D., and Duckworth, R. P. *Business and the Entrepreneurial American City.* Washington, D.C.: U.S. Chamber of Commerce,
1987.

Higher Education
in Partnership
with Industry

PART ONE

Making Partnerships Work: Objectives, Approaches, and Strategies

David R. Powers
Mary F. Powers

We dedicate these chapters to our mothers,

Jennie H. Ferguson
Elouise F. Powers

with love, respect, and gratitude.

M.F.P.
D.R.P.

1

Benefits of Cooperation
Between Higher Education
and Industry

Academia and business are unlikely partners. The two kinds of organizations differ in fundamental ways that, at first glance, seem to preclude, or certainly hinder, cooperation. One key difference lies in their attitudes toward discovery of knowledge. Traditionally, higher education has sought knowledge as an end in itself, whereas business has operated under the profit motive. This difference has several implications. For example, whereas many academics have preferred basic to applied research and are inclined to publish results, businesspeople have valued product-oriented research and are not inclined to make research results public—until the benefits of seeking patents outweigh the risks of disclosure that accompany the filing of patent applications.

Also, as Brown pointed out (1985, p. 13), "In the university, much research is characterized as long-range programmatic effort. . . . With a few notable exceptions, American industry has, during the past few decades, focused on relatively short-range research objectives, closely related to current product lines and foreseeable strategic variables such as raw materials availability and energy costs." However, Brown continued, "There is an emerging recognition that, to maintain technological superiority in the long run, it is essential to make substantial investment in the basic research that will support the 'next generation' technology. . . . It is indeed perhaps this factor more than any other that will provide the rationale for more extensive industrial sponsorship of university research.'' Brown's conclusion regarding the benefits of increased industrial sponsorship of university research is but one of a number of reasons that business–higher education partnerships have been the focus of much attention in the 1980s.

Before exploring further some of the specific reasons for higher education and business seeking partnerships, this chapter will examine some economic factors that will make such cooperation especially advantageous in the foreseeable future.

Higher Education's Role in Economic Development

The economic upheaval that currently is occurring in the United States is commonly described as the transition to a technology-oriented economy, with an increasing percentage of the work force engaged in information and process control, automated production, and services.

Bremer (1985, p. 53) described the present evolutionary stage of the U.S. economy as follows:

1. It is knowledge based—not capital based—although, to be sure, availability of capital is a necessity;
2. It is entrepreneurially based as witnessed by the number of new companies which have been created (600,000 in 1982 alone);
3. It involves world markets. Therefore the international aspect of protection for research technology must be considered;
4. It reflects continuous and often radical technology change;
5. It is becoming decentralized, making the state and local options and initiatives more significant, and, in fact, essential;
6. It is an economy of appropriateness not one of scale— e.g. merely increasing the size of the new production plant will not necessarily reduce the cost of a product or increase its quality.

The importance of higher education to economic development can be understood best against this broad picture of economic change. Services of any agency or organization, including higher education, will be extremely important if they help existing businesses adapt successfully to various conditions and factors characteristic of the changing economy, or if they can promote, directly or indirectly, development of new businesses that have a fair chance of succeeding in the modern marketplace.

SRI International (1986, p. x) has offered a definition of economic development and identified "ideal" college and university involvement in the process:

> Economic development means different things to different people. To some it means helping a failing industry become more competitive. To others it may be recruiting a firm to expand local employment and strengthen the tax base. It can mean developing the capacity of a neighborhood group to generate new enterprises. Increasingly, it connotes high-technology development, or promoting small business and entrepreneurial start-ups, or commercializing new technologies. *Broadly, economic development is a process of innovation that increases the capacity of individuals and organizations to produce goods and services and thereby create wealth.* This, in turn, can lead to jobs, income, and a tax base for communities, states, and regions.
>
> The ideal college and university involvement in economic development is the strategic use of knowledge-based resources to assist in the development of a local, regional, or state economy. Some institutions have resources that can enhance the capacity to produce goods and services and thereby create wealth, jobs, income, and taxes. Appropriate roles can be based on teaching, research, or public service—however an institution can best contribute.

Promoting Business Development. Undertaking economic development activities often is not a clear-cut process. Economic development and prosperity have different roots in different towns or regions, depending on the major firms or organizations that are established locally. Satisfaction of residents with local rates of development and levels of prosperity also vary from community to community and are not necessarily a simple function of numerical formulae depicting growth rates. Depending on variables such as expectations, past conditions, and the size of businesses' investment in the community, growth rates that please one community may be cause for concern in another. In other words, like the "business climate" (the reputation a region has for fostering business success) associated with a region or state, the success of an economic development effort resides to no small degree in the eye of the beholder.

Generally, if trends are toward increasing profits, more persons employed, higher wages, a broader tax base, and greater revenues, residents perceive their economy as sound and current economic development strategies as successful. A sense of well-being prevails. Declines in these factors suggest a problem and a need for action. Governors and state and regional economic development authorities set to work to promote growth, because success in economic development and prosperity are signaled by apparent growth.

In general terms, business development depends on availability of such factors as

- Natural resources.
- Raw and processed materials.
- Energy.
- Capital (at acceptable rates).
- Trained manpower.
- Competitive wage scales.
- Transportation systems.
- Suppliers.
- Acceptable state labor laws.
- Markets.
- Competitive products or services to be marketed.
- Entrepreneurial skills.
- Competitive manufacturing systems.
- Leadership.
- Acceptable tax climate.
- Competitive delivery systems for services.

Not every factor listed here is important to the success of every business or industry. Some factors are more important than others to certain firms, and each firm has needs peculiar to it. In addition, certain of these factors can be modified more easily than others. Thus, state and local efforts to create a competitive business climate often involve initiatives that promise to benefit the broadest possible array of businesses, yet are relatively manageable—for instance, offering loan incentive programs to businesses considering expansion or revising tax laws to include tax-forgiveness clauses for new businesses. Success of such initiatives presupposes that considerable investment has been made in the basic infrastructure required for growth, including roads and transportation systems, sewers, and utilities.

Investing in education is a common mechanism for improving the business climate of a region. The services that educational institutions provide can directly affect such factors as availability of trained manpower and can directly or indirectly affect such factors as availability of competitive products or services to be marketed, leadership, and entrepreneurial skills. Availability of other factors—including processed materials, competitive manufacturing systems, or delivery systems for services—also may be affected by processes or systems discovered or applied by academicians.

The Office of Technology Assessment, or OTA (1984), investigated a number of high-technology development initiatives across the country. Its investigation yielded results relevant not only to high-technology initiatives but to other kinds of development initiatives as well. High-technology initiatives examined by OTA shared three goals: employment, business development, and economic diversification. The OTA stated (p. 5): ''In most cases, strategies attempt to achieve these goals either by mobilizing the necessary local resources or by removing barriers to HTD [high-technology development]. Emphasis of the resulting initiatives fall into six general categories:

- research, development, and technology;
- human capital;
- entrepreneurship training and assistance;
- financial capital;
- physical capital; and
- information gathering and dissemination.''

When high-technology and other kinds of companies choose to locate near campuses, they often do so to have access to campus services, facilities, personnel, and programs. These might include services to identify venture capital for research projects; research laboratories and equipment; personnel capable of providing technical, entrepreneurial, and managerial leadership, training, and assistance; programs offering graduate-level training for employees; services assisting in applications for state matching grants for new companies; space in a university-owned incubator; or information-processing services. Clearly, higher education can be an effective mechanism through which at least some of the initiatives listed by OTA can be undertaken, in support of high-technology as well as other kinds of industries.

In any case, the fact should be borne in mind that strategic planning for economic development generally involves analysis of several key factors before investment in potentially fruitful projects is made. For example, the strengths and weaknesses of the region to be developed need to be assessed, business opportunities need to be identified, and—after capital is accumulated—specific investment alternatives need to be assessed and potential returns need to be calculated. The range of influences that higher education may have on economic development may not fit tidily into the model that is the product of this analysis at clearly defined, discrete points of impact. Instead, higher education may directly and indirectly influence every element and aspect of strategic planning.

SRI International Report on Revitalization at Regional and Local Levels. Particular strategies and incentives to accomplish economic development vary not only by company and type of company but by locale, because each area has different advantages to emphasize and different opportunities to explore. As has been stated, common goals include trying to attract new businesses and future startup companies and assisting local businesses in improving productivity or expanding operations.

An excellent report by SRI International (1984) summarized current research on economic revitalization at the regional and local levels. SRI focused its report on efforts to promote economic development at the regional and state levels—rather than at the national level—for three reasons: (1) regions were adapting to change in different ways, some more successfully than others; (2) in the early 1980s, little attention had been focused on state efforts toward economic revitalization, although many such efforts were under way; and (3) focus on regional or state efforts permitted development of solutions tailored to regional needs.

The report indicated that many factors influence regional growth and decline. Factors that influence a region from within include industry restructuring, entrepreneurship, availability of venture capital, quality of work force, and education. Factors that influence a region from outside include foreign competition and national economic policies. According to SRI (p. 2), of the factors that can be influenced from within a region, four seem to be particularly important:

- *Technology utilization:* The use of technology to increase the competitiveness of existing industries is as critical as the development of new technologies.
- *Management and innovation:* Risk-taking, entrepreneurial management is needed that is willing to invest in new technologies and that recognizes the importance of human resources.
- *Capital investment:* New sources of risk capital are required to help turn new ideas into new products through the rapid commercialization of new technologies.
- *Human resources:* Commitment to education and retraining of the work force is essential to meet changing job needs, as is the development of innovative labor-management relationships that promote adaptation of the work force.

The SRI report emphasized that regardless of the originating causes of changes in industries, technological change often plays a mediating role.

Four economic revitalization strategies that are "known to work" were discussed (pp. 2–3), including

1. *Applying new technologies to renew mature industries.* Older, mature industries can be revitalized by adapting to

new markets, creating more flexible production capacity through the use of new technologies, and adopting new management approaches. Instead of an unproductive conflict between high-tech and traditional manufacturing, what seems to be required is a "marriage of silicon and smokestacks. . . . "

2. *Promoting new enterprises.* The greatest job growth has been in the small and medium-sized firms created by entrepreneurs. Promoting an environment for entrepreneurship involves creating the right incentives in tax and regulatory policy, making venture capital available, and providing management assistance and "incubation" support. . . .

3. *Promoting high technology appropriate to a region.* Development of high technology should be part of an overall economic revitalization strategy that is appropriate to the characteristics of a region. An exclusive focus on high tech is unlikely to create the number of new jobs that might be expected. A key role for high-technology industries can be to play a "catalytic" function because they tend to cluster and grow related businesses in a region. . . .

4. *Investing in human capital.* A strategy that cuts across the preceding three strategies involves the investment in education and retraining that will be required to meet the work force needs of the emerging economy. Human capital has become at least as important as physical capital and will require a constant reinvestment as it depreciates over time. . . .

The report noted that different strategies are appropriate to different regions and to different industries in various stages of development. Here again, services provided by higher education are crucial to the success of each of the strategies identified.

Educational Institutions as a Factor in Locational Decisions. In spite of the varied and numerous factors integral to the success of companies—many of which can be manipulated to serve as incentives to attract businesses—interstate and intercommunity competition for new businesses and industrial plants often revolves around relatively few variables. That is, after a company has developed a marketable product, amassed capital, and identified markets, when the time comes to choose a plant or business location, minor differences in variables such as tax advantages, transportation systems, and materials costs—or preferences of executives—may become crucial to locational decisions.

Prior to the 1980s, many businesspeople would not have considered important in locational decisions factors such as climate and its effect on quality of life. In a 1983 study of considerations used by firms in locating their basic research centers, however, Arizona State University observed that one-third of the factors in the total decision process were related to quality of life—including physical environment, availability of suitable housing, and cultural amenities. States compete for businesses by building stronger research universities and by offering stronger tax forgiveness, low-cost loan, and land acquisition packages— thus tending to equalize, over the long term, some key factors in locational decisions. Climate and other factors essential to quality of life are fixed by nature, however, and they are likely to continue to be relatively important in locational decisions.

In communities that receive high ratings for quality of life, many contributing factors are affected by local colleges and universities and by the efforts and talents of members of their faculties. Cultural events, opportunities for involvement in the arts, and modern social and health services are examples of such factors. As these features tend to attract relatively well-to-do clienteles, they therefore may be of particular importance to businesses that involve delivery of personal services. Accessibility, responsiveness, and academic quality of area colleges and universities may be reported by industries as key factors in locational decisions because, as noted earlier, businesses and industries view educational institutions as major sources of new ideas and as potential sources of technical and managerial personnel (Joint Economic Committee, 1982, p. 34).

It is interesting to note that the availability of academic institutions, highly skilled (technical, skilled, and professional) labor, and favorable taxes were cited by the Joint Economic Committee (p. 32) as the three characteristics of a region most important to high-technology firms. The importance of highly skilled labor in locational decisions suggests that state development strategies that ignore human resource development are not likely to succeed, if attracting high-technology firms is the goal. Other factors reported by the Joint Economic Committee (p. 56) included housing costs, business climate, room for expansion, environmental regulations, and financial inducements.

Since technical and community colleges do not have research missions, the assistance they can offer companies in research and development is limited. The willingness and capability of technical or community colleges to train local manpower to operate sophisticated, specialized equipment can make a significant difference in locational decisions, however. The Joint Economic Committee report stated (p. 24) that high-technology firms ranked need for technical workers even higher than need for skilled labor or professional labor—which themselves were ranked very high. This emphasis on technical workers was explained in the report by perceived differences in mobility; engineers and scientists are viewed as far more mobile than technical workers.

In making locational decisions, businesses may check not only the quality of higher education in an area but the ability of local public schools to produce a work force that is disciplined and well grounded in basic skills. Whether the local public school system is sufficiently attractive that managers and scientists would be willing to enroll their children in it can be an important factor in a locational decision when competing counties are similar in terms of tax and loan packages and other variables. In short, the entire grade through graduate school system of an area may come under scrutiny during locational decisions.

Assisting Existing Companies. As the Joint Economic Committee noted (p. 6), about 75 percent of the net increase in manufacturing jobs from 1955 to 1979 is attributable to expansion in the emerging high-technology industries. Thus, while high-technology industries are an important source of process technology and other industrial innovation that can displace labor, their net impact has been to create jobs. In fact, high-technology industries, particularly the electronics field, have transformed the economies of areas across the country.

Investing in efforts to woo high-technology firms to locate in a state cannot be a productive strategy for economic development, however, if the state cannot compete with other locations in the factors that high-technology companies consider crucial in locational decisions. Likewise, interstate "smokestack chasing" (that is, wooing various kinds of firms, primarily heavy manufacturing) may be counterproductive. For example, when a state legislature decides to grant tax incentives and measures that require cash outlay to lure a large manufacturing company to the state, it should bear in mind that benefits to the state may not equal or exceed costs for some time. Some companies are making it a habit to locate in a state only until incentives are exhausted or a better deal is struck elsewhere before moving on. Fostering development and expansion of existing companies may be a wiser strategy, by far.

Walton (1983, p. 5) reviewed eight studies on job generation by small businesses, and he found that "policies aimed at attracting new businesses will not in general be as successful a regional development tactic as expanding existing businesses. Furthermore, 'global fix' policies that attempt to encourage growth through region-wide tax incentives or special regulations are also likely to have dubious impacts in exchange for high costs. The most successful approaches to regional development appear to be those which are tailored to specific industries or the strengths of a particular location."

If appropriate services can be made available to existing firms, over a period of years they may add employees, obtain more contracts, and have improved records of productivity and quality control. A dozen such successes might have greater payoff in a region with a faltering employment base and numerous marginal, smaller companies struggling to pay state taxes than would the success of one new industry with a large number of new employees. The costs of assistance programs offered by colleges and universities usually are low compared to costs associated with smokestack chasing.

Research programs are expensive and can be an exception to this generality. If research is necessary to devise new or improved products or processes to revitalize an industry, a state may find, however, that the most economical way to subsidize this research is through a state university. On their part, companies also may find that undertaking research partnerships is considerably less expensive than building or maintaining corporate laboratories and purchasing state-of-the-art equipment.

Colleges and universities also can be of assistance to companies throughout the business world—in manufacturing industries, service-based industries, and information-based industries alike—that must become computerized to remain competitive in a technologically oriented economy. Services that can be provided to companies range from systems and software design to the training and retraining required to prepare employees to operate the new systems efficiently.

Because so many products in the modern marketplace are entirely discretionary, companies must be able to respond quickly to consumer demands. Such responsiveness requires knowledge of potential markets and how to create markets. A company also must employ personnel and own production equipment that are sufficiently flexible to meet changes in demands. Since success depends on sound management, responsive and responsible leadership is needed. As ideals of effective management have evolved through the 1980s from authoritarian to more participative styles, universities have organized curricula, consulting services, and executive development programs to help companies modernize and streamline their operations by decentralization of responsibility and elimination of middle-management positions.

Company needs that have just been described—including needs for new and improved products; technologically trained employees, up to date in their fields; computerization of systems; and effective management—all share a common purpose: to increase productivity of the firms. Computerization, for example, may be expected to increase productivity by boosting output, by enhancing delivery of services, by facilitating better quality control—an issue of importance to more and more companies as near-zero-deficit supplier contracts become increasingly common—and by providing a means of avoiding high salary demands of U.S. workers.

In offering services to businesses, colleges and universities should not ignore small businesses. Walton (1983, p. 5) pointed out that "small businesses moderate a region's growth or decline.'' Birch (1979) estimated that about two-thirds of the new jobs created between 1969 and 1976 were in firms of twenty or fewer employees. Walton (1983, pp. 7–9) compared the results of eight studies (including Birch's) that examined data gathered between 1969 and 1980 and found that "the share of net new jobs created by small establishments [fewer than 100 employees] appears to be around 80 percent.''

In many areas of the country, particularly those that are not highly populated, small businesses may be able to provide needed services more cost effectively than chain stores or branch offices, since marketing practices of larger establishments often are designed to succeed in a metropolitan environment. Many small businesses—including cottage industries—are succeeding because they are able to find marketing niches for their products or services through mail-order or modern communications linkages. To help a small business, a college need not have a research mission. Often what is needed is advice on such basics as marketing plans, service-delivery systems, and bookkeeping. New businesses often can benefit as well from such advice. Nurturing new businesses by providing them with space and services at low costs has been undertaken by some educational institutions, usually in business "incubators," which are discussed in Chapter Three.

Categories of Higher Education Services for Promoting Economic Development. As a services-based economy emerges, higher education has assumed increasing potential in economic development. The services that higher education can provide to promote economic development fall into three general categories: Higher education can (1) perform basic and applied research, (2) offer technological and management assistance, and (3) provide appropriate education and training programs. The first two of these categories of service were mentioned by the Joint Economic Committee (1980, p. 279) and the Office of Technology Assessment (1984, p. 28) as ways colleges and universities can contribute to economic development.

1. *Basic and applied research.* Fundamental discoveries by faculty members can lay the groundwork for new applications of technology, which, in turn, can lead to development of mar-

ketable products. Although faculty members traditionally have tended to assign higher status to basic research than to applied research, more recently—perhaps because of the financial rewards that can result from creation of commercial applications—more faculty members seem to be involved in the product creation and development end of the research continuum, rather than leaving that to industry.

Inventions by faculty members can lead to new spinoff enterprises to produce or market the inventions. Because many such startup companies are located near the campuses on which the inventors–faculty members are employed—so that they can conveniently continue to provide ideas and perhaps influence management decisions—research by faculty members can directly affect the economic development of their regions. Large companies also may decide to locate plants or regional service-delivery headquarters near major universities to tap their reservoirs of new information and ideas. Smaller firms may migrate toward campuses for the same reason—and because use of university laboratory facilities, computers, and information systems promises possible savings in investments and opportunities to develop in ways that will allow continued competitiveness.

2. *Technological assistance and advice on updating operations.* Faculty members (often through consulting contracts) can help businesses determine which new technologies, processes, or practices are appropriate to their particular production, service-delivery, or management situations; whether the proposed changes can be initiated cost effectively; and to what extent such innovations can make the companies more productive and competitive. Advice on how to update the operations of companies can focus on improving management techniques, service-delivery systems, production systems and processes, quality control, or product design. Faculty members also can serve as troubleshooters, perform needs assessments and feasibility and marketing studies, and do countless other discrete tasks that are necessary for a company to maintain a competitive edge but which alone do not justify the expense of hiring additional, full-time employees.

3. *Education and training programs.* Hodgkinson observed in 1982 that 90 percent of the 1990 work force was then already at work. This means that while technology is changing, the work force is remaining relatively unchanged; that is, large numbers of young workers with up-to-date technical training are not constantly entering the job market as they did during the Baby Boom era. Since persons already in the work force must continually retrain, therefore, to be able to cope with new technologies, formal education has ceased to be an activity in which one engages only while young; instead, it is becoming a lifelong enterprise. Companies now consider it routine to retrain employees either to fill jobs created by new technologies or to keep current jobs that have changed in nature through adoption of new processes, procedures, systems, techniques, equipment, or practices. Furthermore, such retraining often is not a once-in-a-lifetime event, but may occur at intervals throughout an employee's association with a company. In some occupations, constant updating is essential. In a 1985 report, the Business–Higher Education Forum noted: "A major emphasis of America's educational effort in the coming decades must be to ensure that current workers (about 100 million) receive the necessary training and retraining needed to stay abreast of changing job requirements. . . . Colleges and universities are teaching an increasing number of 'non-traditional' college students—notably older students, women entering the workplace for the first time, and managers and engineers taking short courses. In all, 40 percent of today's college enrollment includes people below 17 or over 25 years of age" (p. 8).

As is discussed in later chapters, many businesses are answering their retraining needs by developing programs themselves. Others are turning to colleges and universities for service. Every kind of college and university is involved, with universities and four-year colleges, for the most part, providing training and updating for professionals and workers skilled in the more complicated or advanced aspects of the new technologies, and with community colleges providing training and updating for technical workers. As investment in employee retraining becomes an integral part of corporate life, employees who once were considered expendable now may be considered among a company's assets. Well-trained, up-to-date employees should be treated carefully, as retention of persons in whom significant resources have been invested can be an important factor in reducing operational costs. In short, higher education can provide services that can help companies remain up to date in terms of products, processes, and personnel.

The preceding division of services by type of higher education institution directly reflects traditional university missions. SRI International has produced a list (1986, p. 10) of university roles in economic development that reveals more detail regarding the spectrum of services being offered:

- Human resource development—tailoring education programs to meet the emerging human resource requirements of the new economy
- Economic policy analysis and research—providing objective information and new knowledge to public and private decision makers about an area's economy
- Capacity building for economic development—assisting a wide variety of community organizations in developing the capacity to participate more effectively in economic development
- Technical assistance to apply existing knowledge to industry—helping firms learn about and adopt effective management and engineering concepts
- Research to develop new knowledge—conducting basic and applied work to produce new knowledge that can result in new products and services or improved forms of production
- Technology transfer of newly developed knowledge to industry—purposefully helping firms to take advantage of state-of-the-art technology developed within the university
- Support for the development of new knowledge-based businesses—having the university take a direct role in promoting new enterprises that utilize knowledge developed within the university.

These roles are illustrated in Table 1.

Table 1. Spectrum of College and University Roles in Economic Development.

Economic Objective	College and University Roles	Examples	Possible Economic Benefits	Possible Institutional Benefits	Some Potential Concerns
Human resources development	New education programs Continuing education Professional development Extension programs	Arizona State Center for Eng. Excellence George Mason Institute of Science & Tech.	Skilled workers Means of updating skills Lifelong learning	New students New programs Revitalized curricula Increased responsiveness	Misreading labor market Vocational orientation Inflexible programs Need to cut some programs
Economic research and analysis	Economic data gathering Economic base analysis Industry analysis Strategy development	Cleveland State College of Urban Affairs Eastern Oregon State Regional Services Inst.	Better information Improved decisions Effective strategies	Public-service mission Community image Student opportunities	Needs not well understood Government/academia conflicts Involvement in local politics Work seen as too academic
Capacity building	Training Technical assistance Building partnerships	Univ. of Colorado–Denver P/P Center Western Carolina WNCT Tri-State Conference	New local capacity New partnerships	Public-service activity Community support Taps faculty skills	Lack of ties to community groups Needs not well understood Involvement in local politics Work seen as too academic
Technical assistance	Small bus. dev. centers Productivity centers Industrial extension Faculty consulting	Georgia Tech. Industrial Extension Service University of Alabama/GM UT–San Antonio CED	Aid to new and small business Knowledge of mgt. and eng. tools	New business support Research opportunities Consulting opportunities Student experiences	Drain on faculty time Not seen as prestigious Faculty resistance Lack of special resources
Research	Centers of excellence Research consortia Cooperative research Industrial affiliates	University of Akron EPIC University of Cal MICRO Michigan State Biotech Center	Technical edge New production processes New products and services	National visibility New research revenues Understanding of needs Access to labs., equip.	Politicization of research Conflicts of interest Threats to academic freedom Economic payoffs are long term Undergrad. education may be hurt
Technology transfer	Tech. transfer program Shared equip./facilities Faculty consulting Sabbaticals	Ben Franklin Partnership Washington Research Foundation Michigan Industrial Technology Institute	Access to technology	New revenues (royalties) Feedback to classroom Student learning Taps technology base	Lack of industry linkages Faculty resistance Competition with private firms Lack of organizational vehicle Academic/industry conflicts
New business development	Incubators Research park Financing program Entrepreneurship	Utah Innovation Center Texas A&M INVENT Ohio University	New startup firms New jobs Increased tax base	New revenues (equity) Faculty income Improved industry ties	Lack of strong research base Requires supportive services Restrictive regulations Detracting from teaching roles Replicating inappropriate models

Source: SRI International, 1986, p. 11. Used by permission.

Advantages of Cooperative
Relationships for Organizations

As a rule, business-campus linkages take the form of activities that complement the traditional instructional, research, and public service missions of higher education. Since different kinds of expertise are available at different colleges and universities, it is predictable that different kinds of institutions collaborate best with businesses in different ways. Community colleges emphasize training and retraining services. Four-year colleges tend to focus on degree-level training and providing technical assistance to small and emerging businesses. Graduate institutions can be a major source of research and technical assistance to large organizations or to smaller businesses with advanced technical requirements.

An outline of many of the advantages that educational institutions and businesses find in cooperative relationships is provided by Powers (1983).

Why Higher Education Seeks Cooperative Relationships with Business. The most fundamental reason that institutions of higher education want to collaborate with businesses is to improve their financial situations. Federal funds available to universities, including funds for medical education, grant programs, facilities, and selected basic research, have declined in absolute terms. Although Bloch (1986, p. 7) noted an "encouraging trend"—that is, that an "increasing fraction of federal support for *domestic* R and D . . . is going for basic research"—Abelson (1986) added a word of caution. Abelson stated (p. 317): "Passage of the Gramm-Rudman legislation, which is aimed at a balanced budget, makes the level of federal support for academic research a chancy business."

The threat that tuition revenues might drop markedly as a result of declines in the traditional college-age population has caused additional financial worries for many colleges and universities. Moreover, in the early 1980s, the country suffered a recession that reduced state allocations and private giving to higher education. At the same time, faculty members of high quality in certain fields in the sciences and engineering were becoming increasingly scarce and expensive to hire—not only because business was luring them away with higher salaries, but because fewer were being trained (Bloch, 1986, pp. 8, 9).

Business–higher education partnerships have provided a means of responding positively to these difficulties. It is not uncommon at research institutions, for example, for faculty members and graduate students to be responsible for technological breakthroughs and new ideas leading to patents and copyrights. Universities can receive large returns not only from royalties but from equity in companies that they found in partnership with private corporations. In such ventures, corporations may provide entrepreneurial skills and capital, and universities may provide research expertise, laboratory support, and patentable concepts, depending on the resources of both parties.

More important for the majority of institutions is the fact that colleges and universities can increase their enrollments and tuition revenues by offering educational and training programs to corporate employees. Moreover, when corporations contribute adjunct faculty members to teach courses in high-demand fields, the need to recruit rare and expensive full-time faculty members can become less urgent. Money saved can be used to improve the programs in which the adjunct faculty members are teaching or to enrich unrelated programs.

In selected fields, faculty salaries can be augmented by consulting agreements with corporations. When corporations are willing to pay some portion of the salaries of faculty members who can provide consulting services, all parties can benefit. Manpower costs to the corporation as well as the university are reduced, and faculty income is improved.

Paring existing university programs to free resources to develop new programs in emerging or fast-breaking specialties is extremely stressful and difficult. By sharing the expenses required to establish new research and training programs, universities and businesses alike can benefit by increasing their abilities to respond quickly to changing markets and to reorder priorities, and they can achieve these goals at a cost lower than either would entail alone.

A second reason educational institutions seek collaborative

relationships with businesses is to promote advancement of knowledge by improving the quality of instruction and research. At most universities, the facilities and instrumentation needed to do research in many fields are aging. Bloch noted (1986, p. 7): "In the past twenty years, federal investment in university research plant (facilities, land, equipment, etc.) has declined in real terms by 95 percent." The Business–Higher Education Forum (1985, p. 8) estimated that repairing the infrastructure of American colleges and universities will cost $50 to $60 billion. The forum added: "A recent survey determined that 25 percent of all research equipment in leading universities is regarded as obsolete and only 16 percent of it is state of the art."

Bloch (1986, p. 11) pointed out that "federal investment in research equipment began to rise significantly in 1984, when it totaled about $335 million or 6.2 percent of total federal R and D support to universities." Bloch also noted that the National Science Foundation planned to spend almost 17 percent of its 1987 budget for research facilities and equipment. He added, however, that although a number of agencies are allocating larger portions of their budgets for such purposes, the need remains significant. This being the case, access to state-of-the-art corporate laboratories would allow many faculty members and graduate students to conduct investigations they otherwise might not be able to perform.

As has been stated, in certain fields quality faculty members are in short supply. Sharing senior staff through joint appointments, dividing financial support, and developing exchange programs can improve the quality of university research and graduate programs and update faculty members. Furthermore, such measures can rejuvenate corporate practitioners and reacquaint them with theoretical and analytical perspectives broader than those on which they rely in their daily routines. An associated result can be evolution of research and development, consulting, and training programs more finely tuned to meet current corporate needs.

A third reason higher education wishes to collaborate with business and industry concerns the need to increase numbers of graduates in high-demand fields such as computer science, physics, engineering, and mathematics. In discussing this subject, Bloch (1986, p. 7) made three important points:

- Two decades ago no competitor had as many scientists and engineers per capita as the United States. This is no longer true.
- Since the early 1970s, the percentage of students entering programs in science and engineering has declined.
- Because the college-age population will continue to decline until nearly the end of the century, the United States will train almost 700,000 fewer scientists over the next two decades even if 1983 college-going rates are maintained.

Shortages of graduates in science and engineering cannot be remedied if universities do not have available enough qualified instructors to teach required courses. Unfortunately, industry salaries for scientists and engineers are high relative to university salaries, and universities often cannot compete. Furthermore, when the best young graduates accept high-paying jobs instead of graduate assistantships, the ranks of the next generation of faculty and senior researchers are diminished. Corporations can help solve these problems by allowing their researchers and staff to become adjunct faculty members. Such adjunct faculty members may teach one or more courses per year without charge, perhaps as part of more comprehensive personnel exchange agreements.

Why Business Seeks Cooperative Relationships with Higher Education. Businesses enter cooperative relationships first of all to meet corporate product, service, or management needs. To make a profit, corporations must seek new products, improve current products, make technological advances in production techniques, package and deliver services more effectively and efficiently, and optimize management. Universities conduct research in fields pertinent to these matters and employ faculty members who can provide expert advice.

Second, corporations working in partnerships with universities can gain access to personnel in fields where talent is rare, such as certain specialties in computer science and engineering.

Corporations that use technical staff are the primary consumers of a university's most visible product—its graduates. By working with universities, corporations not only can increase the number of graduates in needed specialties but can encourage changes in policies and programs to improve the quality of graduates and, thereby, increase their immediate value as employees. Graduate students in cooperative programs frequently become permanent employees of the corporations involved.

Third, such partnerships can result in upgrading the professional development of corporate employees, sometimes through creation of ongoing, comprehensive employee training. Corporations invest vast sums in employee development and training. Most large universities operate noncredit seminars to update professionals or offer courses or even complete undergraduate or graduate degree programs at industrial locations. Community colleges and four-year colleges have become extremely active in offering training and updating programs in subjects appropriate to their curricula and missions.

The need to ease research and development investment is the fourth reason for corporate interest in cooperative programs with universities. Corporations often are faced with uncertain markets and consumer behavior. Investing with universities in shared facilities can help control research and development costs. Public universities often possess ample physical plants, built at state expense and maintained by taxpayers. Aging instrumentation has in many cases, however, precluded state-of-the-art research. Jointly funded efforts based in university buildings with equipment and staff subsidized by government grants can work to mutual advantage.

Fifth, through relationships with universities, corporations can take full advantage of federally sponsored research. Laws passed in recent years empower universities to seek patents on technologies or concepts growing out of federally sponsored research and to sell rights on such patents. The potential value to corporations of the billions invested annually by the federal government in university-based research can be substantial. By engaging jointly in research, with prior agreement on rights to discoveries, both parties can benefit significantly.

Sixth, by working with universities, corporations can keep research cost effective. Hiring staff, investing in research facilities, and dealing with day-to-day problems can be prohibitively expensive. Contracting for external research to meet intermittent needs, speed research on particular problems, or confirm research results can be cost effective.

Perspectives on Business–Higher Education Partnerships. Many of the preceding points were among those made directly or indirectly by respondents to a survey conducted by Peters and Fusfeld (1983, pp. 34–37), which was sponsored by the National Science Foundation. Peters and Fusfeld surveyed thirty-six universities and fifty-six companies to determine their motivations for interaction. The rates at which organizations mentioned the following reasons in their responses are indicated by the percentages in brackets following the items.

Companies mentioned these reasons for choosing to interact with universities (p. 34):

1. To obtain access to manpower. [75 percent]
2. To obtain a window on science and technology. [52 percent]
3. To provide general support of technical excellence. [38 percent]
4. To gain access to university facilities. [36 percent]
5. To obtain prestige or enhance the company's image. [32 percent]
6. To be good local citizens or foster good community relations. [29 percent]
7. To make use of an economical resource. [14 percent]
8. To solve a particular problem or get specific information unavailable elsewhere. [11 percent]

Universities mentioned other reasons for choosing to interact with companies (pp. 36–37):

1. To obtain access to industry as a new source of money and so help diversify the university's funding base. [41 percent]
2. To provide student exposure to real-world research problems. [36 percent]

3. To provide better training for the increasing number of graduates going into industry. [33 percent]
4. To avoid some of the red tape and time-consuming reporting requirements that obtaining government money involves. [28 percent]
5. To work on an intellectually challenging research program that may be of immediate importance to society. [24 percent]
6. To gain access to company research facilities and equipment. [23 percent]
7. To gain access to government funds available for applied research based upon a joint effort between university and industry. [8 percent]

Having pointed out that access to quality manpower was the prime motivation cited by industries for supporting university research, Peters and Fusfeld concluded (p. 34): "Those industries most concerned about the current shortages of technical manpower (chemicals, energy supply, and electronics . . .) are among the most vocal and active in the support of new programs for university/industry research cooperation. Thus, science-based companies that are expanding or have high turnover rates of technical personnel are more likely to support university research vigorously."

Peters and Fusfeld (p. 35) also noted that the second most frequently mentioned reason for collaboration (obtaining a window on science and technology) was particularly important in industries such as genetic engineering and microelectronics that are characterized by high rates of change. Their point (p. 36) that innovation was far down the list of motivations for businesses is interesting because innovation intuitively would seem to be one of the strongest attractions for corporations to university research. The authors explained, however, that although industries do welcome new technical advances that result from university research, they normally do not expect campus research to culminate immediately in usable products or processes—hence their response.

Regarding university motivations for interacting with industry, Peters and Fusfeld (pp. 36–37) pointed out that "far above all the others is the desire to obtain funds to strengthen basic research and graduate training, and to support the facilities that make that research possible.''

Krumbhaar (1985) compiled information drawn from nearly a dozen sources, including reports from the federal government and professional associations and conversations with professionals. In a resulting table (pp. 15–16), he summarized needs that may be met through cooperative relationships as seen by industries and as seen by universities. From this table, the author drew a number of conclusions, two of which are of interest here:

- A wide commonality of interest exists between higher education and business since many of the benefits that a rapidly-evolving, technology-intensive firm would like from a university are the same benefits that a progressive institution wishes to offer (p. 16).
- Many needs of both sides can be satisfied relatively inexpensively (p. 17).

Commonality of interest, as described by Krumbhaar, and low cost of many cooperative ventures (such as some training and technical assistance programs) are factors that should tend to counterbalance a number of the difficulties inherent in university-industry partnerships, giving them a better chance to produce desired results.

Potential Outcomes

A report by the U.S. General Accounting Office (1983, pp. 47–48) listed outcomes higher education services can produce in terms of contributions to industrial innovation. Higher education services can help foster industrial innovation by

- facilitating early recognition of significant breakthroughs in basic research areas which make new products and processes possible;
- increasing the rate at which scientific and technical knowledge and understanding are adapted by industry;

- increasing the availability of sophisticated facilities, equipment and expertise to scientists and engineers in industry and universities;
- orienting university research more toward industrial needs and opportunities (e.g., interdisciplinary research);
- increasing the quality of graduate training of industrial scientists and engineers;
- increasing the rate of founding new businesses that exploit science and technological developments, and improving their capacity to survive; [and]
- increasing the capacity of backward and/or financially constrained businesses or industries to take advantage of scientific and technical developments.

Colleges and universities that can claim to have assisted in accomplishing any of these outcomes can also claim to have done well in fulfilling their service missions. In the future, successful companies in productive areas will be characterized by their ability to engage in technology transfer activities, in turning research into products and more efficient processes and systems. For many companies, that ability will depend to a significant degree on partnerships they have undertaken with higher education.

References

Abelson, P. H. "Evolving State-University Industry Relations." *Science*, 1986, *231* (4736), 317.

Birch, D. L. *The Job Generation Process.* Cambridge, Mass.: MIT Program on Neighborhood and Regional Change, 1979.

Bloch, E. *Basic Research: The Key to Economic Competitiveness.* Washington, D.C.: National Science Foundation, 1986.

Bremer, H. W. "Research Applications and Technology Transfer." *Journal of the Society of Research Administrators,* 1985, *17* (2), 53–65.

Brown, T. L. "University-Industry Research Relations: Is There a Conflict?" *Journal of the Society of Research Administrators,* 1985, *17* (2), 7–17.

Business–Higher Education Forum. *The Second Term: A Report to President Reagan from the Business–Higher Education Forum.* Washington, D.C.: Business–Higher Education Forum, 1985.

Hodgkinson, H. L. *Guess Who's Coming to College?* Washington, D.C.: National Institute of Independent Colleges and Universities, 1982.

Joint Economic Committee of the Congress of the United States. "The Relationship of Federal Support of Basic Research in Universities to Industrial Innovation and Productivity." Report prepared by E. M. Mogee. In *Special Study on Economic Change.* Vol. 3: *Research and Innovation: Developing a Dynamic Nation.* Washington, D.C.: Joint Economic Committee, 1980, pp. 257–279.

Joint Economic Committee of the Congress of the United States, Subcommittee on Monetary and Fiscal Policy. *Location of High-Technology Firms and Regional Economic Development.* Report prepared by R. Premus. Washington, D.C.: Joint Economic Committee, 1982.

Krumbhaar, G. D., Jr. "The Industry-University Connection and State Strategies for Economic Growth." Unpublished paper, Committee for Economic Development, Washington, D.C., 1985.

Office of Technology Assessment, U.S. Congress. *Technology, Innovation, and Regional Economic Development: Encouraging High-Technology Development, Background Paper no. 2.* Washington, D.D.: Office of Technology Assessment, 1984.

Peters, L. S., and Fusfeld, H. I. "Current U.S. University-Industry Research Connections." In National Science Foundation, *University-Industry Research Relationships: Selected Studies.* Washington, D.C.: National Science Foundation, 1983.

Powers, D. R. "University Collaboration with Industry." Remarks to Higher Education Commission of the States, State Higher Education Executive Officers In-Service Education Program, Denver, Colo., Aug. 1983.

SRI International. *Economic Revitalization and Technological Change: Next Steps for Action and Research, Summary Report.* Menlo Park, Calif.: SRI International, 1984.

SRI International. *The Higher Education–Economic Development Connection.* T. Chimura, principal author. Washington, D.C.: American Association of State Colleges and Universities, 1986.

U.S. General Accounting Office. *The Federal Role in Fostering University-Industry Cooperation.* Washington, D.C.: U.S. General Accounting Office, 1983.

Walton, A. L. "How Small Businesses Contribute to Job Generation—The Pitfalls of a Seemingly Simple Question." Paper prepared for the 1983 Conference on Industrial Science and Technological Innovation, Northwestern University, Evanston, Ill., May 1983.

2

Cooperative Approaches
to Education and Research

Although some businesses and institutions of higher education are better suited to certain cooperative relationships than others, successful collaboration occurs across a broad continuum of training, technical assistance, and research partnerships. The Business–Higher Education Forum (1984, pp. 33–34) listed thirteen "traditional" types of business–higher education relationships:

- Corporate financial support of colleges and universities.
- Corporate financial support of students.
- Cooperative education.
- Corporate associate and affiliate programs.
- Research agreements—bilateral and consortial.
- Training programs.
- Personnel exchanges—internships and sabbaticals.
- Conferences, colloquia, and symposia.
- Consultancies, lectureships, and faculty loans.
- Volunteer programs—trusteeships, directorships, and advisory services.
- Corporate access to university resources.
- Corporate recruiting of students.
- Joint projects to address national problems.

The forum recommended that industries consider entering a number of "new and extended" relationships with universities to (1) provide nonconventional support in the form of donated state-of-the-art equipment, incentives for corporations to increase student aid, and loans of staff, administrators, and researchers—the latter two groups to be used as temporary faculty members to make their experience available to university audiences; (2) explore increased use of university facilities and personnel for employee training and contract research; and (3) increase financial investment of all types. These recommended actions may directly or indirectly benefit both partners in the relationship while promoting technology transfer.

Since educational institutions enter cooperative programs in accordance with their missions, community colleges seldom become involved in cooperative research. Universities engage in the full range of programs, however, and the range of programs in which four-year colleges are active also is quite varied. Logan and Stampen (1985) surveyed fifty-seven of the sixty-six leading Class I comprehensive colleges and universities (defined by the Carnegie Council on Higher Education as offering degrees in liberal arts and in at least two professional fields). The fifty-seven respondents reported a total of 684 university-industry program relationships, with 190 consulting relationships "of sufficient size and duration to be monitored by the institution," 56 consortia and 41 industry liaison programs for broader-based consulting, 105 personnel-exchange programs, 13 programs involving shared facilities, and 17 programs to develop industrial parks. Government-funded, joint-effort programs totaled 128, and university-funded research programs totaled 134.

This chapter discusses the two key types of programs that are the basis for business–higher education partnerships: cooperative education and training programs and cooperative research programs.

Cooperative Education and Training Programs

Colleges and universities are by no means an educational monopoly. Training-vendor companies and industrial training departments of large businesses offer hundreds of thousands of courses every year. For example, Zemke (1985, p. 23) noted that only 700 of the 3,000 organizations that offer courses in business and management are actual institutions of higher education.

Many company courses are designed to improve basic communications skills, provide on-the-job training, polish interpersonal skills to improve production or sales, or indoctrinate employees with the company culture. Other courses are more complex, involving professional updating or management training. Zemke (1985) reported that company courses most often are designed to improve supervisory, management and development, communication, or technical skills, or to orient new employees.

A number of corporations even operate degree-granting colleges, which offer state-of-the-art training in specialties important to the sponsors. Eurich (1985, pp. 89–95) identified eighteen industry-based, degree-granting institutions that provided job-related education and training. She stated (p. 118): "The academic degrees being given by corporate colleges range from the associate to the doctorate. Contrary to a generally held assumption, the associate level is not the most prevalent. Instead, eleven institutions offer the master's degree, seven the associate, five have bachelor's degree programs, and three confer the J.D. or Ph.D." An example is National Technological University—established in 1984 through the cooperation of twelve corporations, including IBM, Digital Equipment, Hewlett-Packard, RCA, NCR, Control Data Corporation, and Westinghouse—which offers courses from twenty-four universities via television to employees of corporations nationwide who wish to earn master's degrees in engineering.

Although Eurich noted that businesses spend massive amounts each year to produce education and training programs for their employees, she claimed ("Business and Higher Education Report," 1985) that corporate colleges do not pose a threat to higher education. She was quoted as saying that a task of both higher education and business is to prepare individuals for productive lives, and that this preparation may emphasize job skills or broader, transferable skills.

Anthony Carnevale (in Eveslage, 1986), chief economist for the American Society for Training and Development, pointed out that corporations spend $30 billion a year on formal training and about $180 billion a year on informal training (p. 50). These figures represent an expenditure per employee of $283. Carnevale estimated that corporate expenditures for training nearly equal the total expenditures of primary, secondary, and higher education combined.

Eveslage (p. 50) continued: "As high as these estimates are, corporate training is growing. *Training and Development Journal*'s latest survey of the industry, published in January 1986, reports that training budgets increased by 12.5 percent in 1983. Survey respondents estimated budgets increased by another 14.2 percent in 1985."

Most businesses find it cost effective and productive to enter into relationships with colleges or universities to obtain needed services. Courses can be offered on campuses or at corporate locations; on a credit or noncredit basis; as part of associate, undergraduate, or graduate degree programs; or as part of nondegree enrichment or continuing education series. Payment can be according to a standard fee or according to contract. Tuition may be paid directly by employers or by students who are entirely or partially reimbursed by their employer companies.

Examples of some of the innumerable subjects in demand range from nuts-and-bolts courses in office automation, computer-assisted design (CAD), spreadsheet applications for accounting, and servicing electronic equipment offered by two-year technical or community colleges; to state-of-the-art seminars in computer software design and computer-integrated manufacturing (CIM) offered by schools of engineering; to courses in modern management techniques provided by graduate schools of business and public administration; to professional updating courses offered by schools of social work, law, health professions, and education. Courses in rhetoric for computer software designers, coordinated foreign language and comparative business studies (for persons in import-export industries), and practica in the use of new technologies and materials as arts media are among the innovative courses offered by some universities. Potential students include not only employees of large corporations, but owners, managers, foremen, and other employees of smaller firms; engineers and scientists; teachers; government workers at the federal, state, and local levels; health care professionals, including pharmacists, dentists, nurses, and physicians; social services professionals, including social workers, counselors, gerontologists, and child-care aides; workers in service industries, including insurance agents, real estate brokers, and bank employees; workers in the transportation and warehousing industries; technicians of all kinds in fields from hydraulics to quality control, environmental safety, telecommunications, computer-assisted manufacturing (CAM), and health care laboratory testing; and employees of nonprofit, charitable, and cultural organizations.

The *Chronicle of Higher Education* ("More States Are Requiring Professionals . . . ," 1986, p. 13) reported: "The number of states requiring licensed professionals to attend continuing-education programs has increased in the last few years, particularly for accountants, lawyers, pharmacists, and realtors . . . 47 states now require continuing education of certified public accountants, up from 37 states four years ago. And 36 states require pharmacists, up from 24. Twenty states require continuing education of lawyers, up from 10, and 29 have requirements for realtors, up from 21."

Increasingly, corporations are encouraging employees to develop their talents and are offering incentives to stimulate employee continuity, loyalty, and development. Companies have found that an effective way of increasing employee satisfaction and reducing turnover is to create policies that encourage employees to take courses, either to help them gain the credentials they need for advancement, or for their personal satisfaction. As Eurich (1985, p. 2) pointed out: "Education is as much a business need as running a laboratory or a plant. Gradually, major companies are making human resource investments just as they would make capital investments—in essential education and training that will give employees skills, knowledge and attitudes that will make them more productive and competitive."

Need for Updating and Retraining. Other factors more far reaching than employee satisfaction or human resources investment have given rise to concern among workers, businesspeople, educators, and government officials that more effective means of updating and retraining the country's work force must be provided. These factors include demographic changes, rapid advances in technology, the shift to an automated manufacturing and services-based economy, and the need to compete in international markets and redress the imbalance of trade. At state and regional levels, concern is to attract and retain businesses and jobs and to improve tax bases.

Various organizations have commented on these factors. For example, the *Wall Street Journal* ("Labor Force Changes Expected by 2000 Could Jolt Companies," 1986, p. 1) stated:

> The National Alliance of Business, a non-profit group dedicated to improving the opportunities for the disadvantaged, predicts significant growth over the next 10 to 15 years in the "less well-educated segments of the population that have typically been the least prepared for work," notably minorities, high school dropouts and teen-age mothers.
>
> The population shift will be occurring, the group says, at the same time workers with critical skills will be retiring at an increasingly rapid rate, and when new technologies will be requiring higher skills for entry-level jobs. The result will be "pervasive mismatches between workplace needs and workforce capabilities."
>
> The alliance says business and government must improve training and tackle problems breeding unemployment.

Technological change is an ongoing phenomenon, and as it continues—often rapidly—it creates needs for constant retraining. Both the demand for training to develop new skills in employees and the demand for periodic updating of those skills must determine the content of programs offered to help employees adapt to technological change. Lynton (1984) called this approach "occupational maintenance."

The 1986 report of the Carnegie Forum on Education and the Economy warned that in the future, high standards of living will be achieved only by societies whose economies depend upon activities of highly skilled workers, great in number and in variety of talent and training, who are capable of applying the most advanced technologies. Bringing the matter into a fixed time frame, the National Alliance of Business (Fields, 1986, p. 38) reported that ''by the mid-1990s, about 75 percent of all jobs may require some additional preparation beyond high school.''

Frey (chairman of Bell and Howell) had observed this trend several years earlier in an article (1983) comparing the educational achievements of students in Japan and the United States. He noted that in Japan, 96 percent of youths finish high school, compared to 74 percent in the United States. He observed that the move to the information age was having an unprecedented impact on the labor force and educational system of the United States, factors that were crucial to the competitive success of its economy. Having cited the mean achievement levels of Japanese versus American students in science and math, Frey concluded: ''If a better educated population means a more efficient, imaginative, and productive labor force, then the consequences of this disparity for the American economy are grim to contemplate'' (p. 12).

Effects of changes in demographics, technological advances, and other factors mentioned have been having profound effects on blue-collar workers during the 1980s, and little relief is in sight. The *Wall Street Journal* (Schlesinger and Guiles, 1987, p. 1) stated: ''More than 2.7 million blue-collar workers have permanently lost their traditional jobs since January 1981, according to the Bureau of Labor Statistics. Such losses are continuing as companies face increasing foreign competition, more sophisticated technology and the realization that only efficient concerns will survive.'' Problems have occurred in federally funded retraining and reemployment programs set up to serve workers thus affected, including difficulty in administration, high cost to companies (up to several thousand dollars per worker when retraining is necessary), poorly structured training, and worker apathy. The *Wall Street Journal* continued: "The new jobs often pay less, require relocation or extensive retraining, and force some workers to start over when they should be planning for retirement" (p. 1). In addition, in many new jobs, workers with low-level skills will have to compete with workers in other countries who are willing to accept far lower wages.

What can be done by higher education in response to this situation? Powell (1984, p. 53) provided a succinct response: "Three major categories of activities emerge: Updating American schools through better training and retraining for teachers and a reassessment of the school curriculum; updating the American work force through continuing education and retraining; and updating the American economy through research and development, basic and applied research for inventions in new technologies, increases in productivity, improvements in management, and enhancements in quality. Higher education should position itself as a major technological resource for assisting in these tasks. The once distinct roles of teaching, research, and public service are merging. No longer will education be able to isolate its primary functions of teaching and research from its community role, public service."

Merely to teach particular subjects effectively is not enough. Students must be shown how to keep on learning, how to acquire the habit of relentlessly updating and expanding their knowledge and skills so that they may remain employable in their fields. They must also be well grounded in basic skills and possess sufficient general knowledge to prepare them to change occupations and jobs as necessary. In the course of their careers, most workers now can be expected to change occupations three times and change jobs six times (Choate and Linger, 1987, p. 25). All members of the work force have to be prepared to train or retrain to fill emerging high-technology positions.

In view of the technological change that is profoundly affecting business and industry, what constitutes a better educated population? Ammon and Robertson (1985, pp. 23, 26) reported a Michigan survey conducted in 1984 by the Emerging Technologies Consortium of four Michigan community colleges. In the results of the survey, a number of key issues that business raised for community college action were discussed. The survey (p. 26) revealed that employers were concerned with three levels of basic skills: (1) fundamental work attitude and behavior, (2) competency in language and computation, and (3) technical literacy relating to manufacturing. In addition, the authors noted (p. 27):

> Employers want workers who can function in more than one arena. They speak constantly of the need for crosstraining. It is clear from discussion and employment projections that jobs are being upgraded by technology, not deskilled; the day of the narrowly defined job may be over.
>
> Manufacturing and service firms are struggling to restructure the entire organization, moving traditional, vertically integrated hierarchical organizations toward workers who are also educated to function in these new networking systems. Hence their desire for more systems, more knowledge, more interpersonal and group skills, more crosstraining.

The study also showed that companies are modernizing not only their approach to management, but their design, production, and quality-control systems. Three of four durable-goods manufacturing firms surveyed reported using computer-aided design (CAD) technology. Most reported that CAD would soon replace drafting boards. Twenty-eight percent of the firms indicated that they used formal materials management systems. Half of the durable-goods manufacturers and two-thirds of the nondurable-goods manufacturers reported formal quality-control systems and computer-assisted manufacturing technologies.

Despite a shift to high-technology systems, the Education Commission of the States observed (1986, p. 12), that

> employers interviewed in a recent study . . . reported general satisfaction with their workers' current levels of technical skills but expressed concern about the workers' critical thinking and interpersonal skills. More than one-third felt that workers lack interpersonal skills and agreed that these skills are key factors in hiring decisions and distinguish

superior performance from average performance. Fully
one-half of the employers reported that their workers are
not appropriately motivated; two out of five anticipate that
motivation will become even more important.

The challenge is not simply to prepare students for
work or to improve undergraduate education because of
its contribution to economic development. It is, instead,
to restore the balance between specialized training, aimed
at preparing students for a single career, and general education, aimed at ensuring a common cultural heritage and
preparing students for life.

Jaschick (1986), in the *Chronicle of Higher Education,* reported on the practical side of the matter, stating that focusing
on the needs of students is not enough to satisfy politicians and
business executives; the needs of localities and businesses must
also receive attention. According to Jaschick, the problems colleges face in meeting those needs necessitate the following:

- Experienced instructors who are not academics but are
  employed in industry.
- State-of-the-art equipment, which is often expensive.
- Expanded state support to include the nondegree programs
  and courses needed by businesses.
- Partnerships with developing companies that create the most
  jobs. This is more expensive than delivery to larger companies because the clientele is dispersed and has a wide
  variety of needs (p. 13).

In sum, financial problems may occur for colleges in serving
business clienteles if required programs are expensive and do
not qualify for state support. Businesses that are not thriving
may have particular needs for services that higher education
can provide, yet may be least able to pay.

Challenges Facing Community Colleges. Deegan and Drisko
(1985) conducted a survey of community college involvement
in contract training. They found that two-thirds of respondents
had established contract training programs by early 1983. Three-
fourths of that number had developed some form of centralized

organizational structure for such programs, usually through offices of continuing education or community services. If no centralized structures existed, contract training programs were offered on a decentralized basis through academic deans or directors.

Data from the study suggested that 38 percent of colleges that held contracts held only one to five annually. Twenty percent had six to ten contracts, and 14 percent had eleven to twenty. In the 1981–1982 academic year, 10 percent had more than fifty contracts per year. Over 60 percent of courses were offered at a job site rather than at a school. Also, over 60 percent of contract programs were noncredit, although the majority of institutions provided some mixture of credit and noncredit courses. The Deegan and Drisko study indicated (pp. 16–17) that business and industry were the source of 69 percent of the clients, health care agencies were the source of about 14 percent, and government agencies were the source of about 13 percent.

Not only community colleges engage in contract training. A National Center for Education Statistics study (Cross and McCartan, 1984, p. 19) indicated that 72 percent of the institutions of higher education in the United States offered noncredit programs for adults during the 1970–1980 academic year. The number of programs for nontraditional students continues to increase as colleges and universities become aware of the demand that exists for technological training and retraining programs, for courses for updating professionals, for advanced degree programs tailored to needs of industry employees, and for adult noncredit enrichment courses.

Changes in the industrial sector have clear implications for curricular change at many community colleges and four-year technical and liberal arts institutions. Students cannot continue to be trained in the traditional either/or manner: *either* vocational courses that lead to some specific employment *or* liberal arts courses that lead to no specific employment, but presumably prepare students for many different careers as they adapt to changes in the economy. Instead, as Frey (1983, p. 12) put it: "Neither traditional vocational education nor liberal-arts programs are providing the kind of career preparation our students need for the jobs of the future. We have to expand the scope of both. We must abandon our notion of vocational training as pertaining largely to preparation for the crafts or mechanical tasks. Similarly, the typical liberal education must go beyond arts and letters. If students are to develop job-related skills, courses in computer science, laboratory techniques, electronics, and so forth, will have to be required.''

Feldman (1985) agreed with Frey regarding the traditional division between academic and vocational education. He stated (p. 20): ''Academic and vocational education are *not* in conflict, each has an importance of its own. They are complementary. It is not a question of either/or; it is a question of both/and. Each serves different functions that sometimes overlap.''

Particularly within community colleges, considerable discussion occurred during the mid 1980s regarding changes in mission that might be appropriate to allow community colleges to respond effectively to their ever-increasing responsibility for training, retraining, and continually updating a significant proportion of the country's high-technology work force.

Eaton (1985b, p. 14) described the status of community colleges in the early 1980s. She stated: ''The nation's 1,219 community, technical, and junior colleges form a great training and educational network that enrolled 55 percent of all the first-time freshmen attending college in 1983. . . . Of the almost five million students who are enrolled for credit, 63 percent attend part-time, an indication of the value of these colleges to working students. Occupational/technical programs enroll a majority of credit students in community, technical, and junior colleges. Approximately 70 percent of all credit students in the colleges in the 1983–84 academic year were enrolled in these programs. At last count, the colleges offered more than 1,400 different occupational programs. Alternatively, community colleges have continued to maintain their capacity as a major feeder to four-year colleges and universities.'' Since in the present economy, a well-trained work force appears to be a necessary (although not sufficient) condition of continued development, the importance of the educational services provided by the community-technical-junior college network must not be underestimated.

Eaton also stated (1985a, p. 5) four crucial questions that must be answered as changing needs of society are weighed against traditional values of community colleges:

1. Do training programs lack commitment to general education?
2. In the name of equity, are standards diluted at community colleges?
3. In the name of enrollment growth, are marketplace fads pursued instead of educational substance?
4. Do curricula remain static in the name of tradition, despite extreme changes in our society and the current economy?

Positive answers to any of these questions have significance vis-à-vis the changing economy because such responses imply that graduates of community colleges may be inadequately prepared to be productive members of the modern work force. Eaton argued (p. 9) that the traditional distinction between *academic* and *occupational* curricula must be eliminated, and new curricula must be developed that contain elements of both. Students can learn the skills of an occupation while taking courses that will broaden their general knowledge base and develop their cognitive skills. As Eaton stated (p. 10): "Given our culture's emphasis on multiple occupations, we should ensure that students have the capacity to continue to learn, and the capacity for social, cultural, and civic cognizance and competence. This is part of an overall enabling of the population to deal with societal changes. In this context, the liberal arts and sciences are vocational. In this context, information skills and learning skills are essential. Students need to learn how to think and how to express their thoughts." Standards cannot be diluted, marketplace fads cannot be followed, and curricula cannot remain static if the student is to be served well.

Eaton cautioned (p. 9): "Community college training efforts frequently have been undertaken in partnership with business and industry. While community colleges will continue their productive work in this area, they need to realize that this training effort is distinct from occupational education in its most comprehensive sense. Training speaks to the development of specific skills that may or may not be effective elsewhere. Education provides a generic background of conceptual and general skills that enable students to accommodate many technical skills.'' In other words, the special training requirements of businesses cannot be allowed to dictate general curricula.

Groves (1985, p. 44) described changes that are needed in community and technical college curricula:

> The community and technical college needs a more generic conceptualization of technical/vocational programs. Unique or discrete skill areas should be based upon occupational skill families with instruction focused upon vocationally transferrable psychomotor and cognitive skills that have a strong underpinning of basic literacy skills.
>
> Today's equipment is a combination of electrical, mechanical, fluid, thermal, optical, and microcomputer applications. The operation and repair of this equipment will be impossible without some knowledge of basic principles in all these areas. Future vocational curricula will require a systems-oriented approach firmly rooted in the sciences.
>
> The Center for Occupational Research and Development (CORD) described [Hull and Prescott, 1985] the essential characteristics of the new high-technology curriculum as having (1) a broad knowledge base, (2) heavy involvement with computers, (3) an understanding of rapidly changing technical content, (4) a systems-oriented emphasis, (5) . . . basic understanding of several disciplines, and (6) . . . strong background in the principles and practices of high technology to permit greater employee flexibility. Some of the job skills identified as needed for the new high technology include such things as (1) evaluation and analysis skills, (2) visualization, (3) statistical inference, (4) critical thinking, (5) communications skills in many modes, (6) reference skills, (7) decision making with incomplete information, and (8) responsible behavior.
>
> To incorporate these essential high-tech characteristics and the related job skills into the curriculum, CORD has recommended a core of basic skills subjects stressing math, science, communications, computer literacy, and socioeconomic courses. At the heart of the science courses is physics, which is considered essential because of its general application to all the technical fields. An interdisciplinary technical core of courses is recommended in such areas as electricity, electronics, mechanics, electromechanics,

materials, fluids, thermics, graphics, controls, and computers. Having successfully completed the basic skills core and the interdisciplinary core (this core should be customized to specific areas of specialization), the student would then take specialty courses (e.g., robotics, lasers, CAM).

The *Chronicle of Higher Education* (Fields, 1986, p. 37) reminded community colleges and other institutions of higher education that "Besides advanced education and technical training, postsecondary institutions probably must continue to play a role in remedial education. Although some states are moving to take remedial education out of collegiate institutions, government experts say that many young adults with poor high-school backgrounds and older unemployed workers will continue to rely on community colleges and technical institutes for help in improving their basic skills—or many will never find jobs." Remedial education is a responsibility many institutions would prefer were unnecessary, but as the traditional college-age population has declined, for some it has become not only a matter of service but survival.

Innovative Training and Education Programs. Many retraining/updating/skills-advancement programs made available to employees and businesses involve relatively few special arrangements. An example is tuition-payment programs at colleges and universities that enable employees to advance their educations through enrollment in regular degree programs conducted during evenings or on corporate time—at their employers' expense and to their own and their employers' advantage. Agreements also are common under which employees enroll in graduate programs for a semester or a year to pursue full-time study at their employers' expense. Master's degree programs in business administration designed for executives are becoming popular; many companies are willing to pay full costs of expensive programs for rising middle managers. These programs may be made available partially on company time for individuals willing to spend Fridays and Saturdays of alternate weeks for a several-year period preparing themselves for advancement to more senior posts in their companies. Cooperative education programs also are common in which students in engineering, for example, work half time with companies (or one semester per year) to increase the probability that upon completing their baccaluareate degrees, they will be offered full-time employment with the companies.

Training programs designed by two-year vocational and community colleges to update or upgrade skills of high school–trained employees or to retrain displaced workers also are offered frequently on an ordinary contract basis to companies, state agencies, and unions. Innovative community college–based programs that address emerging technologies also are being sponsored in partnership with business, state government agencies, and unions. Such partnerships represent a closer working relationship among these very different organizations for common advantage. The following are but a few examples.

1. *Keeping America Working (KAW) activities.* The American Association of Community and Junior Colleges/Association of College Trustees' Keeping America Working project is involved in a number of human resource development activities, the best known of which is the Partnership Development Fund. The fund was initiated in 1985 by a grant of nearly $1 million from the Sears-Roebuck Foundation. The Partnership Development Fund is used to provide minigrants to encourage partnerships among colleges and employers, labor unions, and high schools (Choulochas and McKenney, 1986, p. 62). KAW also serves as a clearinghouse for data on partnerships undertaken across the country by independent colleges.

2. *AT&T Retraining Institute.* In 1986, when the Communications Workers of America signed a new contract with the American Telephone and Telegraph Company following a three-week strike, funding for a retraining institute was among the terms. The purpose of the institute is to help workers who face displacement or dislocation find different jobs either within AT&T or with other companies. AT&T workers who can expect to lose their jobs due to changes in the industry receive career counseling and retraining through two-year and four-year colleges. The United Auto Workers Union had negotiated similar clauses in contracts signed earlier with Ford Motor Company and General Motors.

3. *Automotive Service Educational Program.* Choulochas and McKenney also reported (pp. 63–64) on the Automotive Service Educational Program (ASEP), sponsored by General Motors Corporation, which they described as a consortium to meet a single employer's training needs. The consortium grew out of a two-year pilot program for entry-level auto service workers who were students at Delta College in University Center, Michigan. General Motors donated equipment, trained instructors, and helped design the curriculum. Changing technology was bringing with it changes in automobile service requirements and service training. Old-time mechanics were being replaced by persons with the background and training required not only to use electronic and computer technology, but to learn to use even newer equipment as it arrived on the shop floor.

General Motors had found it too expensive to meet its growing training needs by continuing to build classrooms and hire instructors; instead, it approached community colleges that had available classrooms and instructors and were anxious to improve the technical expertise of their faculties and obtain up-to-date training equipment. In some cases, colleges agreed to provide instructors to existing GM training centers; in others, special GM classrooms were established at colleges and staffed by college faculty. The pilot project was such a success that by 1985, thirty-five community, technical, and junior colleges across the country were working with the Automotive Services Educational Program.

4. *State-sponsored programs.* A number of states sponsor programs or units to maximize technology training opportunities. For example, Cross and McCartan (1984, p. 96) described South Carolina's Center for Innovative Training in Microelectronics: "South Carolina's Board for Technical and Comprehensive Education (TEC) initiated a program to improve the resources and instruction available to teachers and industrial personnel in electronics-related areas. TEC established the Center for Innovative Training in Microelectronics, ordered $250,000 worth of state-of-the-art electronics equipment, and hired a director and staff. The center is designed to provide training for industry through customized training courses for specific firms and train-

ing for instructors at the state's 16 technical colleges. The staff expects to train about 500 instructors and industry personnel per year in microelectronics, textiles, machine design, word processing, graphs, and other allied professions.''

Another example of a state effort to maximize technology training opportunities is the Advanced Technology Center at Lorain County Community College in northeastern Ohio. The state government spent $5.4 million to build and equip the center; nearly $2 million of state funds were spent on equipment needed for advanced technology course offerings. Other equipment has been loaned to the center by industry. The *AACJC Journal* ("Learning Spaces . . . ," 1985, pp. 6–8) reported that equipment included a state-of-the-art CAD/CAM system, computerized lathe and vertical mill, industrial robots, and training and electronic test equipment.

The center includes a technology-transfer resource center that provides information to industrial clients, as well as to faculty members and students. Education, training, and retraining programs are available in robotics, CAD/CAM, microelectronics, and process control, with formats and time schedules designed to suit individual companies' needs. The center is also one home of the Ohio Technology Transfer Organization (OTTO), which advises local businesses and industries on ways in which applying research or technological innovation or training company personnel may solve problems or contribute to projects. The center is developing programs to allow faculty members and students to work with industries to apply technology in specific industrial settings. It is also opening an industrial park on an adjacent twenty-six-acre plot.

In Illinois, four programs were started between 1982 and 1986 to help community colleges provide job training for businesses (Jaschik, 1986, p. 14):

- *High-Impact Training Services Program* provided $4 million in 1985–1986 to community colleges that design customized job training programs for companies hiring new workers.
- *Industrial Training Program* provided $3 million to community colleges that design customized job training programs for

companies that intend to move into the state or expand current operations.

- *Prairie State 2000 Authority* provided $1 million in 1985–86 to companies to upgrade workers' skills and $2 million in vocational education scholarships.
- *Economic Development Grant Program* provided $3.5 million in 1986–87 to community colleges to establish offices to acquaint business leaders with college services.

The *Illinois Trustee* ("Excellence in Education . . . ," 1986, p. 8) reported that in 1984–85, community colleges in Illinois provided training to 900 companies and 22,000 employees through 1,500 courses, leading to creation or retention of nearly 3,000 jobs.

5. *Community college consortia.* The consortium approach to providing services also has been described by Choulochas and McKenney (1986, pp. 62–63):

> One development that has gained momentum over the past several years has been the creation of consortia of community colleges as marketing units for training and education. Illinois, for example, has budgeted $2.7 million to create a state-wide community college economic development capacity (averaging $30,000 per institution). Iowa has built its new economic development and training law around the service delivery capacity of state community colleges. There is nothing new in this concept (North and South Carolina have built their reputations on it), but there is every indication of renewed interest in a multicollege partnership-building approach to statewide economic and human resource development.
>
> The partnership-building concept has also taken on a unique local twist, as in the case of the Gulf Coast Consortium of Texas. The Mid-America Training Group replicates the same concept on a regional basis. In this case ten midwestern colleges are marketing themselves to area emloyers for the purpose of providing regional training needs.

Another example of a consortium is the Emerging Technologies Consortium mentioned earlier in this chapter (see Ammon and Robertson, 1985). This consortium was created by Lansing Community College, Macomb Community College, Oakland Community College, and Wayne County Community College. The consortium has examined changes in the workplace resulting from introduction of seven technologies: office automation, telecommunications, computer-aided design, laser applications, quality control, materials management, and computer-assisted manufacturing (CAM). Developments in home health care also have been observed (Ammon and Robertson, 1985, p. 22). Information gathered is used to tailor curricula to the needs of businesses and industries in southeastern and central Michigan.

6. *Quality/Productivity Training Network.* Two national associations—the American Association of Community and Junior Colleges (AACJC) and the American Society for Product Control (ASPC)—established the Quality/Productivity Training Network, which links AACJC's 945 member institutions and ASQC's 200 sections (including 42,000 individual and 400 corporate members). The purposes of this nationwide communication network are to share quality-control and productivity training resources and case histories; develop training programs to help businesses improve quality control and productivity; and expand training resources by disseminating knowledge, materials, and approaches.

The Quality/Productivity Training Network sponsors the Transformation of American Industry National Community Colleges Training Project, which began in 1984. Sponsors include Ford Motor Company, General Motors, Eaton Corporation, TRW, AMCAST Industrial Corporation, the Iowa Productivity Consortium, and the Michigan Department of Education. The project trains trainers to provide instructional support for a video and print training system designed at Jackson Community College in Michigan, which emphasizes the management principles developed by W. Edwards Demming and the use of statistical methods, including statistical process control. By the end of 1986, trainers had been trained in nine states, and plans were being finalized to train trainers in an additional twenty-one states. Quality control and improved productivity training can be crucial to improving the competitiveness of firms. Hansel (1985, p. 40) gave several examples of savings resulting from quality-improvement efforts, including a program at Xerox that decreased overhead costs by 20 percent, and a five-year program at a Hewlett-Packard affiliate that resulted in a 91 percent increase in productivity.

Programs such as these provide opportunities for organizations to consolidate efforts to upgrade employee skills and assist the unemployed. As Cross and McCartan pointed out (1984, p. 98), however, retraining does not provide a solution to all the problems faced by displaced workers. Many displaced workers have lived their entire lives in their communities, own homes there, and do not wish to leave family members and friends behind to seek work elsewhere. Cross and McCartan continued: "Such workers are not prime candidates for [federal] relocation programs. Because states would not typically become involved in such federal retraining and relocation programs, they must be careful to focus retraining programs for displaced workers around high-demand industries near the same location where workers were laid off. Such constraints lead one to believe that state retraining programs for displaced workers, while important, will never become major adult education programs."

Federal Role in Meeting Education and Training Needs. The federal government has accepted responsibility to pay part of the costs of job training for unemployed and dislocated workers in economically disadvantaged regions. Three examples deserve special comment.

1. *Job Training Partnership Act.* In 1982, the Job Training Partnership Act was created, replacing the Comprehensive Employment Training Act. Certain programs named in the act are meant to be operated by the states, with costs matched on a fifty-fifty basis (National Alliance of Business, n.d.). The act requires wide participation by local governments and businesses in a way that ensures shared decision making.

Allocations to the states are based primarily on relative unemployment. In some states, these funds have been viewed as being intended for short training programs of less than one year. Therefore, the majority of these training programs have

been offered by vocational-technical centers or public education systems, instead of by community colleges. Private-industry
councils tend to think of short courses as related to future employment rather than to degree programs, and they are often pres-
sured by public school systems and state education bureaucracies
not to change educational contractors that operated under CETA
grants. As a result, higher education receives relatively few of
the hundreds of millions of dollars in federal funds matched by
an equal amount of state funds that are distributed each year
for JTPA programs. Even so, many community college systems
are taking advantage of this funding source. In 1984, for example, fifteen of the seventeen community colleges in Maryland
ran JTPA-funded programs, enrolling 1,300 unemployed people (Maryland State Board for Community Colleges, 1985).

2. *Cooperative education.* Formal agreements that enable
students to work part time and go to school part time constitute
a well-established type of partnership between higher education
and industry. Federal matching funds to support such agreements are available through a program begun in 1970, for which
appropriations topped $15 million in 1984 (Patterson and
Mahoney, 1985, p. 21). The fact that matching funds are involved encourages colleges to accept responsibility for coordination with companies that participate.

Students who wish to enter such a work-study plan must
be enrolled in degree programs. Some cooperative education
programs have participants alternate working full time for one
semester and studying full time the next. Depending on the
nature of the degree programs, the nature of the businesses involved, and physical proximity of the two, other arrangements
may be made as circumstances require.

Patterson and Mahoney (p. 19) reported findings from
a number of studies of cooperative education programs:

1. Recruitment efforts were thirteen times more successful with cooperative education students than with
recent college graduates;
2. Recruitment costs were much lower ($50) for cooper-
ative education students than they were for recent college graduates ($800);

3. Cooperative education graduates were awarded merit raises more frequently than other college graduates and they were promoted more rapidly to supervisory positions;

4. More than 60 percent of cooperative education students were offered permanent jobs and nearly 80 percent of this group accepted them;

5. Minority recruitment was twice as high for cooperative education students (33 percent) as for recent graduates (16 percent) of other programs.

Patterson and Mahoney also pointed out that 80 percent of the first fifty companies on the Fortune 500 list participate in cooperative education programs.

3. *Federal vocational education funds.* According to the Office of Vocational and Adult Education (1985), hundreds of millions (over $800 million in fiscal year 1986) are allocated to the states each year under matching-fund grants designed to upgrade and update vocational education training offered by the states. Most of the funds are given to public education to buy equipment and pay salaries of instructors in vocational-technical centers. An important goal of vocational education programs is to train individuals for private-sector employment. Vocational education programs tend to focus on youth of high school age—unlike programs funded by the Job Training Partnership Act, which tend to focus on post–high school and adult learners.

Under the Carl D. Perkins Vocational Education Act (P.L. 98-524), the former requirement—that close to one-fifth of vocational education funding must go to career-oriented programs located at community and technical colleges—no longer applies. Instead, states control the amounts that are so delegated. Vocational education funds remain important to many institutions of higher education, however, since in a number of states, such as West Virginia, the percentage delegated has been increased. In state systems, where funds are passed on to institutions without necessarily being identified by source, many community college faculty and staff members may be unaware that as much as 20 percent of their program or departmental budgets may come from federal vocational education funds designated as supplemental in purpose.

Cooperative Research Programs

In any survey of higher education–business relations, research and development partnerships tend to receive much attention. This occurs, in part, because some of the relationships have attracted sizeable investments. Also, research is generally considered a fundamental stimulus to economic development and one of the crucial factors that allows the United States to remain a world leader, politically and economically.

Importance of University-Conducted Research. Lindsey (1985, pp. 85–86) reviewed research funding in the United States:

Of the $60 billion R&D expenditure proposed for the federal government, in the President's budget for 1986, $40.6 billion, or two-thirds, will flow through the Department of Defense. The remaining $20 billion will be spent by other federal agencies and departments.

In *constant* 1972 dollars, it is useful to remember that federal expenditures for R&D now stand to about the same level as in 1967 ($20 billion). Industrial expenditures, however, have more than doubled, rising from $10 billion to $22 billion.

It is important to consider who *conducts* R&D in relation to who *funds* it. Industry now *performs* about 73 percent of all R&D, even though it *funds* only 50 percent. The federal government *performs*—in federal laboratories, etc.— only 12 percent of all R&D, even though it *funds* nearly 47 percent. Universities *perform* about 9 percent of all U.S. R&D, and *fund* from their own sources 2 percent of the U.S. total. But of this 9 percent of all U.S. R&D that universities perform, the federal government *funds* nearly 64 percent, and industry a little more than 5 percent. Thus, universities still rely mainly on the federal government, rather than industry, to fund that 9 percent of the total U.S. R&D that they carry out at present. The relationship is steadily changing, however. In 1981, the federal government funded 70 percent of all university R&D and industry funded about 3 percent.

It is important to note that universities perform about 57 percent of all *basic* R&D conducted in the U.S. Industry, by contrast, performs about 19 percent of all our basic research. Industry . . . concentrates its attention on applied research and development. Of all the R&D that industry *performs,* about 3 percent is basic research, 20 percent applied research and 76 percent for development. With colleges and universities the situation is reversed: 67 percent is basic, 27 percent is applied, and 5 percent is development.

To conclude this review of research funding, it seems clear that the federal government dominates the funding of R&D, and that the lion's share [two-thirds] of federal support flows through DOD [Department of Defense]. Industry concentrates its expenditures on applied research and development; and is funding more than 5 percent of the total R&D conducted by universities. It is also evident that although universities have dominated the basic research field in this country; they have been less involved in applied research, and even less in development pursuits.

The *Wall Street Journal* (Bulkeley, 1986) provided some graphs that offer further understanding of the role of universities in national research. Figure 1 shows the increase in domestic R&D spending over the past two decades. Figure 2 shows how industry, government, and universities divide their research dollars among basic, applied, and developmental research, with universities spending the greatest proportion on basic research.

The *Wall Street Journal* (Lubove, 1986, p. 10D) commented on the current increase in cooperative research: "Universities certainly aren't turning away corporate money. Government support for research is slowing, spurring professors to search for other sponsors. Meanwhile, a 1980 federal law expanding universities' rights to own patents has made academic labs more aggressive about developing patentable products and licensing them to corporations. In all, the National Science Foundation estimates that corporate spending on university research this year will total about $600 million, a 155 percent increase since 1980."

Kinds of Research Partnerships. The range of higher education–business research and development partnerships is extremely diverse. Common types as given by the National Science Foundation are listed in Table 2. Although universities tend to do basic research that advances science, and industries tend to lead in

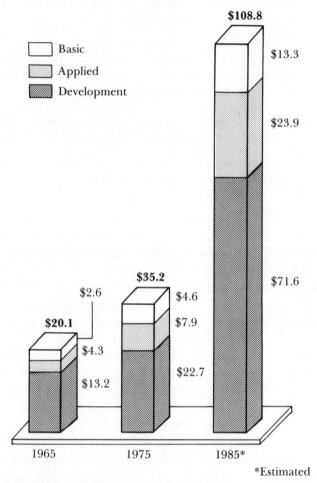

Figure 1. The Research Explosion.

Domestic R&D spending, in billions of dollars

☐ Basic
▨ Applied
▧ Development

$108.8
$13.3
$23.9
$71.6

$35.2
$4.6
$7.9
$22.7

$2.6
$20.1
$4.3
$13.2

1965   1975   1985*

*Estimated

Source: Bulkeley, 1986, p. 5D. Used by permission.

technological advances and their applications in products, in some large universities and businesses the entire spectrum of activity occurs. Physical and financial arrangements between cooperating organizations vary widely. Facilities and personnel connected to cooperative projects may be located at industrial plants, research parks, or hospitals, as well as on college campuses.

Figure 2. A Matter of Priorities.

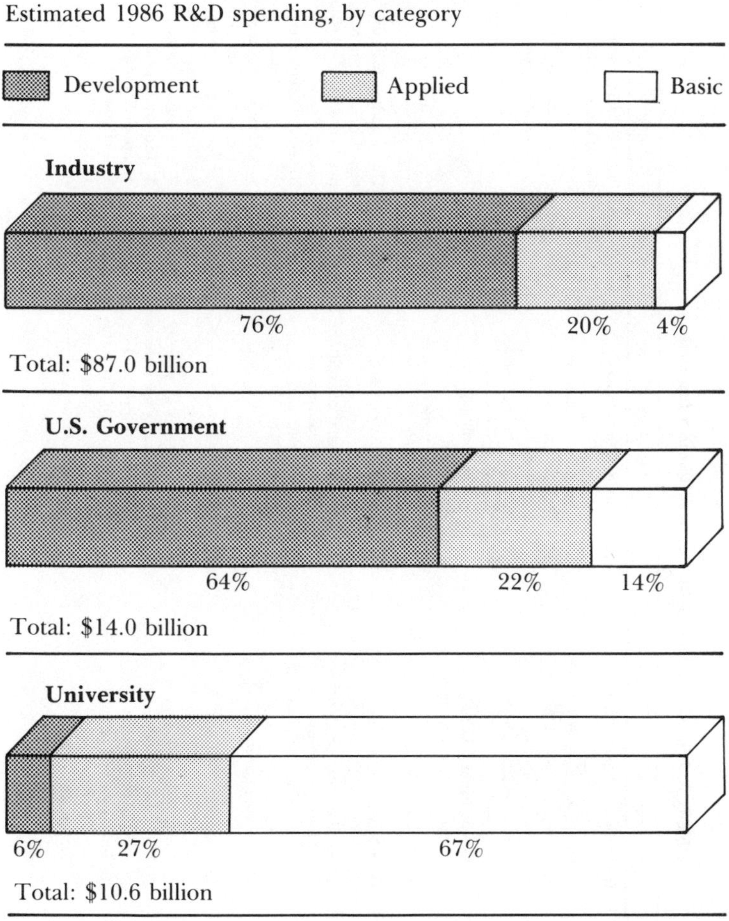

Estimated 1986 R&D spending, by category

▓ Development	▒ Applied	☐ Basic

Industry

76%   20%   4%

Total: $87.0 billion

U.S. Government

64%   22%   14%

Total: $14.0 billion

University

6%   27%   67%

Total: $10.6 billion

Source: Bulkeley, 1986, p. 5D. Used by permission.

The truth of the saying that "ideas travel best with people" is particularly evident in cooperative research and development partnerships. Arrangements allowing researchers to switch
roles with researchers from cooperating organizations, perhaps
spending summers in each other's laboratories, facilitate collaborative research and development of products. Other low-
cost exchanges may involve paying modest fees to consulting
faculty members or adjunct professors drawn from corporate

Table 2. A Typology of University-Business Research Interactions.

General Research Support	Cooperative Research Support	Knowledge Transfer	Formal Technology Transfer
A. Institutional Gifts in Support of Research 1. Monetary gifts 2. Equipment donation 3. Contributions for research facilities	A. Institutional Agreements 1. Contract research 2. Equip. transfer & loans 3. Grants to a professor 4. Graduate fellowships support 5. Gov't.-funded U/I Cooperative research	A. Personal Interactions 1. Personnel exchanges 2. Mechanisms for personal interactions: advisory boards, seminars, speakers programs, publication exchange 3. Adjunct professorships 4. Consulting	A. Product Development and Modification Programs 1. Extension services 2. Innovation centers
B. Endowment/Annuity/Trust Funds 1. Research facilities 2. Endowment chair	B. Group Arrangements 1. Special-purpose industry affiliate programs (focused & discipline programs) 2. Research consortia	B. Institutional Programs 1. Institutional consulting 2. General industry associates programs	B. Univ. and/or Industry Associated Institutions & Activities Serving as Interface and/or Foundation for U/I Research Interactions 1. U/I research coop. & technology brokering & licensing activities 2. University-connected research institutes 3. Industrial parks 4. Spin-off companies & U/I research
	C. Institutional Facilities 1. Coop. research centers 2. Univ.-based institutes serving industrial needs 3. Jointly owned or operated facilities & equipment	C. U/I Cooperation & Educ. 1. Univ. serves as source of graduates for industry: internships, U/I coop. training programs 2. U/I Coop. in graduate curriculum development; alumni initiation of research interactions	

D. Informal cooperative interaction: Coauthored
   papers, equipment sharing

3. Continuing education is
   utilized to initiate
   research collaboration:
   short courses, personal
   contacts
4. Industry-funded
   fellowships

D. Collective Industrial
   Interactions

1. Trade associations
2. Ind. educ. affil.
3. Ind. sponsored R&D org.
4. Ind. res. consortia

Source: National Science Foundation, 1983, p. 68. Used by permission.

ranks. Sometimes formal arrangements are required, as when agreements are negotiated to share laboratories and equipment at either a university or a corporation. Complex legal arrangements concerning patents and confidentiality may be necessary if projects promise commercially valuable results. Some of the problems that may arise in cooperative research projects are discussed in Chapters Four, Five, and Six.

Joint research programs commonly involve long-term collaboration between one or more industries and one or more universities, which share the costs of researchers and laboratories. Well-known examples include the Massachusetts Institute of Technology and Exxon, Carnegie-Mellon and Westinghouse, and Harvard University and Monsanto. In 1982, Monsanto also signed a $23.5 million commitment with Washington University to conduct protein and peptide research. The *Chronicle of Higher Education* (McDonald, 1986) reported an extension of the agreement that provided an additional $39 million to continue the collaborative relationship until 1991. The *Chronicle* noted that in 1986 the project supported about thirty research projects involving about 120 scientists.

Research at the Pennsylvania State University on recombinant DNA technology, sponsored by about twenty companies, is another example of a long-term, joint R&D program. Eastman Kodak, General Foods, and Union Carbide sponsor the Center for Biotechnology in Agriculture at Cornell. Eighteen corporations contributed over $13 million to allow Stanford to create its Center for Integrated Systems. Three universities—Stanford, the University of California, and MIT—are involved in a research consortium called the Center for Biotechnology Research, sponsored by seven companies.

States also have been making sizeable contributions to establish technology centers designed to focus on specific problems in cooperation with industry. For example, the New York State Science and Technology Foundation has funded seven technical centers at state universities. The medical biotechnology center at the State University of New York at Stony Brook works closely with Long Island industries and is sponsored by nearly a dozen corporations. More examples of university-industry cooperative research are described in the next chapter.

As of 1985, the National Science Foundation had granted startup funds to eighteen university-industry research centers, through which dozens of corporations make financial contributions to match government and university investments in research on polymers, ceramics, biotechnology, robotics, microelectronics, computer graphics, welding, materials handling, fluidized bed coal combustion processing, and other fields important to the continued economic development of the nation. In 1984, the National Science Foundation also funded six multidisciplinary engineering-research centers. National Science Foundation–funded cooperative research projects are discussed in Chapters Ten and Eleven by Frederick Betz.

Although a group of small computer or electronics firms may be able to afford to enter into a research partnership with a university, smaller companies usually cannot individually support major investments in research and development. Instead, companies may prefer to participate in a university associates program, through which they gain access to university researchers and up-to-date information for an annual membership fee. Examples of this and other mechanisms for university-industry research interactions, compiled by the National Research Board, are listed in Table 3. Universities encourage associates relationships in part because they support their long-term fund-raising efforts. Development offices always are interested in building networks of friendships and attracting potential donors to fund-raising campaigns.

Speaking on the apparent success of cooperative research agreements, *Business Week* ("The Payoff in Funding University Research," 1986, p. 76) noted:

> This year U.S. companies will shower more than $600 million on universities to finance research that they believe will lead to valuable scientific insights and, ultimately, new products or technologies (*BW*-June 23). In biotechnology, at least, a study by the center for health policy and management at Harvard University's John F. Kennedy School of Government indicates that industry gets its money's worth.
>
> The center polled 100 companies, and they reported that university research results in two to four times as many patent applications as research from any other source—

Table 3. Examples of Selected Mechanisms of Interaction.

Mechanism of Interaction	Examples
University-based institutes serving industrial needs	• Textile Research Institute • University of Michigan Highway Safety Research Institute • University of Minnesota Mineral Resources Research Center • Food Research Institute, University of Wisconsin
Jointly owned or operated laboratory facilities	• Laboratory for Laser Energetics, University of Rochester • Peoples Exchange Program, Purdue University • Synchrotron Light Source, Brookhaven National Laboratory
Research consortia (U/I or U/I/gov't.)	• Michigan Energy and Resource Association • Council for Chemical Research (CCR)
Cooperative research centers	• Case Western Reserve Polymer Program • University of Delaware Catalysis Center
Industry-funded cooperative research programs (partnership contracts)	• Harvard-Monsanto Contracted Research Effort • Exxon-MIT • Celanese-Yale
Government-funded cooperative research programs	• MIT Polymer Processing Program • NSF Industry-University Cooperative Research Program
Industrial liaison programs	• Stanford University • MIT • CalTech • Systems Control, Case Western Reserve University • Physical Electronics Industrial Affiliates, U. of Illinois • Wisconsin Electric Machines & Power Electronics Consortium, U. of Wisconsin
Innovation centers	• Center for Entrepreneurial Development, Carnegie-Mellon U. • Utah Innovation Center

Personnel exchange

- NSF Industrial Research Participation Program
- IBM Faculty Loan Program
- Summer Employment of Professors

Institutional consulting

- School of Chemical Practice, MIT
- Yale-Texaco Program
- Mechanical & Manufacturing Systems Design, Clemson U.

Industrial parks

- Research Triangle Park • Stanford Industrial Park
- MIT Technology Square (Route 128, Boston, MA)
- University of Utah Research Park

Unrestricted grants to universities and/or university departments

- Gifts from industry to departments of chemistry (for example, Columbia University, U. of North Carolina at Chapel Hill, U. Illinois)

Participation on advisory boards

- Visiting committees at most schools of engineering

Collective industrial action (including trade associations support)

- Electric Power Research Institute (EPRI)
- American Petroleum Institute (API)
- Gas Research Institute (GRI)
- Motor Vehicle Manufacturers Association
- Soybean Association
- Council for Chemical Research (CCR)

Source: National Science Foundation, 1983, p. 68. Used by permission.

including their own corporate laboratories. So satisfied are the corporate sponsors that two-thirds say they plan to increase their budgets for research at universities.

"Most companies realized benefits that are important for the birth of the biotech industry," says David Blumenthal, executive director of the center. In a companion survey of 1,240 professors and university researchers, Blumenthal found that they share industry's enthusiasm. The academics said they published more papers, won more patents, and made more money when industry paid for their research.

Figure 3. Production Cycle.

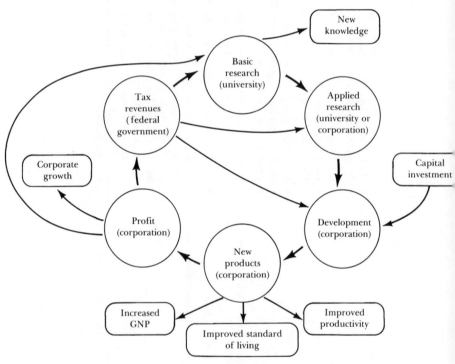

Source: Langfitt, Hackney, Fishman, and Glowasky, 1983, p. 178. Used by permission.

Importance of Promoting Cooperative Research. Langfitt (Langfitt, Hackney, Fishman, and Glowasky, 1983, pp. 177–179) designed a model of the "production cycle" (Figure 3) to illustrate "the importance of linkages between the university, the corporation, and the federal government in promoting economic growth through basic research and technological innovation." Langfitt pointed out that his model demonstrates how knowledge either leaves the cycle or becomes the subject of applied research and eventually the basis of products—and profits. Through taxation and company investment, more knowledge is discovered, and the cycle continues.

One challenge to continued economic development that is illustrated by Langfitt's model is the need for technology transfer. It is not enough that basic research be undertaken and that it generate knowledge. Information must be put into marketable form if it is to affect the economy. Changes in federal laws have been made to encourage such transfers. Reams noted (1986, p. 32): "The foundation for progress in this area was laid by the Carter administration through 1980 legislation offering incentives to corporations by permitting them to market and profit from products developed in part with federal funds. In the Reagan presidency, the National Cooperative Research Act of 1984 clarified the legal status of joint R&D ventures and encouraged their formation." Reams continued: "The R&D tax credit established by Congress, in 1981 [due to expire in 1986], has potential benefits for university-industry relationships. The House-passed tax revision would reduce the present credit to 20 percent from 25 percent, but would extend the credit to corporate donations to universities for basic research."

Putting Industry-Sponsored Research in Perspective. There is no denying that industry-sponsored basic research conducted by university faculty is important to the continued economic development of the United States. The size of the grants and contracts involved can be impressive. Yet several points regarding major partnerships should be kept in mind.

The first point concerns technology transfer, which is essential to economic development. The 1982 report of the Joint Economic Committee of Congress pointed out (p. 22) that 67 percent of high-technology companies surveyed relied on student recruiting as the most important means of technology transfer, 46 percent considered university publications important, and 42 percent valued government distribution of basic research results.

Corporate support of basic research came in fifth, with 25 percent of the companies surveyed considering it important to technology transfer. Assuming that company-financed research in universities is of potential or actual use to the group surveyed, the study seems to reflect an apparent and important point that has been of concern to the National Science Foundation for some time (for example, see National Science Foundation, 1983, p. 18), namely, that financing university-based research is not sufficient in itself to ensure that technology transfer occurs. Because other factors such as processes of information dissemination, invention of applications, entrepreneurism, and capitalization are involved, technology transfer does not necessarily follow investment in basic research. This fact on occasion may be downplayed by university researchers anxious to obtain research grants or contracts.

Because cooperative research programs have received a great deal of publicity, a second point needs to be explored regarding them: namely, the traditionalist concern that emphasis on research leading to economic development may erode the university's commitment to basic research. This concern also was expressed regarding the National Science Foundation's current funding priorities in an article in The *Chronicle of Higher Education* (McDonald, 1985, pp. 23, 27), which stated: "The National Science Foundation's efforts to bolster research in fields that could aid the nation's economic growth could lead to the neglect of other important areas of research. . . . While many researchers applied the foundation's plans to focus greater attention on fields that may encourage industrial innovation, such as engineering and biotechnology, many others believe the agency's basic research programs should not be directed by such eternal pressures." In later chapters of this book, possible effects on university traditions of higher education–business partnerships will be discussed. Here, the point merely will be mentioned that many do not view such relationships in an entirely positive light.

A third point to consider is the fact that although funds for research may occasionally be contributed by businesses in huge amounts, effects of such contracts and grants within the college-university community are concentrated in relatively few institutions. Summarizing information from a survey performed for the American Council on Education, El-Khawas (1985, p. 38) stated: "Research support [by corporations] is heavily concentrated in the nation's large universities. Fully 91 percent of public doctoral institutions and 65 percent of independent doctoral institutions reported having formal ties with corporations. In contrast, only 14 percent of other types of institutions have such research support ties." Similarly, Lindsey noted (1985, p. 86): "It is important to remember that when universities are referred to in relation to R&D, this primarily means the 184 Ph.D.-granting research universities where virtually all university R&D is conducted. In addition, it is important to remember that the other 2,863 institutions of higher education now educate about 75 percent of all undergraduate students." Finally, Smith (1986, pp. 33–34) made the point that "there are fewer than two dozen university-industry collaborations with more than $1 million in funding." In other words, joint research projects may be the wine of university-industry partnerships, but consulting relationships and education and training programs are the meat and potatoes.

Tables 4, 5, 6, and 7 illustrate various aspects of how research money is spent in the United States. All four tables originally appeared in the *Wall Street Journal* (Lubove, 1986, p. 10D). Table 4 shows the sources of research funding of the twenty-five universities with the largest research budgets, and Table 5 shows the research spending of the fifty U.S. companies with the largest R&D budgets. Table 6 shows the basic categories of corporate R&D spending, and Table 7 shows how federal R&D dollars are divided among the states.

In conclusion, a point by Useem may be noted on cooperative programs in general. She cautioned (1986, p. 12):

> For all the talk of the new partnership between educational institutions and industry, relations between the two are uneven and tentative. The much-heralded alliance is occurring primarily at the upper end of the educational system—at the elite colleges and universities. Significant bar-

Table 4. Top Research Colleges and Universities:
Fiscal 1985 R&D Spending, in Millions of Dollars.

Institution	Total Spending	% U.S. Govt.	% State & Local Govts.	% Industry	% Institutional	% Other
1 Johns Hopkins	$ 388.6	94%	a	0%	1%	4%
2 MIT	243.0	78	a	13	a	8
3 Univ. of Wisconsin (Madison)	208.4	60	18%	3	13	6
4 Cornell	203.2	59	14	6	11	10
5 Stanford	199.2	87	a	4	4	5
6 Univ. of Minnesota	173.3	51	11	5	22	11
7 Univ. of Washington	164.0	83	1	5	3	8
8 Univ. of Michigan	163.7	65	1	7	22	5
9 Univ. of Calif., Berkeley	149.9	65	1	0	26	8
10 Univ. of Calif., Los Angeles	149.7	73	a	0	13	13
11 Texas A & M	146.4	49	36	8	2	5
12 Univ. of Calif., San Diego	145.6	79	a	0	10	10
13 Univ. of Illinois (Urbana)	139.6	58	13	5	21	3
14 Harvard	137.7[b]	75	a	4	6	14
15 Columbia (main division)	136.6	88	a	3	1	7
16 Univ. of Calif., San Francisco	131.3	73	2	0	12	13
17 Univ. of Pennsylvania	130.4	71	a	3	11	15
18 Univ. of Texas (Austin)	123.3	51	4	2	33	10
19 Univ. of Calif., Davis	114.9	41	3	0	46	10
20 Penn State	113.2	62	4	14	20	a
21 Yale	107.2	83	3	2	11	2
22 Univ. of Arizona	105.8	49	1	9	36	5
23 Ohio State	103.4	51	12	7	17	13
24 USC	97.3	79	a	6	14	a
25 Univ. of Maryland (College Park)	96.5	41	28	9	22	0
TOTAL (all institutions)	$9,503.7	63%	7%	6%	17%	7%

[a]Less than 1% [b]Estimated

Source: Lubove, 1986, p. 10D. Used by permission.

riers to cooperation still separate most schools from the corporate world. Relations between public schools and businesses usually are fragmentary, weak, and of short duration. Executives are far more willing to donate funds, personnel, and equipment to higher education because funds can be easily targeted to specific programs. Business people want a quick return on their investment, something public schools can rarely deliver. Communication between the

Table 5. The Fifty Biggest U.S. Corporate R&D Spenders: Internally Generated 1985 Funds, in Millions of Dollars.

1985 Rank	Company	Spending	Change from 1984 (in percent)	R&D as Percentage of Sales	1985 Rank	Company	Spending	Change from 1984 (in percent)	R&D as Percentage of Sales
1	General Motors	$3,625.2	17.9%	3.8%	26	Texas Instruments	$402.0	9.5%	8.2%
2	IBM	3,457.0	9.8	6.9	27	Procter & Gamble	400.0	8.4	3.0
3	AT&T	2,209.7	1.0	3.9	28	Eli Lilly	369.8	8.4	11.3
4	Ford	2,018.0	5.4	3.8	29	Rockwell	367.2	21.5	3.2
5	Du Pont	1,144.0	4.3	3.9	30	Allied-Signal	343.0	32.9	3.8
6	ITT	1,085.0	13.7	9.1	31	Control Data	316.1	6.4	8.6
7	General Electric	1,069.0	3.0	3.8	32	GTE	313.0	18.1	2.0
8	Eastman Kodak	976.0	16.5	9.2	33	SmithKline	309.6	10.9	9.5
9	United Technologies	916.2	-1.6	6.1	34	NCR	299.1	3.5	6.9
10	Digital Equipment	717.3	13.7	10.7	35	Goodyear	298.6	6.9	3.1
11	Hewlett-Packard	685.0	15.7	10.5	36	Chevron	296.0	-4.2	0.7
12	Exxon	681.0	-7.5	0.8	37	Northrop	287.5	20.5	5.7
13	Chrysler	609.0	34.7	2.9	38	Pfizer	286.7	12.5	7.1
14	Xerox	603.1	7.4	6.9	39	Burroughs	285.2	3.9	5.7
15	Dow Chemical	547.0	7.9	4.7	40	Upjohn	284.1	15.2	14.1
16	3M	507.0	10.9	6.5	41	Union Carbide	275.0	3.8	3.1
17	Sperry	503.5	9.2	8.8	42	Bristol-Myers	261.7	23.2	5.9
18	Johnson & Johnson	471.1	11.8	7.3	43	Raytheon	260.3	10.3	4.1
19	Monsanto	470.0	27.0	7.0	44	Shell Oil	254.0	17.1	1.2
20	Motorola	464.0	9.2	8.5	45	RCA	251.3	3.5	2.8
21	Honeywell	451.4	7.0	6.8	46	American Cyanamid	250.6	7.9	7.1
22	Lockheed	429.0	13.5	4.5	47	Westinghouse	246.0	3.8	2.3
23	Merck	426.3	8.4	12.0	48	Abbott Labs	240.6	10.0	7.2
24	McDonnell Douglas	423.1	14.2	3.7	49	General Dynamics	228.0	15.7	2.8
25	Boeing	409.0	-19.2	3.0	50	Mobil	224.0	4.2	0.7

Source: Bulkeley, 1986, p. 5D. Used by permission.

Table 6. Where the Corporate Research Money Is: Industry Spending (Includes Funds Provided by Federal Government), in Millions of Dollars.

	1975	% U.S. Funded	1980	% U.S. Funded	1985[a]	% U.S. Funded
Aircraft and missiles	$ 5,713	78%	$ 9,198	72%	$17,801	76%
Electrical equipment	5,105	45	9,175	41	17,313	40
Machinery	3,196	16	5,901	11	11,037	14
Chemicals (and related products)	2,727	9	4,636	8	8,875	3
Motor vehicles (and equipment)	2,340	14	4,955	13	7,058	14
TOTAL FOR ALL INDUSTRIES	$24,187	35%	$44,505	32%	$80,121	34%

[a]Estimated

Source: Bulkeley, 1986, p. 5D. Used by permission.

Table 7. Federal R&D Budget—State by State: Obligations for Fiscal 1985, in Millions of Dollars.

	Allocation	Percentage Change 1980–85		Allocation	Percentage Change 1980–85
1. California	$10,767.6	77%	28. Utah	249.8	2
2. Maryland	4,408.4	79	29. Indiana	226.9	40
3. Massachusetts	3,268.7	60	30. Wisconsin	196.4	61
4. New York	3,123.8	113	31. Mississippi	172.7	58
5. Virginia	2,469.6	133	32. Oregon	153.0	56
6. New Mexico	2,364.5	148	33. Iowa	149.3	23
7. District of Columbia	2,081.5	158	34. Kansas	138.2	-61
8. New Jersey	1,789.7	145	35. New Hampshire	129.7	158
9. Texas	1,654.7	82	36. South Carolina	119.5	37
10. Ohio	1,518.5	44	37. Louisiana	117.3	-40
11. Pennsylvania	1,330.4	26	38. Oklahoma	83.2	-12
12. Florida	1,193.7	7	39. West Virginia	66.1	-57
13. Washington	1,032.3	8	40. Kentucky	65.6	-39
14. Alabama	896.5	97	41. Hawaii	57.9	36
15. Illinois	770.6	28	42. Alaska	50.8	20
16. Connecticut	742.9	58	43. Arkansas	38.5	28
17. Minnesota	714.1	173	44. Vermont	37.8	3
18. Missouri	694.9	-13	45. Maine	36.6	41
19. Colorado	629.3	10	46. Delaware	35.4	70
20. Tennessee	556.3	-23	47. Nebraska	34.6	9
21. Michigan	504.1	34	48. North Dakota	33.0	-15
22. Nevada	490.3	129	49. Montana	27.2	-40
23. North Carolina	477.0	109	50. Wyoming	25.3	-53
24. Arizona	456.7	36	51. South Dakota	14.3	44
25. Rhode Island	334.0	123	U.S. territories	62.4	38
26. Georgia	289.6	71	Foreign offices	35.9	-51
27. Idaho	259.5	76			
			TOTAL	$47,176.2	65%

Source: Bulkeley, 1986, p. 5D. Used by permission.

companies and nonelite colleges and universities is looser and less satisfying than that which exists between corporations and the most prestigious academic institutions. Most of the publicity and activity in the area of company-university relations centers on a relatively small number of schools in America's vast higher education establishment.

Since Useem's study focused on Stanford University and the Massachusetts Institute of Technology, perhaps her bicoastal view of university-industry partnerships is to be expected. The surprise to many is not, however, how much money is going to the elite schools; it has always been thus. The true surprise— and one of the greatest achievements of higher education in the history of this country—is how much the "nonelite" institutions have achieved and continue to achieve with so much less. Examples of training programs discussed earlier on this chapter and technology transfer programs described in the next chapter bear testimony to this fact.

References

Ammon, A., and Robertson, L. "Emerging Technologies in the Workplace." *AACJC Journal,* Mar. 1985, pp. 22–27.

Bulkeley, W. M. "Frontiers of Science: Changing the Ways You'll Live and Work." *Wall Street Journal,* sec. 4, Nov. 10, 1986, p. 5D.

"Business and Higher Education Report." *Educational Record,* Spring 1985, p. 35.

Business-Higher Education Forum. *Corporate and Campus Cooperation: An Agenda.* Washington, D.C.: Business-Higher Education Forum, 1984.

Carnegie Forum on Education and the Economy. *A Nation Prepared: Teachers for the 21st Century.* New York: Carnegie Corporation of New York, 1986.

Choate, P., and Linger, J. K. "Building a High-Flex Work Force." *State Legislators,* Jan. 1987, pp. 24–25.

Choulochas, J., and McKenney, J. "Partnership Building." *AACJC Journal,* Apr.–May 1986, pp. 62–64.

Cross, K. P., and McCartan, A. M. *Adult Learning: State Policies and Institutional Practices.* ASHE-ERIC Higher Education

Research Report, no. 1. Washington, D.C.: Association for the Study of Higher Education, 1984.

Deegan, W. L., and Drisko, R. "Contract Training—Progress and Policy Issues." *AACJC Journal,* Mar. 1985, pp. 14–17.

Eaton, J. "The Challenge for Change at the Community College." *Educational Record,* Fall 1985a, pp. 5–11.

Eaton, J. "Community Colleges and ASQC Join Forces for SPC Training." *Quality Progress,* Mar. 1985b, pp. 14–16.

Education Commission of the States. *Transforming the State Role in Undergraduate Education.* Denver, Colo.: Education Commission of the States, July 1986.

El-Khawas, E. *Campus Trends, 1984.* Higher Education Panel Report, no. 65. Washington, D.C.: American Council on Education, Feb. 1985.

Eurich, N. P. *Corporate Classrooms.* Princeton, N.J.: Carnegie Foundation for the Advancement of Teaching, 1985.

Eveslage, S. A. "Retooling for Tomorrow's Economy with Corporate Outreach Programs." *Educational Record,* Spring–Summer 1986, pp. 48–53.

"Excellence in Education—Economic Development Through Education: The Community College Approach." *Illinois Trustee,* Feb. 1986, pp. 1, 8–13.

Feldman, M. "The Ambush of Vocational Education." *AACJC Journal,* Oct.-Nov. 1985, pp. 16–20.

Fields, C. M. "Need to Retrain People in Changing Fields Confronts Colleges with Creative Challenge." *Chronicle of Higher Education,* Sept. 17, 1986, pp. 37–39.

Frey, D. N. "Executive Exchange." *Industry Week,* Feb. 7, 1983, p. 12.

Groves, C. L. "Quantum Leap: Vocational Education Reform." *AACJC Journal,* Mar. 1985, pp. 42–45.

Hansel, J. L. "The Cult of Technical Rationality." *AACJC Journal,* Mar. 1985, pp. 39–41.

Hull, D. M., and Prescott, C. "Advanced-Technology Core Curriculum Guide." Waco, Tex.: Center for Occupational Research and Development (CORD), 1984.

Jaschik, S. "Community Colleges Are Changing Their Roles to Meet Demands for New Types of Job Training." *Chronicle of Higher Education,* Apr. 2, 1986, pp. 13–15.

Joint Economic Committee of the Congress of the United States, Subcommittee on Monetary and Fiscal Policy. *Location of High-Technology Firms and Regional Economic Development.* Report prepared by R. Premus. Washington, D.C.: Joint Economic Committee, 1982.

"Labor Force Changes Expected by 2000 Could Jolt Companies." *Wall Street Journal,* May 6, 1986, p. 1.

Langfitt, T. W., Hackney, S., Fishman, A. P., and Glowasky, A. W. (eds.). *Partners in the Research Enterprise.* Philadelphia: University of Pennsylvania Press, 1983.

"Learning Spaces: Ohio's First Advanced Technologies Center." *AACJC Journal,* Mar. 1985, pp. 6–8.

Lindsey, Q. W. "Industry-University Research Cooperation: The State Government Role." *Journal of the Society of Research Administrators,* Fall 1985, pp. 85–90.

Logan, L., and Stampen, J. O. "Smoke Stack Meets Ivory Tower: Collaborations with Local Industry." *Educational Record,* Spring 1985, pp. 25–29.

Lubove, S. H. "The Old College Tie." *Wall Street Journal,* sec. 4, Nov. 10, 1986, pp. 10–11D.

Lynton, E. A. *The Missing Connection Between Business and the Universities.* New York: Macmillan, 1984.

McDonald, K. "NSF's Stress on Short-Term Research Goals May Leave Fields Neglected, Scientists Fear." *Chronicle of Higher Education,* Feb. 27, 1985, pp. 23, 27.

McDonald, K. "Biomedical-Research Agreement Signed by Washington University, Monsanto." *Chronicle of Higher Education,* May 7, 1986, p. 8.

Maryland State Board for Community Colleges. "Economic Development Through Education." Unpublished report, Maryland State Board for Community Colleges, Annapolis, 1985.

"More States Are Requiring Professionals to Take Continuing-Education Courses." *Chronicle of Higher Education,* May 21, 1986, pp. 13, 16.

National Alliance of Business. "Allocations for Job Training Partnership Act." Unpublished summary, National Alliance of Business, Washington, D.C., n.d.

National Science Foundation. *University-Industry Research Relationships: Selected Studies.* Washington, D.C.: National Science Foundation, 1983.

Office of Vocational and Adult Education, U.S. Department of Education. "Program Memorandum OVAE/DVE-FY 86-2." Unpublished document, U.S. Department of Education, 1985.

Patterson, S. B., and Mahoney, J. R. "Cooperative Education—Lest We Forget." *AACJC Journal,* Mar. 1985, pp. 18–21.

"The Payoff in Funding University Research." *Business Week,* June 30, 1986, p. 76.

Powell, S. "Higher Education and Industry: Planning and Assessing the New Alliance." In R. A. Scott (ed.), *Determining the Effectiveness of Campus Services.* New Directions for Institutional Research, no. 41. San Francisco: Jossey-Bass, 1984.

Reams, B. D., Jr. *University-Industry Partnerships: The Major Legal Issues in Research and Development Agreements.* Westport, Conn.: Quorum Books, 1986.

Schlesinger, J. M., and Guiles, M. G. "Struggling Back." *Wall Street Journal,* Jan. 16, 1987, pp. 1, 14.

Smith, E. T. "Monsanto's College Alliance Is Getting High Marks." *Business Week,* May 12, 1986, pp. 33–34.

Useem, E. L. *Low-Tech Education in a High-Tech World.* New York: Free Press, 1986.

Zemke, R. "Industry-Education Cooperation: Old Phrase with a Strange New Meaning." *Training,* July 1985, pp. 20–24.

3

Examples of Innovative Alliances

The university seems to be rapidly shedding its ivory tower image. Not only are businesses and industries interested in entering cooperative relationships with institutions of higher education but federal agencies and state governments are interested in promoting such relationships. As was noted in Chapter One, government is showing an increased appreciation of higher education as an important factor in economic development. A number of state governments are investing heavily to enhance higher education's ability to attract new businesses and to improve higher education's ability to provide existing businesses with services that will increase productivity.

State governments are also funding cooperative programs because of their important role in the transition in employment patterns from assembly line manufacturing toward services and automated production: researchers and employees involved in these programs are gaining insight as well as technological and management knowledge and skills necessary for this shift. In states where the transition is occurring rapidly and productively, government and business leaders are striving to ensure that their states retain that lead. Government and business leaders in states that are lagging behind wish to change conditions so that their states may become more prosperous more quickly.

Commenting on the leadership role that state governments have been taking in establishing higher education–business partnerships, Abelson (1986, p. 317) emphasized the importance of technology transfer:

Faltering ability to compete in international trade and attendant industrial employment will not be alleviated soon. An earlier confidence that support of basic research would inevitably guarantee applications and prosperity has faded. Governor Bruce Babbitt of Arizona voiced the opinion of many governors and other politicians when he said, ". . . the application of scientific knowledge is the basis for economic expansion and diversification, the key to formation of new businesses and the competitive survival of old ones." Babbitt further stated that there is a "new awareness that the fruits of university research and development activity have little economic value unless they are systematically harvested in the marketplace."

When the history of this era of science and technology is written, the role of the National Governors' Association will have special attention. This organization was ahead of the federal government in recognizing and indoctrinating in its members the need for greater academic-industrial interactions. . . . Many of the governors concluded that state and local policies could lead to new companies and new jobs through the use of science and technology.

In an effort to create new companies and new jobs, many states have begun to provide funds for a variety of programs to foster applications of research. In a 1983 report, the U.S. Office of Technology Assessment estimated that states and localities had formulated about 150 programs. Today [1986] there are perhaps as many as 500 programs, and virtually all the states are involved. No two states are fostering identical programs, although some common features have emerged. These include research parks located close to universities, incubator facilities on campus or close by, various kinds of financial support for start-up companies, encouragement of faculty to initiate commercial enterprises, cofunding with industry of academic-industrial research centers, and extension services to companies in the state [copyright 1986 by the American Association for the Advancement of Science].

This chapter describes some key innovative cooperative programs and the role of the state in their support.

Key Innovative Cooperative Programs

The kinds of cooperative programs mentioned by Abelson (1986) merit discussion because many of them have been extremely successful and because in some cases their operation has involved avoidable drawbacks and pitfalls.

Research/Industrial Parks. University-industry relationships in the form of research/industrial parks and incubator centers have captured the imaginations of governors, state economic development officers, local government officials, and the popular media. When they are successful, these glamour activities are more visible than conventional cooperative research or educational programs and more profitable for the institutions involved. Their effects in promoting regional economic development also tend to be direct and apparent.

Built on large, grassy sites, many research/industrial parks resemble recreational parks or campuses. Incubator space and services for startup companies often are provided. Tenants of such parks are frequently embryonic advanced technology firms engaged in research and development projects and companies engaged in light, clean manufacturing processes related to advanced technology, applied science, or engineering. Many tenants are service or distribution companies. Research/industrial parks frequently are situated near major university campuses so that the businesses that locate in them can take advantage of university resources.

As the Battelle Institute pointed out (1983a, p. 9), urban institutions are building research parks of a "vertical" nature. These often are called *innovation centers* or *urban research complexes.* They resemble suburban research/industrial parks in providing space for startup firms, but they focus on research and professional services companies and usually avoid manufacturing entirely.

In 1951, Stanford University established the prototype research park, which now houses eighty companies on 660 acres. Establishment of other parks has been led by governors and other public officials and business leaders, as well as by college and university administrators, often working cooperatively. For example, the state of North Carolina, led by a series of governors over a quarter of a century, in collaboration with land developers and university leaders, created the Research Triangle Park, which involves the University of North Carolina at Chapel Hill, North Carolina State University, and Duke University.

Development of a research/industrial park depends fundamentally on a university owning or being able to acquire a suitable site that can provide the basis for aggressive initiatives. High-technology companies also have been crucial to the success of many research/industrial parks. In examining regions in which high-technology companies have been most successful, a study of the Joint Economic Committee of Congress noted (1982, p. 49):

> No single element is responsible for the seemingly spontaneous and spectacular growth of high-technology industries in these regions. Instead a combination of factors, including research and teaching activities at great universities, a rich endowment of labor skills, venture capitalists, high technology entrepreneurs, and Federal procurement activities in the area are intermingled to provide the intricate fabric of a ''creative environment'' that underlies the economic dynamics of the regions. Equilibrium, stability and certainty have been replaced by disequilibrium, change, and uncertainty. The only sense of constancy is change itself, but herein lies the economic strength of the regions. In general, the regions possess a major comparative cost advantage in creating new ideas and an institutional environment that willingly translates these new ideas into marketable commodities and services.

To make the point that developing a successful park may take far longer than many economic development officers and university administrators realize, the 1982 report of the Joint Economic Committee of Congress, in discussing the success of Research Triangle Park, noted that North Carolina was the first state to create—in 1963—a science and technology park. In recent years, North Carolina has continued to be a leader by making additional investments ($46 million in the early 1980s) to create the Microelectronics Center of North Carolina, which is housed in Research Triangle Park. The Microelectronics Center is noted for the basic research it conducts in semiconductors, computer-aided design, and integrated circuit design. Reserves of $16.7 million for 1985–1986 and $12.2 million for 1986–1987 were established by the North Carolina legislature to support the Microelectronics Center. In sum, continued success of a research/industrial park seems to be a function not only of a "creative environment," but of nurturing carefully selected businesses in the park and making additional development funds available to them at crucial times. Wisdom and patience are required to identify and provide long-term, sometimes massive support for businesses that are developing new forms of products that are in great demand or products that in some way promise to be revolutionary.

Since many businesses that occupy research/industrial parks and incubators are founded on venture capital, Crowley's (1985) comment on the success/failure rate of such endeavors is pertinent; that is, Crowley, vice-president of the Massachusetts Technology Development Corporation, estimated that on the average, two out of ten projects funded by venture capitalists may achieve superstardom, but two go bankrupt. A problem with many new companies is that they join the "living dead"; that is, they do not perform well in terms of cash flow—and investors also cannot get their money back out of them. Some venture capitalists specialize in startup efforts and may keep their investments for only a few years until they can sell them or go public by issuing stocks. Other venture capitalists may keep companies in their portfolios more than ten years. Coulter, president of American Research and Development, observed (1985) that founders of research parks must bear in mind that even highly successful research and development projects may not result in marketable products for some time. Aside from commercial applications of research findings, however, research/industrial parks may have a more immediate effect on local economies through creation of jobs. Cazier, president of Utah State University, commented ("Universities and Research Parks," 1986, p. 29), for example, that "development of USU's park is expected to generate 2,000 direct and 1,000 indirect jobs over the next ten years."

1. *Importance of relationship with university.* In examining the effects on regional economic development of the North Carolina, Massachusetts Institute of Technology, and Stanford high-technology centers, the Joint Economic Committee (1982, p. 51) quoted a study by the Research and Planning Institute, Inc.:

In an extraordinary number of cases a university played a major role in the history of the company. There were a number of companies that started to pursue the results of research done at the universities, although generally a significant amount of development work was still required. Often, the original research was performed under government grants. In other cases, especially apparent at MIT, the university encouraged faculty members to do outside consulting work for industry. When the consulting work begins to mushroom, colleagues or students are recruited to help and soon a company is born.

For companies in extremely advanced technologies, a continuing relationship with the academic community not only keeps the senior staff informed of new research developments, but helps the company acquire the most competent technical personnel.

Evidently, relationships with universities are important not only in conducting basic research, but in producing products based on that research, and not only in founding new businesses, but in updating personnel and speeding product development in existing companies.

The 1984 study by the Office of Technology Assessment expanded on these points (p. 30): "Four basic benefits can result from locating a research or science park near a university. First, increased interaction and easier communication between industry and university researchers helps to broaden mutual understanding of problems and needs. Second, business gains quicker access to new developments through increased information and knowledge transfer. Third, business also gains access to student works and faculty consultants, as well as laboratory, computer, library, and other resources. Finally, the increased interaction opens opportunities for creating new businesses and new university/industry programs."

In summarizing their study on economic development, the Joint Economic Committee indicated (1982, p. 56):

The attraction of high technology companies to university-based communities is no accident. Universities contribute significantly to advances in basic science that high technology companies crave, but spawning new ideas is only one step in encouraging high technology industries. Entrepreneurs with the instinctive ability to capitalize on new applications and transfer these new ideas into profitable enterprises are an essential ingredient. . . . High technology entrepreneurs are a breed apart from the entrepreneurs of traditional industries. . . . Success depends upon continuously seeking new applications of science and overcoming the remaining barriers, technical and financial, to the application of new ideas and technology. In short, venture capitalists, high technology entrepreneurs, universities, real estate developers, and aggressive leadership and promotion are the 'infrastructure' for the development of high technology centers.

Engstrom (1987, p. 31) gave an example of the perceived importance of a nearby university to the success of a research park: "If a park lacks a great university nearby, it may be able to find one willing to set up a 'branch office.' When Montgomery County, Maryland officials conceived of R&D Village—a 1200-acre biotechnology research complex that will eventually consist of research facilities, housing, hotels, shopping centers, and a health club—they recognized that a major academic presence was lacking, even though the complex was to be anchored by the Shady Grove Life Sciences Center, home to several government research agencies. So the Montgomery County office of economic development convinced several institutions to initiate programs at the site: Johns Hopkins University is represented by a teaching faculty, while the University of Maryland and the National Bureau of Standards have jointly established a Center for Advanced Research in Biotechnology, specializing in protein engineering and drug design."

　　2. *Success/failure of research/industrial parks.* Examples of successful parks cited by the Office of Technology Assessment include the Stanford Industrial Park, the Research Triangle Park in North Carolina, and the University of Utah Research Park. Other successes include Princeton Forrestal Center, Purdue Industrial Research Park, University City Science Center (involving twenty-eight colleges and universities in or near Philadelphia), Swearingen Research Park (associated with the Univer-

sity of Oklahoma), Ann Arbor Technology Park, Advanced Technology Development Center at Georgia Institute of Technology, New Haven Science Park, Central Florida Research Park, Rensselaer Technology Park, Tennessee Technology Corridor, and Morgantown Industrial and Research Park in West Virginia.

Although a few of these partnerships have been spectacularly successful, not all efforts to copy the achievements of the Research Triangle Park or the Stanford Industrial Park have been equally remarkable. Schmidt (1984, p. 37) reported that only 50 percent of the university-related science parks have been successful. The Battelle Institute (1983a, p. 7), citing Baughman (1982), reported that in a study of "more than two dozen science/research parks that were affiliated with or started by universities in the United States since the 1950's. . . . Approximately six were clearly successful, sixteen to eighteen were failures because they attracted no industries or substantially fewer than planned, and five to six were still in some stage of development."

Table 8. Technology Research Parks:
University-Affiliated Developments.

Arizona State Univ. Research Park 2105 Elliot Rd. Tempe, AZ 85284 Acres 323 Date est. 1983　　　　Tenants 3	New Haven Science Park Yale Univ. Science Park Devel. Corp. 5 Science Park New Haven, CT 06511 Acres 80 Date est. 1981　　　　Tenants 82
Engineering Research Ctr. College of Engineering, Univ. of Arkansas Fayetteville, AR 72701 Acres 23 Date est. 1982　　　　Tenants 0	Univ. Research Park at Lewes Univ. of Delaware Newark, DE 19716 Acres 100 Date est. 1979　　　　Tenants 0
Stanford Industrial Park Lands Management, Stanford Univ. 209 Hamilton Ave. Palo Alto, CA 94301 Acres 660 Date est. 1951　　　　Tenants 80	Innovation Park (Florida State Univ. & Florida A&M) 1673 W. Paul Birac Dr. Tallahassee, FL 32304 Acres 208 Date est. 1979　　　　Tenants 2
Univ. of Connecticut-Storrs 352 Mansfield, Univ. of Connecticut Storrs, CT 06268 Acres 390 Date est. 1982　　　　Tenants 0	Central Florida Research Park Univ. of Central Florida 11800 Research Pkwy.

Table 8. Technology Research Parks:
University-Affiliated Developments, *Cont'd.*

Orlando, FL 32826
Acres 1400
Date est. 1981   Tenants 14

Univ. of Florida Research
& Technology Park
Progress Center, Grinter Hall
Univ. of Florida
Gainesville, FL 32611
Acres 2200
Date est. 1983   Tenants 6

Advanced Technology Devel. Ctr.
Georgia Tech.
Research & Communications
430 Tenth St., NW
Atlanta, GA 30318
Acres 3
Date est. 1980   Tenants 16

Evanston/Univ. Research Park
Northwestern Univ.
Evanston Inventure, 1710 Orrinton Ave.
Evanston, IL 60201
Acres 26
Date est. 1985   Tenants 0

Purdue Industrial Research Park
Purdue Research Foundation
Hovde Hall
W. Lafayette, IN 47907
Acres 177
Date est. 1961   Tenants 25

Northern Kentucky Univ. Foundation
Research/Technology Park
Northern Kentucky Univ. Foundation
Highland Heights, KY 41076
Acres 75
Date est. 1980   Tenants 1

Maryland Science Technology Ctr.
Univ. of Maryland Foundation
Adelphi, MD 20783
Acres 466
Date est. 1983   Tenants 1

University Park
Mass. Inst. of Technology
Cambridge, MA 02139
Acres 27
Date est. 1983   Tenants 0

Geddes Center
Eastern Mich. Univ. & Univ. of Mich.
3040 N. Prospect
Ypsilanti, MI 48197
Acres 508
Date est. 1985   Tenants 0

Ann Arbor Technology Park
Univ. of Michigan
Wood & Co., 21C Ft. Evans Rd.
Leesburg, VA 22075
Acres 820
Date est. 1960   Tenants 15

Dandini Research Park
Univ. of Nevada
Desert Research Inst., Box 60220
Reno, NV 89506
Acres 470
Date est. 1984   Tenants 0

Princeton Forrestal Ctr.
Princeton Univ.
105 College Rd. East
Princeton, NJ 08540
Acres 1750
Date est. 1974   Tenants 50

Univ. of New Mexico Research Park
Scholes Hall
Albuquerque, NM 87131
Acres 90
Date est. 1965   Tenants 2

Rensselaer Technology Park
Rensselaer Polytechnic Inst.
100 Jordan Rd.
Troy, NY 12180
Acres 1200
Date est. 1981   Tenants 26

Research Triangle Park
Univ. of N. Carolina,
Duke U., N. Carolina St.
Research Triangle Foundation
Box 12255
Research Triangle Park, NC 27709
Acres 6551
Date est. 1959   Tenants 47

University Research Park
Univ. of North Carolina–Charlotte

Table 8. Technology Research Parks:
University-Affiliated Developments, *Cont'd.*

Charlotte, NC 28282	Tenn. Technology Foundation, Box 23184
Acres 2800	Knoxville, TN 37933
Date est. 1966 Tenants 11	Acres 2200
	Date est. 1982 Tenants 97
University Research Complex	
Ohio State Univ.	Texas A&M Univ. Research Park
Univ. Research Complex	Research Park, Texas A&M Univ.
200 Sullivant Hall	College Station, TX 77843
Columbus, OH 43210	Acres 434
Acres 200	Date est. 1984 Tenants 0
Date est. 1981 Tenants 3	
	Univ. of Utah Research Park
Miami Valley Research Park	Research Park, 505 Water Way
Wright State U., Univ. of Dayton,	Salt Lake City, UT 84108
Sinclair Comm. College,	Acres 320
Central State Univ.	Date est. 1970 Tenants 51
Mead Corp., Courthouse Plaza	
Dayton, OH 45401	Virginia Tech Corporate Research Ctr.
Acres 1500	220 Burruss Hall, Virginia Tech
Date est. 1980 Tenants 3	Blacksburg, VA 24061
	Acres 120
Swearingen Research Park	Date est. 1985 Tenants 0
Real Estate Devel. Office	
Univ. of Oklahoma	Washington State Univ.
1000 Asp Ave., Rm. 210	Research & Technology Park
Norman, OK 73019	Research Park, 432 French Admin.
Acres 600	Bldg.
Date est. 1958 Tenants 20	Pullman, WA 99164
	Acres 158
Univ. City Science Center	Date est. 1982 Tenants 0
3624 Market St.	
Philadelphia, PA 19104	Morgantown Industrial
Acres 16	& Research Park
Date est. 1964 Tenants 80	W. Virginia Univ.
	1000 Dupont Rd., Bldg. 510
Carolina Research Park	Morgantown, WV 26505
Univ. of South Carolina–Columbia	Acres 670
South Carolina Research Authority	Date est. 1983 Tenants 8
Box 12025	
Columbia, SC 29211	University Research Park
Acres 580	Univ. of Wisconsin–Madison
Date est. 1983 Tenants 1	946 WARF Bldg., 610 Walnut St.
	Madison, WI 53705
Tennessee Technology Corridor	Acres 217
Univ. of Tennessee	Date est. 1982 Tenants 2

Note: The research parks listed here are either operating or under active development, although appropriating funds, gaining neighborhood approval, and completing construction have become a lengthy process for some. Another ten to twenty parks are in early planning stages.

Source: Adapted from Glazer, 1986, p. 44.

High Technology (Glazer, 1986, p. 44) listed the thirty-five university-affiliated technology research parks that currently were operating or under active development (see Table 8), noting that another ten or twenty were in the early planning stages. Ten of the parks were established before 1975, and twenty-five were established after 1975. Only seven of the parks established after 1975 had attracted more than five businesses, a fact that illustrates the patience that may be required to nurture a research park to maturity. *Venture* magazine (Farrell, 1983) included a similar description of research centers. Its list included specialties of the centers and named the universities, government entities, and base companies that were involved. The *Venture* study did not confine itself to research parks only, although research parks were included under its definition of research centers.

Glazer (1986, p. 47) noted that the "perfect combination" for a successful research park is "world class research talent, the infrastructure of a nearby metropolis, and a thriving financial community." She also referred to a statement by Money (director of the Texas A&M University Research Park): "One of the main prerequisites for a development's success is simply staying power . . . [so that] intelligent management can improve the odds. . . . The success of most university parks will depend on how well they are able to identify the university's strengths and market them" (pp. 46–47). Money emphasized the importance of site development, noting that "Arizona State is spending $15 million up front for roads, utilities, and landscaping—before commitment from any tenants—and Texas A&M will spend $6 million for site development before breaking ground for buildings" (p. 42). Glazer explained: "Standards have risen, and with some 40 parks underway nationwide, fledgling companies can be choosier" (p. 42). Regarding the success of research/industrial parks, the Battelle Institute noted (1983b, p. 6):

> The more successful parks involve the university as a core resource, rather than as an "available" activity in the general area. Still, not all such state-generated activities have been successful. Research and science park projects

sponsored by the universities themselves have failed in almost all cases. The projects sponsored [in isolation by major developers] have failed in a majority of cases. The "high technology" parks that have achieved some degree of success usually contain many more distribution, service, light manufacturing, and office jobs than they do positions related to science and technological types of activities. The probabilities of success for these ventures increase dramatically when a community-wide, diversified approach is taken, involving active participation by the university, private developers, representatives of local high technology industries, and community leaders. When any one of these is missing, the chances for success decline rapidly.

On the subject of factors contributing to the success of research parks, Schmidt (1984, p. 37) quoted Orr, vice-chancellor for research and public service at the University of North Carolina at Charlotte, as saying, "It's absolutely critical to get the commitment of a large, well-established company to establish a research park." To explain this position, Schmidt referred to the 1984 Office of Technology Assessment study, which pointed out that 88 percent of high-technology jobs are found in companies with multiple plants and branches. As the second most important criterion for success of research parks, Schmidt cited seeking as occupants "start-up companies offering new products or services." She stated, "Their appeal lies in the possibility that their product will become popular and make employment soar."

Schmidt also listed two main reasons for failure of research parks, saying: "One of the main reasons that about 50 percent of research-park ventures have not succeeded in getting out of the planning stages, or have become little more than high-quality industrial parks . . . is that their locations offer no possibility for interaction with a high technology or scientific community, such as a university, a government facility or an industrial complex. . . . Also, many developers do not realize that a minimum of ten years and as many as twenty are usually needed to establish a base of local employers" (p. 37).

The Battelle Institute (1983a, pp. 7–8) listed a number of common characteristics of successful high-technology sites:

- They often are land-intensive—characterized by suburban locations involving large tracts, deep setbacks, specified low densities, requirements related to off-street parking, and other needs that consume space.
- They all have very definite ties to major universities with recognized science and engineering programs.
- Their periods of development have been much longer than is normally recognized—and in virtually every case have involved fifteen to thirty years.
- They have been very aggressively and professionally marketed by economic development groups, as well as by private firms.
- They have well-developed linkages to a wide range of high technology and traditional industries and activities in their region.
- They boast a number of incentives such as financial inducements, available buildings, and other recognized strengths.
- Their current success is built upon past successes—and their marketing efforts stress the wide range of scientific and high technology activities that they have already attracted—serving as proof of their excellence. . . .
- Many of these successful developments have unique "anchor projects" (such as microelectronics).

The Battelle Institute also listed (1983a, pp. 8–9) a number of reasons for failure of high-technology sites:

- They had no real reasons for being, and were not linked to any other high technology or scientific activity, such as a university with necessary science and engineering programs, a government facility, or an industrial complex.
- The projects were poorly organized, were not well planned, and were limited in terms of funding.
- They received insufficient or poor quality sales promotion to acquaint prospects with their advantages.
- They tended to have high purchase and lease costs.
- Land sale was the main thrust in several cases; no investment was made in starter or incubator space.
- Physical locations were poor, especially in terms of available acreage, types of construction, highway access, utilities, public services, access to air transportation, physical layout, and—especially significant—the types of speculative or available structures.

- Convenants related to zoning and construction were too restrictive.
- The development lacked the type of living and working environment that appeals to scientists and engineers.
- Interaction between the tenants or developers of the park and the nearby academic and/or scientific community was lacking. . . .
- The true science parks have usually failed because their restrictions rigorously defining scientific and technical activities eliminated too many prospects. High technology parks have a much greater chance of success, but even here it is sometimes necessary to accept a wide range of activities (in manufacturing, services, and distribution).

Research and Technical Centers. In addition to research/industrial parks, universities have established research and technical centers, frequently located in campus facilities and funded by the institutions themselves, with some help from federal research grants. Sometimes state legislatures have made special contributions to speed the process of technology transfer, often through building or remodeling facilities.

Typically, research and technical centers have been established so that university-based researchers can explore questions posed by corporations, on the assumption that most direct costs will be offset by corporate support, over time. An instance is Carnegie-Mellon University's Robotics Institute, which, with more than two hundred scientists and engineers, has become the world's largest industry-financed center for research in robotics and manufacturing technology. Some major centers have been funded by state governments in the hope that they will serve as magnets to lure to the areas other corporations interested in particular research topics or will spur growth of companies already located there. The existence of the Microelectronics Center of North Carolina was a major factor in General Electric's decision to build a $50 million integrated circuit plant in Research Triangle Park (Joint Economic Committee, 1982, p. 50), for example. Initial research awards often can be used to attract additional funds, sometimes several times the original amount. As the 1984 Office of Technology Assessement study indicated (p. 30), funding for the University of Minnesota's

Microelectronics and Information Sciences Center included $6 million in corporate money from Control Data, Honeywell, 3-M, and Sperry, in addition to the $1.5 million in federal research awards and $1.5 million from the state legislature that were attracted in 1983.

In 1985, New Mexico entered into a cooperative relationship with local industries and the federal government in an effort to promote high-technology development in the state. The Rio Grande Technology Foundation (Riotech) is a nonprofit corporation allied with the University of New Mexico and Sandia National Laboratory, as well as with three founding corporate sponsors: the *Albuquerque Journal,* Westinghouse Electric Corporation, and Johnson & Johnson ("New Group Bodes Well," 1985). Riotech sponsors engineering research at the University of New Mexico, the New Mexico Institute of Mining and Technology, and New Mexico State University. In this case, funding is from private grants and fees, with no special state allocation involved.

In the 1980s, following relaxation of prohibitive antitrust laws, industrial research consortia began to form in the United States. Examples include the Microelectronics and Computer Technology Corporation, the Semiconductor Research Corporation, the Software Productivity Consortium, International Partners in Glass Research, the Center for Advanced Television Studies, and the Guided Wave Optoelectronics Manufacturing Technology Development Program. Industrial research consortia vary in their involvement in cooperative research projects with universities. Whereas the Semiconductor Research Corporation has funded university-based projects, the Microelectronics and Computer Technology Corporation has its own research facilities, which are staffed in part by member companies.

Technical Assistance and Consulting Services. More modest efforts to broker relationships between on-campus expertise and corporate research and development needs have become extremely common. Some examples are provided here.

1. *Relationships via individual faculty members.* Creation of research parks and centers usually occurs at large and wealthy— or land rich—universities that have research missions and are

already heavily involved in major, federally sponsored research programs. Many faculty members at such universities are also directly involved as individuals in consulting relationships with companies. Faculty consulting services may take the form of providing technical assistance in transferring technology from the laboratory to marketable products or solving specific manufacturing, production, management, or marketing programs. A common university policy is to allow one day per week (usually defined as Monday through Friday) as the limit for outside consulting activities. A few institutions require that consulting be confined to weekends.

In general, consulting arrangements grow out of mutual business–higher education appreciation of needs and values and a common wish to avoid new investment. Faculty members have appreciated the additional personal income and research support generated by work on industrial problems. In many fields, significant support for graduate students has also been generated.

Consulting with businesses or industries is not confined to faculties of research institutions. In reporting the results of a major study, Logan and Stampen (1985, pp. 26–28) noted that about one-fourth of the institutions responding indicated that they had quite extensive and complex relationships with industry. Generally, these institutions regarded consulting activities as consistent with university goals. Most of the institutions had policies that limited faculty time devoted to consulting and required reimbursement for university materials and facilities.

Logan and Stampen pointed out that faculty members at comprehensive institutions may have degrees from highly regarded research universities and may be competent to undertake research efforts, even if research is not part of the missions of their employer institutions, and even if campus facilities are limited. Many of the comprehensive institutions indicated (p. 28) that they viewed consulting as a trigger for other kinds of endeavors, and that consulting activities served the interests of both the educational institutions and the businesses involved by keeping faculty members conversant with recent developments in their fields, better preparing students, improving productivity, and promoting regional economic development. In fact, in

November 1986, the American Association of State Colleges and Universities issued a statement urging its members ''to adopt economic development as a major responsibility'' (p. 1).

2. *Formal arrangements to aid technology transfer through contacts with faculty members.* Consulting services provided by faculty members may be organized in a wide variety of ways. Some examples follow:

a. Centers and laboratories that specialize in problem solving for firms in particular industries have been common for decades within schools of agriculture, pharmacy, engineering, and business at colleges and universities from coast to coast. Industries have not needed to duplicate laboratories, equipment, test plots, or staff when mutually satisfactory arrangements could be made to share university-based personnel and facilities at relatively modest costs.

b. Industrial liaison programs encourage faculty consulting for industrial members. In general, such programs are an excellent means of establishing communications between a department or school and industrial research managers. Industrial firms are invited to become members of a school or department's industrial liaison program for a modest fee. In return, the department solicits research advice and annually presents a research seminar in which their graduates describe their research to the industrial members. This allows industrial participants to observe potential employees. Industrial members often provide grants for graduate support. Industrial liaison programs also may provide short courses for continuing professional education to technical employees of member companies. They are normally most effective when administered at the departmental or school level. The Massachusetts Institute of Technology has had a university-wide industrial liaison program that has operated at a substantial level, but few universities have been able to match this type of success with university-wide liaison programs.

c. A number of states have established university-based advanced technology centers to mobilize the talent and expertise of faculty members to serve business and industry. Challenge grants may be provided for which individual companies can apply jointly with cooperating colleges. Winners of challenge grants receive state funding for projects equal to whatever is pledged by companies. States provide such grants to foster economic development by helping companies become successful and thereby creating—or at least saving—jobs.

A premise underlying state support often is that accommodation to changing technology promotes business success by providing a competitive edge in quality control, productivity of employees, choices of materials, and application of improved production technologies. All companies, not only high-technology companies, can benefit from such changes. Releasing faculty members from some teaching obligations and mobilizing some graduate students to work with companies to define problems, propose alternative solutions, and follow through on implementation may foster success of smaller or outdated companies.

The Benjamin Franklin Partnership in Pennsylvania is an example of a major challenge-grant program. Four advanced technology centers have been established by the state to engage in cooperative research and development projects; provide education, training, and retraining programs in areas crucial to expansion of both established and startup firms; and provide entrepreurial assistance services (Pennsylvania Department of Commerce, 1985):

- North East Tier Advanced Technology Center—located at Lehigh University; involves 69 other private and public colleges, 447 private sector firms, and 70 foundations and other organizations; performs research in CAD/CAM, materials, microelectronics, and biotechnology.
- Advanced Technology Center of Southeastern Pennsylvania—located in the University City Science Center; includes the University of Pennsylvania, Drexel University, Temple University, and over 30 other public and private institutions, plus 350 firms and other private sector organizations; performs research in sensor technologies, space productivity and adaptability, medical/biotechnologies, and materials engineering and processing.
- Western Pennsylvania Advanced Technology Center—located at the University of Pittsburgh/Carnegie-Mellon

University; involves 37 other public and private institutions, and over 250 private firms; performs research in robotics and computers, advanced technology materials, processes and devices, and biotechnology.

• Advanced Technology Center of Central/Northern Pennsylvania—located at the Pennsylvania State University; includes 34 other institutions and 238 private sector firms and other organizations; performs research in food and plant production and processing, coal and mineral production, processing, and utilization, biotechnology, and manufacturing, management, and control systems.

During the 1985–1986 fiscal year, Pennsylvania appropriated $21.3 million to the centers, and consortia members contributed $80.9 million, including $53.8 million in support from the private sector. The total of $102.2 million was used to support 379 projects in 1985–1986.

Ohio's Thomas Edison Program has three main thrusts: the Edison Seed Development Fund, the Edison Technology Centers, and the Edison Incubators. The Edison Seed Development Program offers grants (to be matched by contributions from private sources) of $10,000 to $50,000 for early-stage research projects. Technology centers focus on cooperative research projects in promising areas of research, which currently include welding, integrated manufacturing, polymers, animal genetics, and data base management. Incubators have been established in Akron, Columbus, Miami Valley, Youngstown, Springfield, and Cleveland.

d. As Williams (executive secretary of the National Association of Management and Technical Assistance) noted (Turner, 1987, p. 14), technology-extension services, modeled after agricultural-extension services, have been started by many state universities and land-grant colleges. Some—such as the University of Tennessee's Center for Industrial Services—call upon regular faculty members to diagnose problems and recommend solutions, and others—such as the Georgia Institute of Technology's Research Institute—employ technicians full time. Services are free and focus on short-term projects.

Marlow (director of the Pennsylvania Technical Assistance Program at the Pennsylvania State University) reported benefits from the program's services "of $17.1 to 1 on a dollar-to-dollar ratio"; that is, the $775,000 annual program budget yielded more than $13 million in benefits. Center staff included eight engineers, two information coordinators, and two librarians. Marlow estimated that the center solves "1,000 to 1,400 technical problems a year, half for small businesses and half for local governments, hospitals, and state agencies" (Turner, 1987, p. 14).

The Ohio Technology Transfer Organization (OTTO), started in 1978, commits Ohio's two- and four-year colleges to provide technological assistance in their service regions through a network of thirty-four agents located across the state. Information provided often is related to new technologies, materials, equipment, and management methods. Linking the network through Ohio State University enables a broad-based pool of talent to be tapped as required.

The University of Nebraska operates the Nebraska Technical Assistance Center with help from grants from the Department of Economic Development and the Economic Development Administration of the U.S. Department of Commerce. Center staff travel across the state calling on businesses to offer assistance and bring in appropriate faculty members, as required.

e. The Illinois Research Network (IRN) is a statewide electronic directory of faculty resources (Illinois Research Network, n.d.). The directory can identify faculty at seven Illinois universities who have the expertise to meet particular needs of business, government, and education across the nation. A glossary of 6,500 subject terms helps to identify faculty members with needed talents from among thousands of profiles on line. Eight IRN search offices help locate talent to consult on special projects, conduct research and development, speak at conferences, develop proposals, identify testing facilities and laboratories, conduct employee training and in-service seminars, provide expert testimony, evaluate applications of new technologies, provide technical assistance, stage artistic performances, and conduct community programs. The network states that it "does not enter into the interview or negotiation process between faculty and interested parties. It does not evaluate or make judgments about faculty or the information contained in their profiles.''

f. Small business training and research centers such as the Center for Entrepreneurship and Small Business Management at Wichita State University and the Center for Entrepreneurial Studies and Development, Inc., at West Virginia University not only advise owners of established businesses, but help persons with marketable ideas develop plans for founding new businesses, including providing information about how to get venture capital, how to build management teams, and how to deal with problems of production and marketing.

g. The National Aeronautics and Space Administration (NASA) sponsors a number of centers to inform business about technology resulting from NASA-sponsored research. The NIAC (NASA Industrial Applications Center) at the University of Pittsburgh has broadened its services to include not only access to some 400 data bases worldwide, but access to faculty members to advise on technology-transfer problems. In 1984, more than 130 faculty members served the Pittsburgh NIAC and its clients as consultants or solicited information for their own research in technical and nontechnical subject areas, activities that led to generation of $11.39 from external funding sources for every dollar invested in the NIAC by the university. More than 750 clients in industry; health care systems; federal, state, and local governments; and education forwarded requests for assistance in 1984 from throughout the Northeast and a number of foreign countries. The Pittsburgh NIAC also organizes seminars and conferences and engages in electronic publishing.

h. Small business development centers (SBDCs), subsidized by the Small Business Administration of the U.S. Department of Commerce, are located on several hundred college campuses to provide advisors to small businesses on a wide array of subjects. Faculty members may advise owners of small businesses on designing business plans, analyzing markets, and devising advertising strategies. They also provide up-to-date information on legal issues; management, accounting, and employment practices; and other important matters. In 1985, according to the *Chronicle of Higher Education* ("U.S. Programs That Help Colleges . . . ," 1986, p. 22), the centers received $18.2 million from universities, $13.1 million from state governments, $5.9 million from private sources, and $3.4 million users fees to more than match the $28.5 million federal allocation, as required by law.

Incubator Centers. Incubator centers are intended to provide an environment in which small or newly emerging businesses may be nurtured during the difficult embryonic years when company failures are common. Incubators usually charge modest rents and typically are located in existing, vacant buildings. So that fledgling companies need not pay high overhead costs during their formative stages, incubator facilities often provide centralized services that can be called upon by any of the occupants of the building, as required. Secretarial services, mailing lists, photocopying facilities, accounting services, legal advice, library services, computer use, and access to graduate students as researchers are among the services available at reasonable costs, so that companies need not divert limited start-up funds until cash flow can support fuller staffing. Faculty members at nearby sponsoring universities may provide fledgling companies with management advice concerning development of business plans, alternative sources of financing, or marketing studies. They also may assist by solving technical problems or teaching needed courses. Some of the businesses served by a university in an incubator center may be founded by members of its faculty.

Businesses remain in incubators for various lengths of time, depending on their success and the rules of the individual facility. Some incubators encourage companies to remain, if space permits, even after they have emerged from the embryonic stage. A 1985 study by the National Council for Urban Economic Development (NCUED) surveyed seventy incubator facilities and determined that "almost twice as many firms survive to move out as failed while there. This compares favorably to the general business environment, where roughly four times as many fail as succeed during their first five years" (p. 3).

Most incubators are organized as collaborative efforts by local governments and colleges or universities, although private corporations may play a role in providing facilities. The Battelle Institute (1983b, p. 6) commented on the success of incubators: ''Some of the most successful incubator projects have involved guaranteed demands for goods and services—such as computer support. A majority of the incubator projects found across the United States are still based largely on the endowments provided by their parent universities.'' The moral is, of course, that universities that hope to make significant sums of money by opening incubators may be disappointed, unless they are canny and lucky enough to sponsor firms that turn out to be great successes.

State funds also are being allocated to develop incubators— as, for example, at the Georgia Institute of Technology, which operates the Advanced Technology Development Center, one of the first state-sponsored incubator facilities. Not only are states appropriating funds to state-owned educational institutions to operate incubators, they are sponsoring loan programs serving other kinds of organizations interested in developing incubators as a means of improving the employment bases in their communities. By 1985, after a state-funded Small Business Incubator Loan Program had been established in Pennsylvania, for example, nearly forty incubators had been developed, more than in any other state.

1. *RPI incubator.* A successful incubator has been developed at Rensselaer Polytechnic Institute by remodeling an old building and renting space to startup companies (LeMaistre, 1984, p. 8). The management department at Rensselaer helps inexperienced companies develop plans and seek financing. The engineering and science faculties assist in resolving technical problems. When a company expands sufficiently, it may move into a 1,200-acre technology park owned by Rensselaer. The university has also developed a Center for Interactive Graphics, a Center for Manufacturing Productivity and Technology Transfer, and a Center for Integrated Electronics—all of which serve the advanced technology needs of the companies that support them financially. An interest-free loan from the state of New

York is allowing Rensselaer to build a Center for Industrial Innovation, which will house the three centers and help the institution initiate programs—such as courses in computer-assisted design and manufacturing—to serve businesses and help industries retain professionals. An incubator that is focused on high-technology firms, has a strong faculty in the sciences at an associated institution, and supports research centers cosponsored by industry and the institution can be expected to provide an environment conducive to economic development of the surrounding area.

According to Mahone (director of the Rensselaer Incubator Program), growth has been rapid; although the incubator started in a basement in 1980, by 1982 it had acquired an Economic Development Administration grant and was occupying 40,000 square feet. Its goal is simple: to "grow" successful companies. Mahone (1985) observed that many faculty members did not unite in favor of the incubator until some company successes indicated that fruitful ideas could be nourished effectively in such a setting. The institute requires a 2 percent or larger equity interest in all companies in the incubator. Rensselaer has variable rent, starting at $6.00 per square foot during the first two years of tenancy, with increases thereafter. Occupants are asked to sign one-year leases and draw up business plans, formalities that are not required by some other incubators, such as the science park in New Haven.

Investors constantly visit incubator centers that are associated with universities. At Rensselaer, they ask about products and technologies being developed and visit with founders of companies in residence. The director of the incubator encourages faculty members to develop consulting relationships at whatever rates they can negotiate. Relationships of faculty members with companies inevitably are limited by university policy; for example, one day per week is allowed for consulting. Some departments or schools are quite conservative and do less to encourage these relationships.

2. *New Haven Science Park.* In New Haven, Connecticut, a nonprofit corporation called the Science Park Development Corporation was founded in 1982, sponsored by Olin Corporation,

Yale University, and the city of New Haven. The state of Connecticut also has provided major support. Each founder has one representative on the twelve-member board of directors. As of November 1985, according to Chauncey (president of the corporation), eighty entrepreneurial companies were occupying 200,000 square feet in two incubator buildings. A new building for a subsidiary of the Southern New England Telephone Company and several additional buildings for new tenants requiring larger quarters were under development. The Economic Development Administration of the federal government had granted funds to be matched by the city and state for rehabilitation programs. As of January 1986, the city had invested $1 million, the state over $2 million, and private sources over $5 million in the centers. Increased federal and private investments were anticipated.

Chauncey (1985) indicated that the incubator centers have low rents ($7.50 to $10.50 per square foot per year), including heat, electricity, and air conditioning. Various services, such as telephone answering, typing, copying, and computer rental, are for sale as used. Companies are given access to resources at Yale, including library, purchasing, and faculty consulting services; insurance; student employees; and proximity to other companies started in New Haven by faculty members. Chauncey noted that contacts with alumni are of particularly great value to companies in the incubators because many ideas and referrals important to their success have come through such contacts. Although the corporation is independent, Yale has loaned it money—at usual interest and terms. Chauncey made an important point when he called Science Park (Science Park Development Corp., 1984, pp. 8–9) "first and foremost a real estate development . . . [since] it is income from land leases, development fees and related real estate activity that will be the main source of our funding for the future."

Importance of State Support to Cooperative Programs

A 1984 report by the Office of Technology Assessment of the U.S. Congress identified (pp. 44–45) a number of initiatives used by regional and local organizations to attract high-technology industry. These include land-use actions—planning and zoning regulations—vocational-technical training, incubator buildings, marketing programs, high-technology task forces, and venture capital funds. State government also may become productively involved in many of these efforts.

In addition, the desire for university improvements was cited as an important incentive. For example, investment in engineering schools was favored by a number of state legislatures during the early 1980s. Arizona sought $50 million over five years to establish Arizona State University as a high-quality engineering center; the state has appropriated $20 million for new buildings, and industry has contributed $10 million for equipment. Most of the funds raised by the $90 million bond issue approved in 1984 by New Jersey voters was designated to improve engineering programs in state educational institutions. In 1985, the Nevada legislature appropriated almost $15 million for a new engineering building at the University of Nevada. Florida allocated $7.7 million to engineering schools in 1985, in addition to $4 million for high-technology and research development.

State funding of research and advanced training opportunities is another highly effective incentive. An instance is the ongoing support for research and graduate student training in microelectronics and computer sciences and their applications provided in California by the Microelectronics Innovation and Computer Opportunities Program (MICRO), initiated in 1981. In 1985, $3.4 million in state funds and $8.0 million in industrial contributions supported some ninety projects.

The Office of Technology Assessment reported (1984, pp. 48–49) that providing sustained local effort over a period of decades; identifying local needs and resources; adapting to external constraints; linking initiatives to other broader development efforts; and taking local initiatives and forming partnerships to establish, implement, and operate programs are factors affecting success in attracting high-technology industries. These factors and others such as tax policies; leadership by governors and mayors; and influence by legislators, university presidents, and boards of trustees also have direct bearing on the success of university-industry partnerships in effecting economic change.

Figure 4 shows the "bootstrap effect" that states hope their funding of university research will have on economic development.

Figure 4. "Bootstrap" Effect of State Actions.

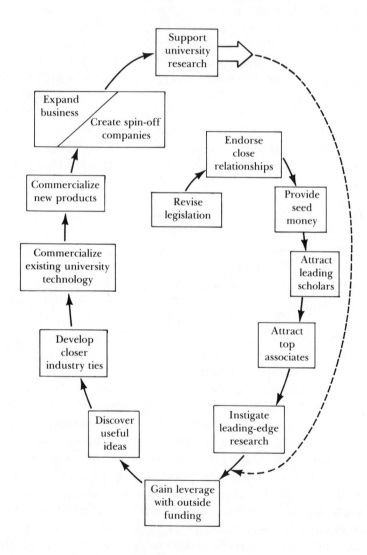

Source: Advisory Committee to the Texas Senate Committee on Business, Technology, and Education, 1985, p. 3. Used by permission.

As the 1983 U.S. General Accounting Office Report (p. 50) implies, leadership by those with power over policy and appropriations is required to nourish potentially fruitful program initiatives, and absence of leadership can guarantee that initiatives will never be created. For this reason, strong leadership is required at the campus, corporate, and local and state government levels to initiate and sustain networks of efforts of maximum productivity between universities and businesses.

Of course, action can be taken by colleges and universities to cooperate with companies without significant involvement or assistance from political leaders and government. Most programs that have been successful in inducing large-scale, regional economic change, however, have required direct, sustained action by political leaders to support legislation, appropriate funds, and record priorities. In fact, in case after case, programs having an investment multiplier effect and marked impact on economic development (often, by tapping into the generative cycle described in Figure 4) occur in states and institutions where public leaders have proved their commitment by designating significant funds. This is not surprising, given the fact that successful research partnerships require first-tier faculties and up-to-date facilities. Involvement at the state level also can be important in strengthening programs of technical colleges and vocational training schools to allow them to respond faster and with better quality to the needs of emerging industries.

A State-Level Organization to Promote Partnerships. According to the Maryland State Board for Higher Education (1986, p. 9), state initiatives for promoting technological innovation should include "(1) sponsoring research and development at universities and companies; (2) improving the educational system from elementary education to graduate school; (3) training workers in the technical skills required by high technology companies; (4) encouraging university/industry linkages so that industrial innovators can draw on academic resources; and (5) economically supporting and providing incentives for growth of technology based firms."

Using North Carolina as a model, Lindsey (1985, p. 88) described university-industry-government partnerships as "essential to economic growth." It follows, according to Lindsey, that states need to create organizations to design policies and strategies that will ensure that scientific and engineering resources are directed effectively to meet state needs. Lindsey recommended that such organizations include representatives from research and education institutions, business and industry, state and local governments, and other interest groups.

In addition to promoting partnerships, Lindsey noted, such a state-level organization must consult with people statewide to identify public and private sector needs and opportunities, particularly those that are affected by scientific and engineering resources, and devise immediate and long-term objectives. Lindsey gave as examples of projects the creation by North Carolina of the North Carolina School of Science and Mathematics to promote improvements in education, and the creation of the Microelectronics Center of North Carolina and the North Carolina Biotechnology Center to strengthen research in fields on the frontier of scientific advance.

Lindsey also recommended that the state-level organization must decide how to meet crucial needs when no organization currently exists in the government structure for that purpose. As examples, he noted North Carolina's development organizations, incubator facilities, and venture capital firms, which were designed to meet the needs of fledgling companies. He emphasized: "The common feature of state efforts should be the *identification* and *removal* of public barriers and disincentives to industry/university cooperation and technological innovation; and the *creation* of incentives" (1985, p. 89). Lindsey also recommended that the state organization foster cooperation between universities and industrial firms.

Lindsey gave several reasons why state government plays an essential catalytic and supportive role in promoting use of scientific research by the public and private sectors to meet their needs:

1. Most university research and development is conducted at the 184 research universities, of which 119 are public institutions. Many of the 65 private institutions also receive state support in some form.

2. Community colleges and elementary and secondary schools are entirely supported by state and local governments.

3. Most forms of economic activity "exist and function within state boundaries and relate closely to state and local governments. These units of government are the prime points of contact with respect to locational issues, labor relations, environmental management, provision of capital, living conditions for employees, and other facets of economic activity that entail industry-government interaction" (p. 90).

4. The governor of a state can play a unique role in bringing together representatives of state and local governments, businesses and industries, and colleges and universities.

Lindsey made a key point when he emphasized (p. 88): "Fostering effective and expeditious use of scientific and engineering resources in relation to the civilian economy of our nation is the role of state governments . . . the partnership relations among industry, universities and government, relations essential to innovative institutional development and economic growth, are best fostered at state and local levels of government."

Financial Incentives and Examples of State Initiatives. A variety of federal, state, local, and private financial incentives have contributed to university-industry and economic development partnerships. The Office of Technology Assessment study (1984, p. 47) gave examples of key federal programs, such as Urban Development Action Grants, Industrial Development Bonds, Economic Development Administration Grants, and Community Development Block Grants. Federal funds have also been available for university-industry partnerships through the Jobs Training Partnership Act, Small Business Administration loan programs, and Small Business Development Centers, funded by the U.S. Department of Commerce Small Business Administration. In some states, projects have been assisted by such programs as the Appalachian Regional Commission.

Most states provide a variety of economic development financing strategies, such as economic development bonds, low-interest loans to corporations, and funds for building roads, and strategies for obtaining utilities for new plants and facilities. In certain states, research parks have been built with public funds, with utilities and development costs involved in preparing sites met at public expense. State tax monies have been used to build technical colleges and to operate programs designed to serve employees of existing industries or attract additional industries with promises of fully trained work forces. Increasingly, states have been willing to loan money to for-profit corporations at less than the prime rate of interest, a practice that provides, in effect, a subsidy to companies that promise to add jobs or save jobs—at the cost of reducing interest income to the state from public dollars available for investment.

A survey published in *High Technology* magazine (Brody, 1985, pp. 20–23) showed that by the end of 1984 more than a dozen states had established state grant programs that provided capital assistance for startup or expanding companies, and over forty states had started some form of state loan program to such companies, either through loan authorities or departments of economic development. A similar number of states were funding training programs and technical assistance centers for industry. More than a dozen were providing specific research and development tax incentives.

In addition, according to the survey, a few states had authorized creation of state-chartered venture capital corporations and were offering a 25 to 50 percent tax credit to investors. The *High Technology* survey noted public venture capital programs, because they often are a crucial factor in developing high-technology firms. It reported that some states provide seed or venture capital funds by investing a portion of the state's retirement fund—1 percent in the case of Pennsylvania. In actions that did not involve use of retirement funds, Colorado established five regional venture capital funds totaling $2.25 million. Utah created the Utah Technology Finance Corporation and designated $1 million to the corporation's venture fund, to be matched four to one. New Hampshire established a Venture Capital Network, which matches entries on two data bases: It matches entrepreneurs and their proposals with venture capitalists who wish to invest up to $500,000 in startup companies. Availability of venture capital is a necessary but not sufficient condition for entrepreneurism, however. In New Mexico, a state venture capital fund ($90 million in severance tax money) was not immediately successful; no applications for below-market-rate loans were filed during the first year of its existence (Crawford, 1985, p. A4).

In an article in the *New York Times* on state-operated venture capital investment, Farrell (1985, p. 12F) noted that "most of the state operations are small: $10 million is the maximum amount usually appropriated by a legislature as a venture capital fund. Investments are modest, generally $100,000 to $500,000 per company, and almost always limited to new, high-technology companies in the belief they have the greatest potential to grow and create jobs. Entrepreneurs seeking equity investments from the funds almost always agree to operate within a state's borders. They usually have to demonstrate a prototype product ready for marketing, pass stringent reviews and agree to secure additional financing from private sources. Only about one in 20 pass this sort of screening."

Even so, state and university venture funds are extremely important, considering the fact pointed out by Engstrom (1987, p. 31): "Venture capital tends to concentrate near the coasts. In 1985, 44 percent of the $2.6 billion in all venture capital went to California, two-thirds of that amount was concentrated in the northern section of the state, according to *Venture Capital Journal*. Another 13 percent of the total went to Massachusetts, and Texas took third place with 6 percent." The problem of scarcity of venture capital for Middle-American investment is compounded, according to Engstrom, by venture capitalists' tendency to invest predominantly in projects that are close to home.

Investment of university endowment or foundation funds in spin-off ventures is not only a means of solving the venture capital problem but, in the case of successful ventures, a means of making money for the institution. For example, the Michigan State University Foundation has invested in a for-profit corporation created by its own faculty. As Carroll reported (1985, pp. 22–23), Neogen Corporation was founded in 1981 with money from the foundation and private venture capital. Creation of the company stimulated concern within the university about losing top researchers and generating funds to support research on subjects of interest to industry. Neogen's first product was a mycotoxin detection kit, and the corporation has acquired three subsidiaries producing a variety of products. In 1985, according to Carroll, Neogen employed about 130 people, including 51 scientists.

The University of Pittsburgh also decided to invest part of its endowment funds in high-technology companies that grew out of discoveries made by members of its faculty. Toward this end, it invested in a Foundation for Advanced Science and Technology (FAST). The foundation is empowered, like a venture capitalist, to invest in specific programs, in return gaining equity in each project or company. FAST is a nonprofit subsidiary of the University of Pittsburgh Trust. It has access to university facilities and faculties, including the Pittsburgh University Research Center (formerly the Gulf Oil Research and Development Center) and a 30,000-square-foot incubator facility.

State initiatives to promote economic development partnerships have been wide-ranging and often creative, as illustrated by the following examples:

1. *Initiatives in Michigan.* According to Anuskiewicz (1985), Michigan has provided an exception to Farrell's generalization that state venture capital operations tend to be small by instituting a number of sizeable investment funds. Eighty million dollars is available in the Michigan Strategic Fund for investment in research and development and product development. In addition, Michigan makes available 5 percent of the state pension fund as venture capital. Since its creation in 1983, the Michigan Venture Capital Fund has invested $42 million in twenty-five companies. Michigan also has provided seed money for several university-based research institutes, including $25 million in fiscal year 1985. Among the institutes it has supported is the Molecular Biology Institute at Michigan State University in East Lansing.

The Michigan Research Corporation is an invention of members of the faculty of the University of Michigan, but it bears no legal relationship to that institution. Harker, president of Michigan Research Corporation, noted (1985) that the for-profit corporation was formed by faculty members to allow them to retain equity in the products they discover, play a central role in management and sale of their ideas, and obtain larger royalties than is possible through university mechanisms. Formation of the corporation was possible after a Michigan law prohibiting faculty members from holding significant equity in such a company was changed. Tenured and tenure-stream faculty members who are principal investigators on projects continue their primary appointments with the university, but research faculty in similar positions may receive half or more of their salaries from the corporation. To generate capital, the corporation sold stock in itself to companies and banks. Capital for particular projects comes from venture funds, research and development limited partnerships, or other sources such as the federal government's Small Business Innovation Research Program.

2. *Initiatives in Illinois.* Illinois has established a Governor's Commission on Science and Technology charged with developing a comprehensive long-range plan to advance high technology in the state. Peterson (executive director of the commission) reported (1985) that the prevailing culture in Illinois had favored developing strategies to increase employment by big corporations, rather than encouraging people to spin off and become self-employed in their own small companies. The steps Illinois has taken to encourage faculty initiatives include revising patent policies and developing the Illinois Resource Network as an electronic directory of faculty resources available to corporations.

Illinois has also created a venture capital fund, whereby several million dollars in general-fund appropriations can be invested as seed capital in return for some equity in startup firms. A special fund—the Business Innovation Fund—was created so that the state could match private investor and small business loans to small high-technology firms, investing perhaps $100,000 in each company. The state has been convinced it can recruit business in the traditional smokestack-chasing mode and encourage retention and growth of existing businesses. In addition, providing seed capital is meant to help the state grow new businesses by providing an environment that supports entrepreneurial activity. By working with corporations, national labs such as Argonne and Fermi, and a dozen universities in the state, Illinois has appropriated funds to develop advanced technology centers and materials technology, supercomputers, a software center, and similar projects.

3. *Initiatives in Massachusetts.* The Massachusetts Technology Development Corporation provides venture capital to new or small high-technology companies. According to Crowley (1985), vice-president of the corporation, its purpose is to help new businesses or inventors achieve commercial success by providing debt, equity, or royalty agreement capital and assist small companies in finding venture capital. The corporation coinvests with private funding sources in promising firms. Crowley reported that by late 1985 the corporation had a fund of $8 million and had made thirty-four deals. The corporation is a quasi-public state agency, but operates as a separate organization with an independent board of directors, six of the eleven members of which are from private companies.

After the corporation provides first-round financing to start a company, it typically does not extend second-round financing to expand a company. The goal is to serve as a catalyst rather than obtain maximum return for each dollar invested. The Massachusetts Technology Development Corporation does try, however, to stimulate success in the companies it supports by requiring development of sound business plans, marketing plans, and sales plans. Crowley (1985) stated that high-quality boards of directors and professional managers are crucial to the success of these companies.

It must be noted that Massachusetts was a wonder in jobs creation during the mid 1980s. *Time* ("A Tale of Two States," 1986, p. 14) reported that in the period 1984 to 1986 nearly 50,000 businesses were started in the state, creating some 160,000 jobs. Between 1975 and 1985, the population of Massachusetts rose by 1 percent, while jobs increased by 28 percent. More than half a million jobs were created between 1976 and 1984, a quarter by high-technology companies (p. 15). Talent associated with the excellent universities in the state contributed significantly to this expansion.

4. *Initiatives in New Jersey.* The New Jersey Commission on Science and Technology has led in the creation of four advanced technology centers in biotechnology, food technology, ceramics, and hazardous waste management. Fifty-seven million dollars (derived from a 1984 bond issue) were appropriated to build the four centers. Funding opportunities provided by the commission also include an award of $40,000 to any business that receives a federal Small Business Innovation Research (SBIR) Phase I grant, according to Fenway (1985), a member of the commission. The commission believes that subsidy of Phase I efforts bolsters the success of startup firms and increases the probability of their receiving SBIR Phase II and Phase III support. New Jersey is contemplating subsidy through grants and centers of research and training efforts in several new fields, including computer aids to industrial productivity, telematics, and aerospace. A ceramics center has been established with thirty-two industrial partners, who paid $35,000 each to join the cooperative research and development program. In 1985, the Biotechnology Center (Rutgers University) had twenty industrial partners, and the Center on Hazardous and Toxic Substances (New Jersey Institute of Technology) had seventeen partners. Each of the centers had a $3 to $4 million annual operating budget.

5. *Initiatives in New York.* New York is supporting a variety of programs to stimulate university-industry cooperation, under the direction of the New York State Science and Technology Foundation. Jones, executive director, pointed out (1985) that the foundation promotes statewide scientific and technological education, as well as basic and applied research and development, and serves as a conduit between the private sector and the academic community. It oversees New York's seven Centers for Advanced Technology, which are sponsored jointly by the state and industry to enhance technology transfer. Originally, nineteen universities responded to a request for proposals to establish such centers. Seven centers were designated: the Columbia University Center for Computers and University Systems, the Cornell University Center for Biotechnology in Agriculture, the Center for Advanced Technology in Telecommuni-

cations at the Polytechnic Institute of New York, the Center for Health-Care Instruments and Devices at the State University of New York at Buffalo, the Center for Biotechnology at the State University of New York at Stony Brook, the Syracuse University Center for Advanced Technology in Computer Applications and Software Engineering, and the University of Rochester Center for Advanced Optical Technology. Currently, each center is supported by $1 million from the state, which must be matched by private funds and federal grants. Since 1983, the state has contributed $25 million to the centers, and $50 million has been contributed in private funds (Engstrom, 1987, p. 27). Another program supervised by the New York State Science and Technology Foundation is the New York Corporation for Innovation Development, which provides financial assistance to new technology-based business ventures and has invested $50 to $100 thousand in such new companies.

6. *Initiatives in Indiana.* The Indiana Council on Science and Technology has as its goal linking industries, universities, entrepreneurs, and the state government. It is a private, not-for-profit corporation with a $20 million initial state appropriation. It plans to spend $150 million over a ten-year period. Hague, president of the council, noted (1985) that the board of directors consists of eight university presidents; eight industrialists representing small, medium, and large corporations; and eight persons from the public sector. Included in the public sector appointees are a senator, a state representative, a labor representative, and a superintendent of public instruction.

The council targeted thirteen diverse technologies that it thought would be conducive to economic development of the state and established a complex committee structure involving over five hundred people to encourage investments or take other actions needed to support the thirteen technologies. By early 1985, financial support had reached $10 million per annum. Payback of investment is required through a percentage of gross sales of associated products, processes, or services, according to Hague. If a university holds the company, one-third of the gross proceeds must go to repay the investment until two times the original investment has been repaid.

The goal of the Council on Science and Technology is to help companies through the sometimes drawn-out, high-risk stages of development—to bridge the gap between forming a company to market an idea and the point at which risk becomes reasonably low and conventional funding can be arranged. Projects that will result in products that cannot be produced in Indiana are not eligible for funding. Among the university-based initiatives supported by the council are biotechnology programs at Indiana University and Purdue. Half of available funding has been used to support joint university-industry cooperative research, such as an artificial intelligence project at Indiana State, a ceramics project at Notre Dame, and a robotics project at Purdue. Thus far, matching funds have not been required to qualify for council support. The council invests in incubators, new products, and entrepreneurial activity, but all projects are monitored very closely. The fact that the council is private has particularly helped it achieve its goals, because it can move faster than state government—more nearly on the time schedule required in private industry—and it can invest resources realistically, as needed.

7. *Initiatives in other states.* A fine report compiled by Maryland's State Board for Higher Education (1986) provides a wealth of information about initiatives under way in forty-one states. In addition, Mingle and Walker (1985), in a report sponsored by the State Higher Education Executive Officers, described three categories of state initiatives: (1) programs to endow faculty chairs (eminent scholars programs); (2) funding for special program initiatives or "centers of excellence"; and (3) initiatives to promote applied research centers or other types of university-business linkages. Eminent scholars programs provide permanent sources of funds to attract outstanding faculty members, usually by matching private donations with state funds. Mingle and Walker noted that Florida is presently in the process of endowing eighty-four chairs. The Battelle Institute examined the impact of centers of excellence (1983b. p. 6):

The centers of excellence concept, emerging in numerous state strategies, is based on the philosophy that individual universities and their graduate education programs should be selectively supported in line with their traditional (but perhaps declining) areas of recognized expertise. The consequences of such action can be both positive and negative. This kind of specialization does not necessarily support the growth and responsiveness of the university to the widely diverse needs of modern industrial society. Given limited resources to develop and sustain broad ranges of full-service educational and research facilities, states may choose to pursue the centers for excellence concept, but they must also seek to develop those kinds of interinstitutional relationships that provide both the breadth and depth required by new technology industry.

Centers of applied research are extremely diverse and may receive state funds on a competitive proposal basis or as a result of specific legislative action. Mingle and Walker reported (1985, p. ii) that such centers are "often tailored to the particular economic structure and climate of the region." Some states provide matching grants to cooperative research projects; that is, the state awards grants on a competitive proposal basis that must be matched by corporate money. Other states, such as North Carolina, have invested in centers of research in particular fields, such as microelectronics. Mingle and Walker point out that this promotes entrepreneurial activities.

Taking Advantage of All Resources. Although in many states economic development has been stimulated by challenge grants, applied research centers, or venture capital from state sources, it can also be promoted by other means. The state of Oregon, for example, in addition to approving funding for an Oregon Center for Advanced Technology in Portland and allocating $2 million to the University of Oregon for new faculty positions in high-technology fields and $12 million for science buildings (Engstrom, 1987, p. 26), has been promoting economic development in a more distinctive way. *High Technology* magazine reported (Brody, 1985, p. 28): "Although it offers little in the way of official incentives, Oregon has aggressively courted companies running out of room in Silicon Valley . . . [which] once ensconced in the state . . . spin-off new ventures at a steady clip." Oregon "promotes cheap land and housing, natural beauty, clean water (lessening the need for pretreatment), and overall livability.'' In 1984, Oregon repealed its unitary tax requiring foreign companies with plants in Oregon to pay tax on their worldwide holdings. Now that income earned in the United States need only be reported, Japanese firms are moving into Oregon. Officials and legislators in other states may learn from Oregon's example that a state may prosper that makes the most of the opportunities and resources available to it.

References

Abelson, P. H. "Evolving State-University Industry Relations." *Science,* 1986, *231* (4736), 317.

Advisory Committee to the Texas Senate Committee on Business, Technology, and Education. "Report on Fostering Emerging Technologies in Texas." In I. Fink, "The Role of Land and Facilities in Fostering Linkages Between Universities and High Technology Industries." *Planning for Higher Education,* 1985, *13* (3), 1–12.

American Association of State Colleges and Universities. "Economic Development—A Major Responsibility for AASCU Institutions." Position paper presented by the Task Force on Economic Development, AASCU, 1986.

Anuskiewicz, T. Remarks at "Federal High Tech '86." National Science Foundation/Department of Energy Interagency Conference on Federal Research and Development for High-Technology Firms with 500 or Fewer Employees, Boston, Nov. 25–26, 1985.

Battelle Institute. "Sites for High-Technology Activities." Special report to Southern Regional Education Board. Atlanta, Ga.: Southern Region Education Board, June 1983a.

Battelle Institute. "Universities and High-Technology Development." Special report to Southern Region Education Board. Atlanta, Ga.: Southern Region Education Board, June 1983b.

Baughman, G. W. "Twenty-seven University-Related Research Parks in U.S." In *Development of High-Technology Industries in New York State,* Battelle-Columbus, Apr. 1982.

Brody, H. "The High-Tech Sweepstakes: States Vie for a Slice of the Pie." *High Technology,* Jan. 1985, pp. 16–28.

Carroll, J. "The Higher Education–Economic Development Link." *State Legislatures,* Sept. 1985, pp. 22–23.

Chauncey, H., Jr. Remarks at "Federal High Tech '86." National Science Foundation/Department of Energy Interagency Conference on Federal Research and Development for High-Technology Firms with 500 or Fewer Employees, Boston, Nov. 25–26, 1985.

Coulter, C. Remarks at "Federal High Tech '86." National Science Foundation/Department of Energy Interagency Conference on Federal Research and Development for High-Technology Firms with 500 or Fewer Employees, Boston, Nov. 25–26, 1985.

Crawford, G. J. "Let's Invest *Your* Money." *Albuquerque Journal,* Oct. 17, 1985, p. A4.

Crowley, R. Remarks at "Federal High Tech '86." National Science Foundation/Department of Energy Interagency Conference on Federal Research and Development for High-Technology Firms with 500 or Fewer Employees, Boston, Nov. 25–26, 1985.

Engstrom, T. "Little Silicon Valleys." *High Technology,* Jan. 1987, pp. 24–32.

Farrell, K. "High-Tech Highways." *Venture,* Sept. 1983, pp. 38–50.

Farrell, K. "The States Enter Venture Capital Game." *New York Times,* Jan. 27, 1985, p. 12F.

Fenway, H. Remarks at "Federal High Tech '86." National Science Foundation/Department of Energy Interagency Conference on Federal Research and Development for High-Technology Firms with 500 or Fewer Employees, Boston, Nov. 25–26, 1985.

Glazer, S. "Businesses Take Root in University Parks." *High Technology,* Jan. 1986, pp. 40–47.

Hague, J. Remarks at "Federal High Tech '86." National Science Foundation/Department of Energy Interagency Conference on Federal Research and Development for High-Technology Firms with 500 or Fewer Employees, Boston, Nov. 25–26, 1985.

Harker, R. Remarks at "Federal High Tech '86." National Science Foundation/Department of Energy Interagency Conference on Federal Research and Development for High-Technology Firms with 500 or Fewer Employees, Boston, Nov. 25–26, 1985.

Illinois Research Network. "Expertise, Talents, and Opportunities for Business, Government, and Education." Promotional material, n.d.

Joint Economic Committee of the Congress of the United States, Subcommittee on Monetary and Fiscal Policy. *Location of High-Technology Firms and Regional Economic Development.* Report prepared by R. Premus. Washington, D.C.: Joint Economic Committee, 1982.

Jones, H. G. Remarks at "Federal High Tech '86." National Science Foundation/Department of Energy Interagency Conference on Federal Research and Development for High-Technology Firms with 500 or Fewer Employees, Boston, Nov. 25–26, 1985.

LeMaistre, C. W. "Partnerships for Research and Development." In *Forging Links for a Productive Economy: Partnerships Among Government, Business, and Education.* Lexington, Ky.: Council of State Governments, 1984.

Lindsey, Q. W. "Industry-University Research Cooperation: The State Government Role." *Journal of the Society of Research Administrators,* Fall 1985, pp. 85–90.

Logan, L., and Stampen, J. O. "Smoke Stack Meets Ivory Tower: Collaborations with Local Industry." *Educational Record,* Spring 1985, pp. 25–29.

Mahone, J. Remarks at "Federal High Tech '86." National Science Foundation/Department of Energy Interagency Conference on Federal Research and Development for High-Technology Firms with 500 or Fewer Employees, Boston, Nov. 25–26, 1985.

Maryland State Board for Higher Education. "State Initiatives to Promote Technological Innovation and Economic Growth." In *Postsecondary Education Research Reports.* Annapolis, Md.: State Board for Higher Education, 1986.

Mingle, J. R., and Walker, C. "State Incentive Programs for Graduate Education: A Survey of the States." Unpublished report of the State Higher Education Executive Officers, Denver, Colo., 1985.

National Council for Urban Economic Development. *Creating Jobs by Creating Business Incubators.* Washington, D.C.: National Council for Urban Economic Development, Nov. 1985.

"New Group Bodes Well." *Albuquerque Journal,* Jan. 23, 1985, p. 4.

Office of Technology Assessment, U.S. Congress. *Technology, Innovation, and Regional Economic Development: Encouraging High-Technology Development, Background Paper no. 2.* Washington, D.C.: Office of Technology Assessment, 1984.

Pennsylvania Department of Commerce. *The Ben Franklin Partnership Programs: Advanced Technology Initiatives.* Harrisburg: Pennsylvania Department of Commerce, 1985.

Peterson, N. Remarks at "Federal High Tech '86." National Science Foundation/Department of Energy Interagency Conference on Federal Research and Development for High-Technology Firms with 500 or Fewer Employees, Boston, Nov. 25-26, 1985.

Schmidt, P. "The Greening of Research Parks." In "National Employment Report," a special edition of the *New York Times Magazine,* sec. 12, Oct. 14, 1984, p. 37.

Science Park Development Corp. *Science Park Third Annual Review.* New Haven, Conn.: Science Park Development Corp., 1984.

"A Tale of Two States." *Time,* May 26, 1986, pp. 14-18.

Turner, J. A. "Little-Known Extension Services Enable Universities to Help Industry." *Chronicle of Higher Education,* Jan. 7, 1987, pp. 11, 14.

U.S. General Accounting Office. *The Federal Role in Fostering University-Industry Cooperation.* Washington, D.C.: U.S. General Accounting Office, 1983.

"U.S. Programs That Help Colleges Aid Business May Survive Threat." *Chronicle of Higher Education,* Apr. 16, 1986, p. 22.

"Universities and Research Parks." *Business Facilities,* Feb. 1986, pp. 28-38, 76-78.

4

Creating Successful Partnerships

Many elements contribute to the making of a successful partnership. For example, the 1986 SRI-AASCU study of higher education–business partnerships recommended that to take advantage of current challenges and opportunities, colleges and universities should become more entrepreneurial and engage in strategic planning (SRI International, 1986, p. 58). The study listed eight steps in "strategically developing an institutional role in economic development":

1. *Decide on an institutional commitment.* An institution must decide what it wants to gain from economic development activities, according to SRI (p. 58), and build consensus among institutional constituencies regarding general goals and the internal changes that would be needed to meet them. Revising the institutional mission statement may be appropriate.

2. *Analyze the external environment.* An institution must assess community and industrial needs. SRI pointed out that this step involves tasks new to many institutions, including understanding how the local economy is changing; the key economic needs facing state and local government; and the needs in the area for training, research, and technical and technological assistance. Current challenges and opportunities must be clearly understood.

3. *Assess institutional strengths and weaknesses.* An institution must decide how to marshal its strengths to meet the needs identified in step 2, and how to strengthen certain capacities that

seem likely to contribute the most. If neighboring institutions already have developed certain strengths, it may be sensible to complement rather than try to duplicate them.

4. *Determine targets of opportunity where involvement makes sense.* As SRI pointed out, "Every institution needs to determine its economic development niche" (p. 59). Current programs may be strengthened, additional faculty involvement may be encouraged, and new programs may be developed as efforts are intensified to inform businesses and government of services available.

5. *Define appropriate new roles.* Decisions regarding new roles must be appropriate in terms of an institution's mission. Two rules of thumb are (1) always capitalize on institutional strengths, and (2) the institution must be ready to make the necessary investment in the effort.

6. *Organize for new roles.* New activities may logically fit into existing institutional organizational structures, or they may require creation of new structures.

7. *Establish new policies as necessary.* The institution must revise or develop the policies necessary to operate cooperative programs with businesses and develop an institutional climate that supports the faculty members and administrators involved. Policies may deal with faculty consulting or with financial matters such as patents, licensing, and royalties.

8. *Implement and follow through.* The institution must select leaders, make assignments, develop monitoring and evaluation procedures, and publicize its efforts. SRI emphasizes that credit must be given to the college or university for its contributions. A wise institution duplicates and builds on successes. Table 9 is a checklist devised by SRI for institutions to follow in pursuing a role in regional economic development.

A key to effective strategic planning is consultation and consensus building (Powers and Powers, 1983). A productive role for an institution in economic development, like the strategic planning process itself, constantly evolves as external conditions and internal resources change and give rise to new possibilities and difficulties. Therefore, SRI's list of eight steps should be viewed as iterative, a series of acts to be constantly reperformed.

Table 9. Checklist of Questions for Colleges and Universities
Pursuing a Role in Economic Development.

- *Institutional commitment*
  How do the board of trustees, administrators, faculty members, students see the institution's mission?
  How do the community, the state, local industry, and other key actors see its mission?
  How does that mission relate (or how could it relate) to economic development?
  Should explicit recognition be given to economic development in the mission statement?
  What processes can be used to develop a consensus on the college or university role?

- *Community and industry needs*
  What is the nature of the local/regional/state economy?
  What are its key industrial sectors?
  How is the economy changing? What are its future prospects?
  What economic development issues face local/state government?
  What are the manpower needs of the economy?
  What are the technical assistance needs of firms?
  What are the research needs of firms?
  What are the technology development needs of firms?
  What are the opportunities for new business development?

- *Internal strengths and weaknesses*
  What unique resources does the college or university have that relate to community and industry needs?
  How do the academic areas relate to the economy's manpower needs? Is there a match or mismatch?
  How does the research program relate to local firms' technology needs?
  How do technical capacities relate to local needs for technical and analytic assistance?
  How do public service and outreach activities relate?
  Are there new capacities that ought to be developed?
  Are there strategic new investments that need to be made?

- *Determining involvement*
  Are there local needs that can be met by existing college or university resources and programs?
  Are there local needs that could be met by new programs that would be appropriate for the college or university?
  Are there areas of strength/excellence that could be developed as an economic asset?
  Are there current areas of collaboration that could be enhanced?

- *Defining roles*
  What are the institution's competitive strengths?
  Where can it make unique contributions to the local community and industry?
  How do its capacities compare with those of other colleges or universities in the area? Which roles should be left to others?

Table 9. Checklist of Questions for Colleges and Universities
Pursuing a Role in Economic Development, Cont'd.

What resources are available to help the institution carry out new roles?
Which roles are most supportive of the core missions?

- *Organizing*
  How well is the college or university organized to carry out new roles?
  Are new organizational arrangements required?

- *Establishing new policies*
  Do current college or university policies support moving in new directions?
  How do policies affect faculty involvement with the community and with
  industry?
  Are public-service activities given sufficient recognition?
  Do consulting policies balance the use of faculty expertise with academic
  responsibilities?
  Are patent, licensing, and royalty policies in place?

- *Implementation*
  Who will take the lead in implementing new economic development initiatives?
  How will linkages with government and industry be maintained?
  How will the initiative be monitored?
  How will it be evaluated?
  How will it be publicized?
  How can successes be replicated or amplified?

Source: SRI International, 1986, pp. 61–62. Used by permission.

Eveslage (1986, pp. 48–51) also listed steps to be followed
in setting up an outreach program: (1) set goals; (2) preserve
academic integrity; (3) identify academic services that can be
marketed as "products"; (4) review the institutional mission,
identify strengths, and make appropriate changes that will allow
maximum benefit to accrue to the institution from outreach programs and, in turn, will provide maximum support for those
programs; (5) review academic policies to determine whether
they support or pose barriers to service of existing client groups;
(6) review academic practices to streamline bureaucratic hurdles
involved in registration and other routines; and (7) assess internal support, encourage it, and direct it appropriately. This
list does not contain the emphasis on strategic planning that
characterizes the SRI-AASCU list, but it is a compact statement of the major internal changes that must be undertaken
by an institution embarking on cooperative programs.

As Matthews and Norgaard recommended (1984, p. 170),

regional needs assessments may be useful in determining what services might be productive if undertaken by local colleges and universities. In conducting such assessments, it is important to learn not only about present needs but about future needs of companies. Some companies are unwilling to speak directly of future needs, believing that to do so will reveal more than they care to of their plans for development. Broader but well-chosen questions may reveal enough information for planning sound educational responses, without tapping into confidential information. For example, asking employers to describe the effects that changes in technology are having on their companies and how these effects will evolve in the foreseeable future may elicit responses that are extremely useful in academic program planning and in identifying possible subjects for consulting and training contracts. In urban areas with high concentrations of businesses of various types, enough potential clients for research services may be identified through needs analyses to justify organizing a departmental or interdepartmental structure to undertake appropriate projects.

Successful Partnerships

The *Chronicle of Higher Education* (Jaschik, 1986, p. 13) reported that community colleges have joined universities and four-year colleges in directing their services not only to individual students, but to particular businesses and localities. Eveslage (1986, p. 48) noted that all educational insitutions that redirect their services may encounter difficulties when businesses and government agencies as well as individual students become clients. Eveslage stated: "The first needs that must be met are those of the organization." Since the organization is paying for an institution's services, it will go elsewhere if its needs are not met. Nevertheless, Roy's "PGR" (perverted Golden Rule)—which states that "them that has the gold makes the rules" (1980, p. 82)—cannot be allowed to dictate institutional behavior. The needs of the students, the professional standards of the faculty members, standards of quality, and the traditions of the institution also must be satisfied.

Elements of Successful Programs. The 1986 SRI-AASCU study reported a survey exploring involvement in economic development to which 300 AASCU member institutions responded. Respondents identified ten factors as key to the success of efforts related to economic development (SRI International, 1986, pp. 44–56):

1. *Entrepreneurial leadership.* Nine out of ten AASCU institutions surveyed reported that entrepreneurial leadership is required to identify and respond effectively to new opportunities.

2. *A clear mission.* An institution's mission must support its economic development efforts so that they are not in conflict with other programs.

3. *Well-defined and understood community needs.* Institutions must clearly understand local needs to develop appropriate, evolving programs that not only meet current needs but continue to meet them as they change over time.

4. *Institutional capacity.* In describing the results of the AASCU survey, SRI stressed the importance of quality. To be successful in economic development, an institution must match its strengths with the needs of its service region and do well what it claims it can accomplish.

5. *Strategic location.* Institutions that are located near major economic centers should take advantage of the opportunities their locations provide, and institutions that are not so located may need to create opportunities.

6. *Effective relations with public and private sectors.* Ties with the public and private sectors were identified by respondents to the AASCU survey as providing key support for economic development efforts. Overcoming cultural differences between academic institutions and public and private organizations is essential to productive relationships.

7. *Availability of resources.* Respondents to the survey identified lack of resources as the most important factor hindering involvement in economic development efforts. Resources may be sought from government, industry, or other public or private sources. Internal conflict for resources sometimes can be ameliorated by redirecting departmental expansion plans to include an economic development thrust.

8. *Supportive culture.* Institutions can build cultures that

support economic development by hiring administrators and faculty members who have positive outlooks and by modifying mission statements, policies, and campus reward structures.

9. *Supportive policies.* The second most important barrier to involvement named by AASCU respondents was lack of institutional rewards for faculty and staff.

10. *Facilitative organizational arrangements.* The AASCU survey noted (SRI International, 1986, p. 54) that structures within institutions are needed to coordinate involvement in economic development activities, promote interdisciplinary approaches to economic development challenges, allow institutions to be more responsive by freeing them of state bureaucratic restraints, and promote communication with industry.

Economic development efforts may be centralized—directed from the president's office, for example—or decentralized—directed by individual departments or other organizational units. Internal structures designed to oversee economic development efforts by colleges and universities include special centers, industrial extension programs, centers of excellence, research institutes, legally independent structures, and interuniversity arrangements, examples of most of which have been discussed in previous chapters.

Whatever particular structures are adopted, Gerstenfeld (1983, p. 9) preferred university-wide to departmentally based approaches: "A disadvantage of the departmental programs is that a company may not know which of several programs, if any, is the correct one for a given need. Or, the company may need to belong to a number of programs to fulfill its several needs. Also, a faculty member in a departmental program may not have the time or interest in performing a liaison role." Gerstenfeld added that university-wide programs require liaison staff who understand both industry needs and university capabilities. Otherwise, a company may end up with a convenient point of initial contact in the university that leads nowhere.

Matthews and Norgaard (1984, pp. 128–129) emphasized the importance of third-party facilitators in establishing higher education–business partnerships. They stated: "The purpose . . . of third parties is not necessarily to erase differences but to coordinate them and develop from them effective alliances. Third parties are frequently in a position to mediate effectively, dispel distrust, and help the partners sort through their different goals and values as they search for common ground. . . . Third parties can provide invaluable assistance to industry and higher education on two fronts: gaining access, and matching needs with resources.'' That is, third-party facilitators can identify organizations with compatible goals and needs along with individuals within the organizations who are in positions to authorize establishment of cooperative relationships. They can undertake needs assessments for both parties and carry out evaluation and quality-control measures.

To this should be added the observation that colleges and universities that are initiating cooperative programs often are more successful if considerable decision-making and negotiating authority is delegated to reliable representatives, including not only third-party facilitators but project initiators, deans, and other personnel involved in project design and implementation. These individuals may be responsible to a committee or task force or to the academic vice-president or the vice-president for research, as well as serve as liaison with the president, the council of deans, and the faculty senate; however, they also should have the authority to move events along.

Beder (1984, pp. 85–90) drew four conclusions regarding successful partnerships between continuing education agencies and business or government organizations that are important to any type of partnership among higher education, business, and government. Beder stated (p. 90): ''Continuing education agencies that have flexible, adaptive structures, adopt a posture of openness to the external environment, operate with a sense of commitment that engenders trust, and adhere to the principle of reciprocal benefit will find it easy to establish successful collaborative relationships.'' High standards and sound administrative practices are vital for program continuation.

Creating Successful Training Programs for Businesses

The point should be made, at the risk of repeating information emphasized in earlier chapters and in the chapters on contract training by Aslanian, that employers have become educators for a number of excellent reasons. Educators who wish to expand their institutions' training services to businesses and industries are wise to begin by understanding why companies have felt a need to organize training programs themselves. Craig and Evers (1981, p. 33) provided a concise list of reasons:

- To compensate for inadequacies of traditional education, not only in skills of secondary school graduates, but also to train many college-educated employees who lack abilities in a wide range of generic areas such as communication, decision making and interpersonal relations
- To cope with economic and social changes that affect the workplace
- To provide upward mobility for employees through training for technical or managerial responsibility
- To cope with the changes in technology that make job skills and knowledge obsolete
- For proprietary reasons (this is how we want you to do it here) or for competitive reasons (sales training for company-specific product knowledge)
- Because of inconvenience (scheduling, administrative, distance) or unavailability of suitable traditional education services.

In designing training programs, educators should attempt to address one or more of these points if they expect their programs to be favorably received by employers. Courses to orient new employees, instill corporate philosophy, or promote employee enthusiasm should be avoided, however, because their content and goals are not sufficiently compatible with those of higher education.

Craig and Evers continued (p. 33): ". . . need is the basic motivation for employers to assume education and training roles . . . employer roles have expanded . . . from transmittal of basic technical skills to a broad concern for human resource development (HRD). . . . Corporations look to the development of their human resources (employees) as an investment necessary to ensure economic success." It follows that educational institutions may expect to find customers for their services if they provide quality programs at reasonable cost that meet actual employer needs that have been identified as crucial to economic success.

Lynton (1981, pp. 66–67) added a further dimension to the assessment by business of higher education: "Most employers complain that graduates of colleges and universities are simply not prepared to be effective members of an organization." Academic curricula are viewed as "too narrowly focused on [theoretical, abstract] cognitive content," according to Lynton, with the result that students receive too little guidance regarding behavioral or affective factors, too little practical experience, too little practice in dealing with complex situations, and too little participation in problem-solving teams. Lynton stated (pp. 66–67): "All of this adds up to a pervasive feeling that academic institutions provide inadequate preparation for the transition from theory to practice and that even technically well-prepared graduates are not employable without further training. . . . Related to this corporate criticism is the widespread view that most faculty members simply do not know how to teach adults, especially those who return to the classroom with a great deal of prior work experience." Lynton's point is not only that degree programs should be improved and made more useful, but that educational institutions should not expect to be called upon for additional human resource development services if their deficiencies have been partly responsible for creating the need in the first place, and if they seem either unable or unwilling to become more consumer oriented.

Career and vocationally oriented programs tend to have similar objectives, whether they are offered by proprietary technical schools, community colleges, unions, or industries. In general, however, objectives and expectations of universities and colleges are quite different from objectives and expectations of employer-sponsored programs. Four-year colleges and universities typically design programs or curricula so that they foster the ability to learn and enable individuals to research questions, think independently, analyze information, and make judgments. Ideally, educational programs should go beyond mere mastery of material. Students must develop the skills required to update information over time and continually advance their knowledge. As noted in Chapter Two, many community colleges are modifying their curricula so that their students also may be prepared to update their skills or even change careers as technology becomes more complex.

Most employees engage in far less creative and independent activities than they would be prepared for by classic university training, however. That is, they are expected to perform repetitive, cyclical, or patterned functions within fairly narrow limits, under supervision. As a result, the majority of training programs in business and industry are focused on mastery of specific skills such as word processing, on specific kinds or models of equipment such as injection molding production equipment, or on specific processes such as using accounting software. Many employees must work cooperatively to perform defined segments of complex tasks in increasingly horizontal organizations, a kind of milieu that requires an ability to communicate effectively, both orally and in writing, and the knack of getting along with others.

Despite differences in overall goals between companies and colleges, some of the specific skills that companies require of their employees can be mastered through conventionally designed credit courses—taught on site at companies or on campuses—which are part of usual collegiate curricula. Thus, offering customized short-term training courses is not always the best way of meeting corporate goals. The point remains, however, that differences in organizational values and goals may require significant accommodation in course design and management of classroom assignments if company goals for training programs are to be met.

Advantages of Providing Training Programs to Business. Colleges and universities have not been discouraged by criticisms such as those summarized by Lynton; on the contrary, training programs designed for business clienteles have continued to proliferate—partly out of a desire to serve, and partly out of a desire to profit. Kopecek provides an excellent review for administrators who are uncertain of the advantages of providing customized job training programs to business and industry

(Kopecek and Clarke, 1984, pp. 10–13). According to Kopecek, potential benefits include (1) expansion of the university's service mission, (2) expansion of economic revitalization efforts, (3) more advantageous relationships with businesses, (4) professional development of staff, (5) increased use of the college, (6) expanded access to additional education to update and increase knowledge and skills directly related to employment, (7) personalized service for employer-students to better meet their particular needs, (8) new or expanded funding sources, (9) increased employer-student productivity, resulting in increased company profits and competitiveness in the marketplace, and (10) a program that may serve as a mechanism to attract government funding. Deegan and Drisko (1985, pp. 14–17) listed benefits as including (1) improved relationships between the parties, (2) job placement opportunities, (3) identification of potential part-time faculty, (4) increased revenue to the college, (5) opportunities to meet the training needs of the community, (6) increased visibility resulting in greater community support and increased enrollments, (7) faculty development, and (8) positive public relations.

Important financial benefits to a college or university may result from providing companies with education or training programs, as when corporations pleased with such services donate major equipment to the institution or develop a more permanent philanthropic interest in its future. Also, an institution usually expects some profit in addition to full reimbursement for its services. Increased tuition revenues may result from enrolling new clienteles of students from the workplace, retaining more students as a result of the combined work and study opportunities available when relationships with companies are established, and receiving additional state subsidies as a result of increased enrollments. Such advantages can provide considerable motivation for designing training programs for businesses, even if significant adjustments in institutional policies and practices are required.

Initiating Training Programs. In reading Aslanian's advice later in this book on initiating training programs, it is well to bear in mind not only the advantages that can occur for colleges and universities as a result of offering training for businesses, but the profit orientation of the business clients in such arrangements. Sound educational programs can affect human resource planning and productivity, which, in turn, can affect company expenses and company growth. Such programs can reduce expensive employee turnover by increasing employee satisfaction: by opening doors to promotions, increased wages, higher titles, and more interesting responsibilities. Programs also can reduce turnover by providing opportunities for workers in businesses affected by technological change to upgrade their outdated skills and remain employable. For many employers, courses must provide immediately usable skills, however, or they will not feel they are realizing sufficient return on their investment. Pointing out long-term or indirect benefits of training to such employers may not convince them of the need to sign a training contract. Evidence of past successes always is the best advertisement of training programs. Satisfied customers—employers and employees—singing the praises of programs are the best guarantee of continued success. In addition to professional pride, therefore, every reason exists for emphasizing quality in program development, implementation, and evaluation.

Eveslage (1986, pp. 51–52) gave more specific advice regarding program initiation by pointing out steps to be taken in conducting market research to determine potential client groups who might enroll in training programs. She recommended (1) making a list of every conceivable potential client in the region; (2) collecting information about the potential clients that reveals their current and evolving training needs; (3) developing a list of top prospects by matching client needs against the educational services that can be provided; and (4) again reviewing how, precisely, a proposed program can meet specific client needs so that the program can be marketed more effectively.

Kaplan (1984, pp. 87–88) defined five elements that are contained in all programs and courses, no matter how sophisticated.

> *Element 1.* The company and the college must agree on the identification of the training need and the outcomes that are to occur from the program. The agreement (usually formally documented in some type of contract or memorandum of understanding) should specify the terms of the proposed program or course, including initial determination

of the type or scope of training, numbers of individuals to be involved, time, price parameters, evaluation methods, and provisions that specify the mechanism through which parties may agree to new or adjusted conditions to their contract.

Element 2. An instructor-trainer with the required experience, knowledge, and skills available during the time specified by the company must be identified . . . more sophisticated or larger programs with several components may use a curriculum specialist to conduct a task analysis and develop a training plan and curriculum. A program coordinator to administer, coordinate, and serve as a liaison between the company and the college also may be employed.

Element 3. A meeting between the instructor and company representatives is held for information gathering and to begin the specific course planning process. It is important for the instructor to speak to all individuals at the company directly related to the programs. During these conversations, the instructor can ascertain first hand the competencies needed to be learned as well as the skill level of the participants to be taught. A visit to the work site and observations of the company's ongoing operation are also important to instructional planning.

Element 4. The design and development of the course should be completed by the instructor whose knowledge of the subject area helps determine the course length and content. The resources of the college—library, audiovisual department, handouts, overhead transparencies, slides, course outlines, and test material—are made available to the instructor. Access to instructors in the same or related fields, if available, can be a tremendous asset.

Element 5. Course outlines should be reviewed by appropriate college personnel and shared with company representatives. At this point the company has an opportunity to review the program and verify that the outline and the stated objectives will meet its specific needs.

Kaplan (p. 89) also provided a checklist of items to include in training contracts: program title, description of course content, schedule, location of training site, equipment required and who will supply it, name of instructor and brief biography, number of participants, fee schedule, method and time of payment, and signatures. In Chapters Eight and Nine, Aslanian gives examples of agreements that illustrate these points.

Some Problems and Responses. Deegan and Drisko (1985, pp. 14–17) identified some common problems encountered by campus administrators when offering contract courses, namely: unqualified instructors, inadequate facilities for training (especially in high-technology areas), difficulty in scheduling courses around work shifts, faculty reluctance to participate, short time period for course development, and lack of suitable marketing strategies.

Problems related to the traditional credit-hour and semester were identified by Ammon and Robertson (1985, p. 27). They pointed out that business training systems are tailored to an eight-hour day and a forty-hour week, and that traditional course designs and schedules do not deal adequately with business needs. That is, a standard college or university syllabus designed to include over the period of a semester forty-five contact hours in a lecture setting and an additional ninety hours of independent reading of textbooks, library research, and study, with the emphasis on theory rather than practical applications, may not fit a company's needs, which are more likely to be for skills training and review of specific applications accomplished in twenty hours of tightly controlled instruction. Employees enrolled in a course may not have access to a library or laboratory or time to do research and write term papers. When such is the case, community colleges and technical colleges may be more successful in meeting the needs of businesses than are colleges that do not offer career-oriented programs below the graduate or managerial level.

Luther (1984, p. 79) reported that some businesses have had bad experiences in arranging for off-the-shelf courses to be offered to their employees. Problems that were reported included inconvenient scheduling, teaching approaches that did not treat students as customers, insufficient flexibility, courses that did not teach state-of-the-art knowledge about industry-specific technology, lack of interest in the specific needs of employers and employee-students, and lack of emphasis on establishing credibility as an agent able to provide quality services.

Luther also noted a tendency on the part of industry to underrate the need for teaching skills. More frustrating was a lack of understanding by some businesspeople of the need to improve quality to improve competitiveness, and the relationship between intensified training and quality improvement.

Without compromising their traditions, colleges and universities can do much to produce courses—customized or standard—that better meet the needs of businesses. For example, courses can emphasize practical applications of subject matter of immediate interest to the business contracting for courses. Instead of requiring students to work independently and rewarding only individual achievement, teaching techniques can be used that require students to work in cooperative groups, as they will on the job. Teams of teachers—some of them, if necessary, from other institutions—can be used if no single faculty member possesses the cutting-edge knowledge required to teach a state-of-the-art course in science and technology or the range of skills required to teach a highly specialized, applied course that is needed by a company. Appropriate company employees can be consulted during course design to avoid assigning inappropriate instructors or using an inappropriate syllabus or approach. Campus routines can be modified to deal with requirements of industrial clients, such as designing class meeting times and places to complement the working schedules of employees or changing policies to allow tuition payment by contract. If institutional facilities are considered inadequate, courses may be offered at business sites.

In all cases, the ability of a faculty member to provide what a company needs should determine his or her assignments to teach courses for that company. This point may seem too obvious to bear mentioning, yet it is not uncommon for a college to offer to have a regular faculty member conduct an existing three-credit course on site at a company, only to have the company's director of personnel or human resource development respond that the faculty member's experience or the program content he or she proposed is not a good fit with company requirements for employee training. Flexibility is absolutely required of faculty members assigned to teach courses for businesses, since most faculty members, especially those at large universities, are accustomed to defining goals and objectives of courses in terms that make sense to curriculum committees of their peers and are not accustomed to asking employers to define their objectives regarding training contracts.

In fact, if any point is predominant in designing or operating successful training programs for business, that point must be choice of teaching faculty. Anyone operating a training program must learn to know well every faculty member in every specialty for which demand for instruction exists. Their strengths and weaknesses must be explored, not only regarding their areas of expertise, but their teaching skills, their ability to make clear the implications in the workplace of the principles they describe in class, and their understanding of the needs of the businesses being served and how their courses may be modified subtly to meet those needs. Many faculty members have no interest in teaching courses for businesses, and many are not qualified in terms of state-of-the-art technological knowledge, flexibility, understanding of business needs, teaching skills, or motivation rooted in a desire to have direct, practical effects on employees' skills and performance. If faculty members have previously taught or consulted under contract, the businesspeople who employed them should be questioned about their performance. Modern classrooms and technologically advanced teaching aids are not necessary for courses to be successful, but knowledgeable, skilled, and motivated faculty members are.

Luther (1984, pp. 80–81) provided five commonsense guidelines to follow in developing customized training programs: (1) get to know the customer, (2) learn about the customer's problems and needs, (3) develop a strategy for satisfying the customer's needs, (4) do a good job, and (5) follow up on evaluations for improvements. Again, these points may seem obvious, yet failures too often may be traced to them. Paris (1985, p. 30) strongly recommended involving employers in course and curriculum evaluation. Payoff can be significant, she argued, in terms of improvement in instruction, production of graduates in numbers and with skills actually in demand locally, improvement of program marketing, and increase in employer interest in the program and in the parent institution.

Advice offered by Kopecek (Kopecek and Clarke, 1984, p. 14) is more general, but is straightforward and practical.

Regarding contract training, he warned that program integrity must be maintained by controlling what is taught and levels of achievement, comprehensiveness of the institution's curriculum must be maintained by controlling the magnitude of the institution's involvement in customized training, and program quality must be guarded by careful evaluation and continued faculty development. In other words, care must be taken to ensure that engaging in contract training does not erode missions and standards, instead of benefiting the institution.

In sum, success of contract training programs is often influenced significantly by basic factors such as choice of instructor, whether the institution is flexible or choking in red tape, and whether the institution is qualified to provide the particular training needed by the contracting business. Many such factors can be controlled to some degree by the institutions.

On their part, businesses can take some fairly simple steps to become more responsive so that educational institutions are given a fair chance to succeed. For example, businesses may make crucial adjustments internally by assigning appropriate personnel to serve as contacts with higher education; make decisions regarding programs and contracts; evaluate programs; and evaluate the return on the investment that the company is making by paying full costs for employees, providing tuition assistance, or allowing time off with pay to attend classes. In addition, businesses should be reminded to support education programs by recognizing graduates at company events and modifying policies, if necessary, to add appropriate training to the criteria that determine promotions and raises; identify clearly such matters as what constitutes job-related training, standards that must be met for employee students to qualify for tuition reimbursements, conditions under which tuition must be repaid the employer, and so forth; and establish guidelines for education programs, including such basic points as requiring institutions offering services to be accredited and permitting delivery of services via modern technology, such as televised lectures and seminars conducted via satellite with professors and classmates in distant studios.

Creating Successful Cooperative Research Programs

Development of university-industry research partnerships, as Matthews and Norgaard pointed out (1984, pp. 166–168), often is not a matter of simple linear progression. An atmosphere of trust is not built quickly. Political and economic conditions can create—or obliterate—goals around which partnerships form. Whereas most cooperative relationships occur because university personnel initiate them, research partnerships often are the culmination of years of repeated contacts among university and industry personnel, perhaps involving extensions of student-student or professor-student relationships formed while in graduate school, perhaps involving personnel exchange programs, continuing education or employee development programs for technical or scientific personnel, equipment donations, conferences, symposia or graduate-level seminars, or other contacts requiring less serious commitments, lower levels of funding, and more modest expectations.

Industry employees who are alumni are often effective resources in initiating research contracts, because they may be willing to argue within the company for new relationships and work with diligence and persistence to overcome obstacles. Many research relationships evolve out of consulting work performed by university scientists under contract to a corporation. Consulting relationships are most often initiated by companies (Peters and Fusfeld, 1983, p. 40). Sometimes their purpose is technical assistance, as, for example, when faculty members are asked to analyze a company's product or service line and recommend appropriate diversification or to study the feasibility of diversifications in terms of effects on current procedures and facilities. In any case, if sound advice is provided by a university, over time a climate may be created that is beneficial to formation of a more extensive research partnership or one that is focused on investigation of more fundamental matters. Essential to such a climate is understanding on both sides that potential partners have strong interests in common and that joining forces may bring benefits to both.

Initiating a Cooperative Research Program. Rosenbloom and Kantrow (1982, p. 121) quote Pake, vice-president of corporate research at Xerox, who describes three criteria used by Xerox's own corporate research centers in selecting research areas:

1. *Business importance.* In a seminar offered jointly by the Harvard Business School and MIT's Sloan School of Management, and reported by Rosenbloom and Kantrow, Pake described this criterion as "estimated relevance to projected Xerox business areas." Rosenbloom and Kantrow emphasized the word *projected* in Pake's phrase, saying: "It signals that, because investments in research pay off far into the future, managers must make their decisions according to where the company is headed, not just where the company stands. It is this decision that links research management to corporate planning."

2. *Technical opportunity.* To judge this criterion, Pake asks

- Are the ideas any good?
- Are first-class researchers (at Xerox or elsewhere) available to pursue them?
- Is major investment likely to yield advances, or is the technology mature and stable?
- How many years will it take before we see useful results?
- How many failures and successes have others had in this area?

3. *Additional questions.* If an idea passes the first two tests, additional questions must be asked:

- Can the target technology be obtained from vendors or through acquisition?
- What costs would be incurred by despacing [eliminating] an existing research program to implement the new proposal?
- Is there enough hope that a successful result can be transferred downstream?
- Will the necessary capital be available?

If such questions are asked by corporate executives regarding research undertaken in their own laboratories, similar questions may be on their minds when considering sponsorship of university-based projects.

Frye (1983, p. 6) recommended to university researchers and administrators interested in initiating cooperative research programs that a direct approach may work well. That is, university representatives should visit companies, attempt to analyze their needs, and describe programs in which the university is strong that may meet those needs. Frye reminded universities that "the golden rule of selling is to 'Know Your Customer.'" He noted: "A new approach or a niche is most likely to interest such a company." Another approach is to contact "sleeping" industries and convince them to allow their product and processing lines to be examined. Such an examination may result in no progress, Frye warned, even if recommendations are sound. A good approach to stimulate activity is to convince company representatives that the analysis was their idea.

Salsbury (1983, pp. 9–13) outlined important steps in seeking industry sponsorships of university research:

1. *Make key decisions.* Decide whether the university really wants to do industrial research—and if it is willing to give up some academic freedom to do so.

2. *Determine whether the university has a product to sell.* List the kinds of research—by department and by professor, including only those professors who want to be involved—in which industry may be interested. Industry's response will depend in part on whether the university's researchers are better than those of its competitors.

3. *Set up and fund a university structure to handle industry-sponsored research.* According to Salsbury, such a structure should have the authority to coordinate faculty "sales efforts"; arrange contracts and handle finances; and recommend and administer policies regarding cost of services, overhead, publication of results, patents, and income sharing.

4. *Develop a marketing plan.* Develop a marketing plan based on university inventory results and a target area based on who the university's competitors are and their targets, the university's areas of excellence, and geography. "Sales literature" also must be prepared.

5. *Enlist assistance in finding industrial support.* Include university officials, faculty members, alumni, personnel officers, consultants, the state development office, scientific meetings, patent literature, and directories of major laboratories. Departmental advisory councils may be very helpful.

6. *Make contacts with industries.* Telephone acquaintances at industries, send followup letters, and then make appointments. Write to contacts you do not know and then make appointments. If you cannot identify a contact within a company, get in touch with either its director of research or president. At the first meeting, repeatedly describe how the university can help the company, while discussing major problem areas, new areas, how the two organizations' capabilities complement each other, and how much money is available for research. Salsbury emphasized how important it is to listen: ''If you talk more than one-third of the time, you are talking too much and not listening enough.'' Don't discuss particular projects at the first meeting.

7. *Develop ideas for proposals.* Consider proposing basic research similar to one of the university's current projects, product or process improvements, innovations based on discoveries made in different fields, research requiring expertise the company lacks, or use of new equipment or approaches.

8. *Develop a proposal.* Be positive and be brief. In a few pages, explain the idea, how it will help the company, how long the project will take, and how much it will cost. Make a second appointment to discuss the proposal. When technical details have been agreed upon, settle all issues regarding costs, policies, patents, and publication rights to avoid problems later. Salsbury warned that getting contracts to the signature stage in less than six months is unusual. Patience, persistence, a positive attitude, and an understanding of how the university can help the industry are key factors.

Roberts (1983, p. 27) echoed several of Salsbury's points when he emphasized that key factors in research program development are aggressive marketing and follow-up by university researchers; willingness to work with industry in designing and performing research; and concentration, if possible, on a major research growth area, with investigations conducted by distinguished researchers. Roberts recommended (p. 28) that development of detailed research plans can help avoid many problems. Roberts identified the "key consideration" in launching a successful program as defining a focused program with mutually acceptable objectives. In addition, partners must respect each other as scientists, communications must be open, and both parties must be committed to the success of the endeavor.

Matthews and Norgaard (1984, p. 119) made a noteworthy point regarding establishment of research partnerships when they stated: "The obstacles to partnerships created by a corporation's outmoded policies and procedures have a severe effect on all but the most elite educational institutions. It is one thing if you are the president of a front-rank research institution and you have a good relationship with the vice-president of a large high-tech company. But it is quite another if you are the president of a small community college or of a regional state university that is attempting to get an engineering program off the ground. The problems encountered by these less elite institutions are symptoms that alert us to barriers in the corporate structure—internal barriers that hinder a company from forming the very partnerships that will enable it to meet its own needs."

Matthews and Norgaard continued: "The competing demands of long- and short-range outlooks have a substantial effect not only on a firm's philosophical outlook but on its daily operation." A firm that focuses only on immediate payoff will not be inclined to finance basic research. Over the long term, the firm may suffer the consequences, but that is no solace to university personnel trying to establish mutual-benefit research programs. Instigating change in policies to encourage research and human resource development can be extremely difficult in the face of market pressures, company mergers, administrative streamlining, and the ever-present concern with the immediate state of the company balance sheet. Companies must be constantly concerned with profits to survive, but their viability in future years must also be of interest. By the time significant changes in demands for company products or services have occurred, it may be too late to plan how to meet them.

Additional substantial barriers to university research cooperation that occur with smaller companies were listed by Peters and Fusfeld (1983, p. 49): problems of smaller companies tend to be specific and of insufficient challenge to university researchers, smaller companies lack the research structure and personnel to develop university contacts, and smaller companies cannot spend money on research. As has been noted, the research needs of many small companies can be met through consulting contracts with faculty members from four-year colleges, who often are well trained and are willing to deal with problems that are too limited in scope for large university research programs to consider.

Some Considerations for Business. A common rule of thumb is that development costs are ten times the cost of creating an invention, and commercialization and marketing costs are ten times the cost of development. Nevertheless, the relatively lesser amounts spent on research are of considerable concern to companies when balance sheets are examined, particularly if no discernible results have yet been forthcoming from projects already under way. Businesses must ask if potential payoffs make it worthwhile to contract research to universities, especially when the process thereby passes out of their direct control in terms of precise directions of research, deadlines to be met, and use of information gained. Advice of authors from business as well as academe may be of value to those interested in establishing cooperative research projects.

Weiss and White (1980, p. 11), for example, recommend that all industrial research executives ask five key questions when deciding whether or not to sponsor university research:

1. What direct benefit from this research could accrue to the firm compared to that resulting from doing the research in house, elsewhere, or not at all?
2. Who—what individuals—will be responsible for the research?
3. Will commitments—of personnel, cost, time, quality, scope—be met?
4. Will the firm's interests and information be protected?
5. Does the firm have confidence in the competence, and trust in the ethics, of the key people involved?

Weiss and White pointed out that (1) a university must have skills or facilities that the industry does not have to make the price of doing the research competitive; (2) since a university does not guarantee proper performance of the research, the personal responsibility and skills of the researchers are crucial; (3) since "university researchers are too often lax about scrupulous adherence to commitments," some reassurance on this score is necessary; (4) although the university needs freedom of inquiry, businesses need to guard proprietary information, and an agreement must be reached that protects both positions; and (5) the firm must have faith in the competence and ethics of the persons involved because these characteristics are the only reliable guarantee that its money will be well spent.

Sparks (1985, p. 20) noted a number of basic issues important to businesses that are considering sponsoring university-based research: (1) decide which research activities should be delegated and which should be performed in house; (2) do not automatically object to cooperative projects on the basis of supposed cost alone, as delegation may turn out to be cheaper; (3) make industrial needs and values "known and felt," so that universities become willing to perform research actually needed by industry; (4) promote frequent interaction between university and industry personnel working on projects; and (5) provide flexibility in the relationship to deal with "sometimes-sticky problems," such as proprietary information and credit for discoveries.

Barker (1985, p. 24) also gave some advice to industries entering research partnerships:

> You will have to spend some dollars, but people are, in the long-term, more important. If you try to form an affiliation with the expectation that all you need to contribute is dollars . . . very little is going to happen. You have to put people into the project. A corporation that is going to do this must change its sociology. It must change its reward system, it must change the way it integrates its basic research and development of programs, and it must build the university link as an integral part of its R&D structure. The sum of these changes should be a changed social system within the organization. The linkage with the uni-

versity must become close, industry scientists must be expected to use the industry resource effectively, they must become an accepted part of the extended university community. The management of the R&D program will have to reflect these expectations and find ways within the corporation to involve university scientists and to assimilate the university resource.

Promoting Successful Research Partnerships. Johnson and Tornatzky (1984) studied 118 cooperative research projects that had been partially sponsored by the National Science Foundation to determine "how projects develop, how they are implemented . . . and what project features contributed to successful technical and organizational outcomes" (p. v).

Regarding the 118 projects, the authors observed (p. 12) that

- There had been extensive contacts between university and industry scientists, most frequently through consulting relationships, before the cooperative research projects took on formal standing and received National Science Foundation support.
- University scientists had led in initiating projects.
- Both university and industrial participants expressed a high degree of general satisfaction with projects and their technical quality.
- Most participants felt that the cooperative projects would not have been undertaken in the absence of the National Science Foundation program.
- University-industry researchers involved in the projects were senior scientists with "considerable prestige and authority in their institutions."
- Project management and decision making resided with university and industry principal investigators in the majority of cases.
- Communication and coordination between teams were frequent, through telephone conversations or meetings.
- Most university and industry researchers felt that improvement in projects, instrumentation, and methods had resulted from participation in the foundation-sponsored program.

• University researchers were more optimistic than their industrial colleagues that the firm would benefit from the projects.

The National Science Foundation study focused on foundation-supported projects that involved numerous senior researchers engaged in scientific investigations that had survived peer review before federal funding was awarded. It is not clear how satisfactory or successful cooperative projects might have been that lacked foundation support and were less well structured or conducted by less senior personnel. Foundation evaluators reported that exchanges of personnel between corporate and university sites seemed to be associated with commercial outcomes (Johnson and Tornatzky, 1984, p. v). They also reported that "industry scientists with prior personal links to the participating university (for instance, as former students) seemed to be attached to projects in which there were greater expectations of commercial outcomes." The evaluators concluded: "In general the variables that seemed to contribute to all aspects of project success were those related to interpersonal interaction. The I/UCR [Industry/University Cooperative Research program] was conceived as building on dialogue between university and industry scientists; this study uncovered abundant evidence that this design approach was realized in practice."

The National Science Foundation's evaluation suggests a number of general observations that may be helpful to those who wish to start cooperative relationships or make existing relationships more successful:

1. The payoff from university-industry partnerships tends to be fairly slow in coming and to extend over the long term. Therefore, expectations should not be for immediate results, with dramatic, marketable advances in products or processes, except when projects have focused on providing technical assistance to companies to solve immediate problems. Research and development takes time.

2. Successful research and development connections often are based on such fundamental factors as common research interests, trust, and good interpersonal relationships. The National Science Foundation evaluation implied a point made earlier in

this chapter, which should be emphasized: A good way of initiating university-industry partnerships is by organizing a consulting service to provide technical assistance to companies. The short-term, cooperative relationships that result may quickly yield useful solutions to narrowly defined problems. Over time, as advice repeatedly provides some immediate payoff and confidence is built, more substantial, longer-term cooperative projects may develop.

3. As with all research and development projects, sustained financial support of cooperative projects over a period of years is likely to be necessary if major progress is to be made. A sound financial base may already exist if salaries of faculty members and costs of laboratory equipment and support staff have been built into the university's budget, and if the research budget of the corporation regularly contains sizeable funding for consultants. Short-term funding is not likely to yield significant payoff unless university leaders free faculty members from other duties or agree to house cooperative projects in campus laboratories at minimal or no charge to the project.

As Peters and Fusfeld noted (1983, pp. 41–42) the majority of large, industrially funded programs receive government seed money during their developmental stages. Sometimes, university foundation or endowment funds are used to attract matching state funds or federal support, which is used to leverage industrial support of a program.

4. Promoting a sense of commitment by the president of a company or its chairman of the board so that leadership will be provided from the top is likely to be especially helpful in developing regional partnerships in which civic responsibility and improving productivity to encourage economic development are more important than advancing science. Just as good technical research questions often are best developed by scientists talking to their peers, initiating economic development projects, committing resources, implementing necessary policy changes and organizational structures, and simplifying procedures often are more effectively undertaken by senior leaders of universities, corporations, and state government. Senior leaders have the authority to remove barriers and lift prohibitions. They can change policy so that it fosters, not hampers, cooperation.

Cooperative higher education–business partnerships of all types have a factor in common: They may not be sustained over time, and results may not be significant or beneficial to any party involved, unless the scientists, trainers, or managers who actually conduct the research, training, or technical assistance that comprise the projects want them to be successful. If researchers are put to work on projects that do not interest them, do not promise to be fruitful, or cannot serve corporate needs; if the corporate director of training doesn't want faculty members teaching employees; or if production managers don't want technical assistance, likelihood of sustaining success is poor. In short, successful cooperative projects must be developed both from the top down and the bottom up.

5. University researchers feel rewarded when their research questions raise further questions as part of a natural progression in the advancement of science and technology. Industries, on the other hand, do research on particular, closely defined problems—such as improving products or improving productivity of manufacturing processes—which must be solved if they are to maintain a competitive edge. Because of the pragmatic orientation of the for-profit company, success of cooperative projects is likely to be greater if early efforts focus on solving problems actually facing companies, problems that their boards of directors or executives consider critical to corporate success.

As has been noted, many smaller companies are not involved in basic research because they cannot afford a significant research and development division. A regional university may consider broadening the assistance it provides to smaller companies to include some basic research and development projects, especially if it has been building confidence in its quality by providing needed technical assistance as part of an institutional mission to promote transfer of technology to the private sector. If smaller businesses individually cannot pay for needed research, a grant may be sought, or a group of smaller businesses of the same type may contribute, perhaps through associations.

Additional opinions by observers of cooperative research projects may be helpful in making such partnerships successful. Johnson and Tornatzky (1981, pp. 50–53), for example, discussed three university-industry "integrating concepts" that seem to promote more effective interaction: goal congruity and compatibility, boundary-spanning structures, and organizational incentives and rewards. Organizations with goal congruity and compatibility interact more successfully. The success or sterility of cooperative projects may also be directly related to the effectiveness of "boundary-spanning units" which may be located in the educational institution or the business or may be independent, and which are capable not merely of initiating cooperative projects, but of managing them successfully. In addition, Johnson and Tornatzky emphasized the great importance of organizational incentives and rewards, without which participants lose interest.

Tornatzky and others (1982) provided some information developed from the establishment of National Science Foundation–sponsored centers that is generally applicable. Although they also noted that viability of research programs is of central importance, they emphasized that good management, healthy relationships with the rest of the university, cooperation with industrial partnerships, and marketing capabilities also are essential. Other conditions include association of distinguished researchers with the center; existence of a "critical mass" of faculty members, staff, and students; physical capability for conducting the research; and experience among university researchers in conducting major research projects and in working cooperatively with industry.

Peters and Fusfeld (1983, p. 42) warned that cooperative research projects may not succeed if either partner fails to have realistic expectations. A university may count on continuing support that may not be forthcoming when personnel shifts occur in the company, or the company may have unrealistic expectations regarding the amount of time or financial investment necessary to produce results. Sometimes scientists promise more than they can deliver. Disagreements over patent rights, licensing, and delay of publication of results also mar some partnerships.

In an article on a collaborative effort between a university and a utility that owned a nuclear power plant, Fingeret (1984, pp. 61–62) warned that faculty members with backgrounds in collaborative relationships should be appointed to play central roles; that contacts with businesses should be broadened so that whatever units of the university (including continuing education units) that actually are capable of forming productive relationships have opportunities to do so; that the project director—if the director is a faculty member—must have institutional support to avoid potential conflict and harm to the project; that "a broad base of relationships should be established between the cooperating organizations, and multiple opportunities for social as well as professional interaction should be provided"; that team members should share information about their cultures (business and university) to overcome differences, rather than confine themselves to discussing only information related to the project; and that ability to work as part of a team, in addition to technical expertise, should be a criterion in choosing researchers.

High Technology (Ploch, 1983, p. 18) reported an interview with R. M. Davis, vice-president of Martin Marietta's Michoud division. The Polymer Processing Center (PPC) of the Massachusetts Institute of Technology had developed a vented screen molding process for the company. Davis listed six principles of successful technology transfer, which are good advice for businesses sponsoring university-based research of any kind:

1. Define the problem early.
2. Allow a reasonable period of time for the university lab to identify the real issue and to generate ideas.
3. Continue to support the working relationship.
4. Check the feasibility of the lab's theories regularly (PPC has quarterly project reviews).
5. Ensure management's commitment to technology transfer.
6. Promote cooperative effort between the lab and the industrial user (the contractor brought MIT scientists onto the factory floor to study the problem).

Managing Cooperative Research Projects. Managing any large research project is a challenge. Complications can occur because researchers loathe bureaucratic details; because research centers and departments can be viciously competitive regarding laboratory space, equipment budgets, and staff positions; because departments may enter into major brouhahas concerning tenure decisions and appointment of research associates, which have implications regarding what areas of research expertise are to be maintained or developed intra- or interdepartmentally; or for innumerable other reasons, all of which are serious if they affect the success of projects.

Budnick and Mojena (1983, p. 3) recommended, in managing large research projects, appointment of both an associate administrative director and an associate technical director to deal with conflicts between business-related and research-related functions. They also recommended that conflicts with departments may be reduced by granting research centers autonomy regarding purchasing, hiring, and space allocations.

Hall (1983, p. 30) took a different approach. He prefaced some charges to managers of cooperative research projects with the statement, "Less administration is better." He added, "Administrators can serve to facilitate the projects, but must seek to ease the burdens of the researchers rather than their own." He claimed that "the two biggest problems researchers have with administrators are: 'You cannot do that' and 'Write me a justification.'" He told administrators to avoid four acts:

- Do not apply rigid governmental rules to industrial projects unless requested by the industrial partner.
- Do not create paperwork (it infuriates researchers and keeps them from doing research).
- Do not call the pompous prima donna a pompous prima donna and vow vengeance.
- To whatever extent possible, keep lawyers away from researchers.

Peters and Fusfeld (1983, p. 40) noted that management of most industry-sponsored programs is the responsibility of the faculty scientist, who has "final say on the program design, project selection, and allocation of resources. On occasion, the faculty member will also have a consulting arrangement with the company to help manage or give advice regarding the company programs related to the university sponsored research." According to Peters and Fusfeld, although many larger projects have advisory boards, most project directors feel that actual management functions cannot be carried out by a committee, but must be the responsibility of a single individual, if progress is to be made. They noted (p. 40) that difficulties may occur because "in industry, the ultimate responsibility for management normally resides at a level above the research scientist." In universities, responsibility resides in individuals who must be skilled in management as well as in science.

Unfortunately, identifying good scientists who also are good managers can be difficult. Some bully staff associates into compliance, some are true absent-minded professors who forget that they're supposed to be in charge, some fear responsibility and turn everything over to assistants or committees, some turn simple issues into pawns in larger political games, and some have no notion whatsoever of how to orchestrate a group project. Department chairs, deans, and vice-presidents for academic affairs and for research must keep an eye on research centers and large projects and may intervene if unprofessional decisions are made, if institutional policies and practices are violated, or if acts are committed that might damage the reputation of the university. Researchers eager to acquire funding learn to cut deals with industry, learn their needs and how to define reasonable projects, and learn how to manage projects so that research outcomes may be delivered as specified by contracts. Some defaults are unavoidable; others may be cause for shuffling personnel into more suitable positions of responsibility.

Friedman and Friedman (1984) discussed management of "organized research units" (ORUs), which they defined as nondepartmental structures, including centers and institutes, created as homes for research endavors, often supported by external sponsors. They noted (p. 27) that ORUs have existed since before the turn of the century, and that more than 6,000 exist at present. ORUs may be established to consolidate resources, pool expertise to attract funding, provide a focus for interdisciplinary research, and promote interdisciplinary collaboration. Because ORUs are often created specifically as homes for industry-sponsored research, Friedman and Friedman's advice on how to improve their effectiveness is central to this discussion.

According to Friedman and Friedman (p. 28), a fundamental problem with ORUs is that "unlike most departments, ORUs tend to lack universally agreed-upon intellectual cores and consistent nomenclature across the academic tier. Because of their idiosyncratic nature, there are no accreditation standards, no externally imposed conventions, and frequently, no peers. In other words, their strength is their weakness."

The central administration of a university must be responsible not only for authorizing creation of ORUs but for monitoring their performance and terminating them when their purposes have been accomplished. An ORU may command attention both because of the resources it may attract to campus and because of the problems it may create. Potential problems include fostering extreme rivalry among departments for funds and prestige, which can be damaging to the institution; serving as power bases for ambitious faculty and administrators who are primarily interested in their own success; and not being sufficiently high in quality to add to the prestige of the university.

Friedman and Friedman recommended that no center be created unless its goals complement university missions and strengths. When creating a center, organizational and bureaucratic policies must be examined to be sure they will promote effective operation. Commitments must be identified regarding internal and external support, joint appointments, faculty and departmental support, space, equipment and personnel, and funding (p. 29). Because ORUs are not part of departments, the central administration must set up internal mechanisms to accomplish a number of functions that departments usually provide. For example, procedures for evaluation of the center and the director should be established, and an academic advisory committee should be appointed to oversee the center.

According to Friedman and Friedman (p. 29): "Successful ORUs require initial and continuing support from three sources: sponsor(s), university administration, and interested faculty members." No center can survive unless the faculty support it. An ORU usually should be centrally located because that signals to funding agencies and clients a broad base of internal support and encourages participation by faculty members from more than one department. Choice of a leader is crucial; Friedman and Friedman recommended that professional status be the key criterion. They also recommended that ORUs not accept contracts to perform tasks that lower their prestige. If scholarly accomplishment is the goal, then ORUs should not also attempt to provide training and client services.

To ensure good relations with the parent university, ORUs should share their resources—specialized equipment and personnel—with departments. They may provide research opportunities for faculty members on release time, as well as opportunities for summer employment. Faculty members associated with an ORU should bear their fair share of teaching, advising, governance, and ambassadorial duties. Directors should avoid acting like dictators, give credit where due, remain in constant communication with departments, define a research emphasis for the center that is accepted in the parent institution and complements its goals, and encourage ORU faculty members to publish in refereed journals and participate in academic activities on campus.

Changes in Faculty-Related Policies and Practices to Promote Successful Partnerships

Some college and university policies and practices are intended to ensure that matters such as purchasing, accounting, and fair employment are conducted according to standard practices, as specified by state and federal statutes and regulations. Other policies and practices have been developed to safeguard interests of faculty members and students. Since most university policies and practices were designed before complex partnerships and other relationships with the private sector became common, they often need to be modified to protect the interests of all parties entering collaborative relationships. Usually, not only the colleges and universities but the businesses and industries involved must make accommodations.

University communities jealously guard their fundamental traditions and values. Although policies and practices must be restructured periodically to serve institutional goals more effectively, they must not be changed so radically that fundamental university traditions and values are violated. On the other hand, they need not be formulated so restrictively that they preclude cooperative relationships by standing in direct conflict with corporate research and development principles.

Overload Compensation and Release Time. Linnell (1982) noted that often the fields that are effecting rapid changes in society are those in which innovative corporate products or processes are giving companies a competitive edge. Such fields currently include information and computer sciences and advanced technology fields such as biotechnology and computer-assisted manufacturing, composite materials, signal processing, electronics, and microprocessing, as well as business management and industrial engineering management. Faculty members who are experts in such fields have the greatest opportunities to be involved in corporate research and generate the most profits.

At the same time, many faculty members are not in demand by corporations to conduct research because they are out of date, have few innovative ideas to offer, do not seem able to communicate ideas effectively, or do not have personalities that contribute to close working relationships. In technical assistance and consulting, certain qualities and attributes of faculty members are less important than they are in contract teaching, however. For example, when providing technical assistance, faculty members come in contact with fewer corporate employees. A company may gladly endure an abrasive, agrumentative personality for a short period if the information he or she provides meets company needs.

In any case, at major universities, perhaps 10 percent of the faculty may be involved with industry in research and development efforts. Faculty members in engineering, science, and business are among the most likely to be heavily involved in consulting and may generate substantial outside income through multiple agreements with one or more companies. The vast majority of faculty members in most fields, however, are involved in partnerships with corporations only through instruction, if at all.

Linnell (1982) also described changes in sources and levels of research support and personal income among professors. Relationships entered into by professors are influenced by sources of income and apparent profitability of spending time in certain activities. Seeking reduced teaching loads and becoming less accessible to students can be very rewarding economically if time thus gained is used in consulting or in starting for-profit, spin-off enterprises. No one should be surprised if professors choose to spend time in activities that promise greater economic return.

The response by institutions to faculty members assuming additional, money-making responsibilities has been to change policies and regulations to make certain that faculty members do not spend so much time in extracurricular activities that they default in rendering the services for which the universities are paying them. Thus, most institutions now require reporting of all outside teaching, consulting, and other employment and commonly limit external activities to one day of the five-day week. Although universities usually do not limit activities during the three summer months for faculty members who are not under twelve-month contracts, they may require that training, consulting, and research grants and contracts for that period be managed through institutional accounts, according to institutional policies.

College and university time-and-effort reporting requirements for research, consulting, public service, or other outside employment vary greatly from institution to institution and range from casual, unwritten assumptions to codified reporting procedures. The federal government requires that reports be submitted stating how personnel who are compensated partly or wholly on federal grants expend their efforts. Federal grants usually prohibit overload compensation or payment from grant sources that exceeds full-time base salaries. State-owned or private institutions may choose, however, to pay additional overload compensation with money obtained from external sources. Such compensation should be carefully reviewed and usually is undertaken only for short, fixed periods. When developing budgets for research projects, the fact must be borne in mind that if a project entails loss of service of full-time faculty members, full costs of part-time faculty to replace the services usually must be included in budget calculations.

The time that a faculty member spends on external activities is essentially self-determined. A faculty member who is less interested in working with companies may carry a heavier instructional burden than one who secures release time by attracting to his or her department external grants or contracts. Since some institutions make no distinction between federal contracts and corporate contracts, they may require that the fraction of time to be devoted to a corporate project be designated, overhead be charged, direct costs be charged to an institutional account number, and other practices be fulfilled that originally were devised for managing federal grants. This red tape can be discouraging to business sponsors.

Many faculty members tend to undervalue their work and accept modest compensation from corporations for services rendered, often far below levels corporations are accustomed to paying external consultants. When consulting is performed on an overload basis, for example, administrators should set overload compensation for faculty members and graduate students for a sixth day of work per week at a rate no less than 20 percent of their regular weekly salaries and encourage them to request at least such minimum rates when they independently engage in consulting activities. Sometimes a daily rate is calculated as 1/180 or 1/200 of an individual's nine-month university salary. Compensation for research conducted during summer break also should be calculated at an appropriate rate, perhaps at a weekly rate of at least 1/36 of the base academic year salary. By limiting summer earnings to the equivalent of two or two and a half months of full-time income, some institutions in effect require that vacations be taken.

Compensation for faculty members teaching courses for companies often is best arranged by having the courses made part of regular, full-time work loads. Where short, intensive courses are involved, however, or where contracts and assignments are not predictable, faculty members commonly are compensated on a per course of overload basis. To avoid interference with scholarly work and other responsibilities and to avoid generating expectations of extra income on a regular basis, contract instruction should be distributed among faculty members.

Development of an externally funded course may require unusual effort by a faculty member. When course development does not bear any direct or long-term relationship to the regular instructional programs of the college, the faculty member developing the course may be compensated from funds derived from the course contract. Even if compensation for days spent identifying objectives for the course, becoming familiar with the employee setting and expectations, and preparing a course outline and lectures must be from institutional funds, the investment should be worthwhile because it should have a long-term multiplier effect in terms of company satisfaction and faculty performance. In any case, quality is always important.

When entering a cooperative relationship with industry, a university need not change policies governing conduct of ordinary business, such as recruitment of employees, purchasing, or expenditure of funds. Other policies, if unchanged, not only may cause conflict within the university community, however, but may attract the attention of state legislators, if the institution is state-owned. Problems commonly arise when cooperative projects promise to generate significant proceeds.

One potentially controversial policy involves the question of whether faculty members should receive equity in products and processes they develop—or even overload compensation— when development is undertaken in university facilities with assistance from technical staff employed by the institution. If terms and conditions of faculty appointments are controlled by legislation or state-wide union contracts, then legislative or executive action may be required to resolve the matter. Likewise, legislation may be required to change state policies or statutes governing the kinds of activities that are permitted at state-owned universities. Accommodations usually can be made to mutual satisfaction when organizing a cooperative project, but since red tape can be tiresome to corporate leaders unaccustomed to dealing with state bureaucratic requirements, in the interest of good relations university officials should take appropriate action to keep it from becoming an issue.

Quality of Teaching and Research. Usually, full-time faculty members are assumed to be of suitable quality, since they have pursued graduate degrees, passed tenure and promotion reviews, and satisfied peers on a variety of important criteria on a periodic basis. Even so, faculty members may be out of touch with state-of-the-art applications, in corporate settings, of discoveries in their fields, and this may be reflected in the corporate training programs they design. Faculty members may not be familiar with what employees do on the job or how they need to improve or update their skills. As a result, contracting companies may express dissatisfaction that their objectives have not been met. In such cases, faculty members may be augmented with part-time instructors who are familiar with various applications of the subject matter in the workplace, and who, in fact, may be employees of the company for which the courses are being offered. Such an approach has the salutary effect of updating regular full-time faculty members and making them more valuable to traditional students, as well as immediately improving course content.

Hiring adjunct faculty members can be the best way to fulfill certain training contracts, especially when full-time faculty members are overscheduled and persons uniquely qualified to teach the particular courses can be identified. Relying excessively on adjunct faculty members often is not a sound practice, however. Regional accreditation bodies or specialized professional accreditation associations may have established minimum standards concerning the precentage of courses offered that may be taught by adjunct faculty members. More important, use of excessive numbers of adjunct faculty members, regardless of their excellence or prestige, can produce quality-control problems and subtly erode institutional traditions and professional standards. To avoid problems, departments—as well as deans—must bear responsibility for oversight and include adjunct faculty members in their activities, as appropriate.

For credit courses, every effort should be made to ensure that the quality of courses offered at business sites is comparable to the quality of courses offered on campus. Quality of courses and faculty members is of greater concern to corporate audiences than academics may assume. In fact, corporations may be more concerned with such matters than are some college officials, whose main goal is to solve the problem of processing enrollees as quickly as possibly by identifying adjunct faculty members to teach the contract courses. Growth in numbers of clients and expansion to other companies is more dependent on quality than on course cost, because corporations are accustomed to paying for quality and to evaluating it routinely.

In educational and training programs, style, relevance of approach to subject matter, satisfaction of student or client, flexibility in covering material that is desired, and willingness to try to meet each other's needs on a course-by-course basis are very important. If a company has certain training needs that it does not wish to meet in house, it may sign a contract with a local college without bothering to inquire in depth about the qualifications of faculty members assigned to the project. On the other hand, if it is investing in what it hopes will be a prestigious executive development or management training program, it may require as teachers nationally significant figures from a prestigious institution. Because so many variables exist in expectations by contracting companies and attributes of faculty members available to teach contract courses, deans of colleges who want to establish records for providing excellent service must make it a habit to discuss with corporate personnel officers the outcomes of contract courses that not only are desired, but are likely to result.

Occasionally, a corporation requests that a faculty member be relieved of all instructional obligations so that he or she will be free to concentrate fully on cooperative research activities. This is flattering and alluring to those faculty members who are more interested in research than teaching. Faculty members should be cautioned, however, to do their part to protect the quality and continuity of their departmental instructional programs by continuing some involvement in teaching, if only at the level of one course per year. Faculty members also must seek ways of involving students in research efforts, both to contribute

to the education and experience of the students and to provide
financial support for them.

A survey by Blumenthel and others (1986, pp. 1361–1366)
of 1,200 faculty members engaged in biotechnology research
at forty of the fifty universities receiving the largest amounts
of federal research funds revealed that "biotechnology researchers with industrial support publish at higher rates, patent more
frequently, participate in more administrative and professional
activities and earn more than colleagues without such support"
(p. 1361). According to the authors, "the most obvious explana-
tion for this observed relation between faculty accomplishments
and industry support is that companies selectively support tal-
ented and energetic faculty who were already highly productive
before they received industry funds" (p. 1364). The authors include this observation: "At the same time, faculty with industry
funds are much more likely than other biotechnology faculty
to report that their research has resulted in trade secrets and
that commercial considerations have influenced their choice of
research projects. Although the data do not establish a causal
connection between industrial support and these faculty behav-
iors, our findings strongly suggest that university-industry research relationships have both benefits and risks for academic
institutions. The challenge for universities is to find ways to
manage these relationships that will preserve the benefits while
minimizing the risks" (p. 1361).

Salary Increases, Promotion, and Tenure. An institution that
establishes criteria and standards for salary increases, promotion, and tenure decisions often does so in response to a series
of predictable questions. What does the faculty member do with
his or her time? What contributions to scholarship are evident?
What is the quality of such work?

The long-term impact of lucrative contracts and their potential for distorting the missions of institutions and faculty reward
systems may require new ground rules. Traditional criteria for
promotion and tenure should remain in place, but evidence of
scholarship could be redefined to include corporate product
development in addition to publication in refereed journals.
Service may be redefined to include not only uncompensated

assistance to the university or community, but paid consulting in faculty members' areas of expertise.

Extra income is attractive, particularly to faculty members in the lower ranks who have young children. Under present regulations at many institutions, however, providing technical assistance or performing contract research for industrial sponsors can interfere with a faculty member's production of sufficient numbers of publications in refereed journals to be considered worthy of tenure, and it is considered detrimental to a faculty member's professional development as a researcher. The fact that industry most often supports projects of leading researchers, not young scientists, saves many from the temptation of spending time on lucrative projects that would not be viewed favorably during tenure review.

On the other hand, when senior researchers do attract a grant and ask young scientists to join their teams, those who refuse may be ignoring an important research opportunity they otherwise might never have. Senior scientists who attract assistants from graduate student ranks must treat them fairly. They must not exploit them by overworking them, assigning them excessive responsibility for conducting repetitive laboratory routines, allowing them insufficient time to prepare for teaching assignments, taking credit for their discoveries, or depriving them of time for family life. Departmental oversight of graduate student activities is essential, particularly when students are working in research fiefdoms.

Companies' assessments of faculty members' performance in teaching contract courses at corporate sites and the utility of courses to their employees may add another dimension to traditional indicators of teaching quality. Policies regarding compensation increases might also change. For example, external work need not lead to permanent changes in base salaries for nine-month faculty appointments, thereby distorting relative salaries compared to peers, if that work is treated in the same way as consulting, overload, or summer income and handled through third-party payments.

Academic salaries and raises commonly are influenced by success in conducting research, providing public service, and obtaining external support. Most universities require that whenever feasible, significant proportions of researchers' salaries be charged to external grants and contracts, even when disproportionately low fractions of the researchers' time are invested in the activities. With overhead on external grants set above 40 percent at many universities, successful grantsmen not only relieve their institutions of salary requirements but provide substantial contributions to general operating budgets. Universities commonly reward grantsmen by giving them appropriate merit pay increases, tenure, promotion, or awards. The question arises, however, of whether raises, promotion, and tenure should be a function of how much grant money a faculty member brings to the institution.

Questions arise at some universities, moreover, regarding the relative value of applied research and development versus basic research. Should a faculty member's success in securing corporate funds for applied research and development—such as designing or refining a marketable product—be considered as important in promotion and tenure decisions as success in securing funds for basic research?

Furthermore, what if a best-selling product developed by a university researcher were manufactured under an agreement that would bring a third or more of the considerable profits to the coffers of the university? Should that fact be allowed to influence promotion or tenure decisions, not only regarding the inventor but other members of his or her department whose ideas have not been commercially successful? Some may argue against allowing success in gadgetry or marketing to be a factor in promotion and tenure decisions, whereas others tend not to quibble about the means required to ensure continued support if funds gained thereby can be used to improve program quality. Sometimes faculty members who are envious or fearful of not being able to compete with those who attain commercial success object to tenure decisions or promotions of successful colleagues on grounds intended to disguise their true motives.

Even more disturbing questions arise concerning faculty appointment procedures when corporations provide the funds that allow personnel to be hired. Should candidates for certain faculty appointments be required to pass corporate as well as departmental review?

The SRI-AASCU study (SRI International, 1986, pp. 53–54) reported that "lack of rewards for faculty and staff involvement was identified as a major barrier to institutional involvement by 41 percent of institutions in the AASCU survey, making it the second most mentioned barrier" (the first being lack of resources). SRI noted (p. 53) that institutions that are most actively working with industry often have changed their policies to encourage involvement of faculty. In the area of promotion, salary, and tenure policy, SRI pointed out (p. 54): "The university's reward system can include explicit consideration for involvement in public service or industry activities, as well as for traditional teaching, research, and publication. Credit can be given in such systems for public service, consulting activities, applied research, and the like."

Special Considerations. Whatever policy changes are made to promote faculty involvement in industry-sponsored activities, the integrity of the academic process and the interests of students must always be protected. Faculty members must not become so focused on grant hunting and earning extra money through consulting or spin-off ventures that they neglect their teaching responsibilities. University researchers who have industrial contracts must not—consciously or unconsciously—influence graduate students to do research that could be more valuable commercially than scientifically.

Furthermore, a question arises regarding graduate students who wish to conduct dissertation research as part of university-industry cooperative research projects; that is, should such students be required to sign pledges of confidentiality concerning use of proprietary data provided by the companies involved? Such a requirement would have considerable impact on the composition of dissertation committees, which might have to consist of faculty members also willing to sign such a pledge. It also might hinder completion of degree programs and publication of dissertations. No department or faculty adviser should allow a graduate student to become involved in such a project unless the company affirms in writing the student's freedom to publish the results of his or her research, and unless the university has established clear guidelines to protect the student in case problems occur.

In addition to meticulous conduct regarding the welfare of students, faculty members who spend much time in consulting or starting their own businesses must not impose on colleagues in their departments teaching and other duties that should be their responsibility. Other members of the department may help, rather than allow students or the reputation of the department to suffer, but the practice is unfair. Some institutions have policies to prevent such abuses. Professors who spend unusual amounts of time in external activities become part-time faculty members, and part of the proceeds from commercialization of their research flows to their departments.

Professional behavior is required not only of researchers who have been successful in obtaining contracts to perform industry-sponsored research, but of personnel not so fortunate, in the same departments and in others. Personnel may be jealous or feel slighted or frustrated by allocation of federal and institutional funds or at not having an equal opportunity to become rich and famous.

Whitburn (1984, pp. 37–39) wrote about the negative effects that conservatism—unwillingness to accommodate to change—may be having on English departments across the country. He called attention to a trend on the part of companies that deal in information and information technology to ask university-based rhetoric teachers and researchers to work on applied research projects. Whitburn described such projects: "Typically, applied research is designed to improve the information that either constitutes a product (for example, computer messages that appear on a screen) or enables customers to use a product (for example, a manual about assembling the components of a personal computer)."

The lure of engaging in such company-defined, applied research is described by Whitburn (p. 37): ". . . faculty members with corporate ties tend to be rewarded with status, salary and other kinds of support. . . . As a rule, academic departments with corporate support have remained stable or gained faculty lines while departments lacking such support have been cut.'' Whitburn claimed, however, that literary specialists on curriculum committees and appointments committees refuse to hire faculty members or approve new courses in composition and communication that would allow ties to be formed with the business community. Whitburn warned that if universities do not respond to industry's training and research needs in rhetoric, industry will devise programs itself to fill the gap. He concluded that the dangers of refusing to work with industry outweigh the dangers of working with it.

Changing curricula and updating programs to make them more useful in preparing students for the modern workplace can occur only if faculty members are conversant with technological changes in their specialties and in broader society. Tenured faculty members sometimes grow stale and stop keeping up with developments in their fields, as do some instructors at vocational-technical centers after they have earned enough seniority to ensure job security. Since better faculties design better curricula, faculty development is one key to better training. A second key is having up-to-date equipment in training facilities, or failing that, access to a videocenter that can bring demonstrations to the training centers via satellite from businesses or laboratories using modern devices in their day-to-day operations.

Curriculum change and faculty development often require adding to library collections, updating laboratory facilities and equipment, and so forth; eventually, much of the plant and resources of an institution are affected by technological change. Investments must be weighed carefully, especially because thoughts of building new classrooms or laboratories seem to strike many people as the only answer when updating a program. Very frequently, such an approach is not the best. People must always be the number one priority; that is, funds must first be allocated to hire the best faculty members possible. Second, investment must be made in up-to-date equipment, of the type trainees actually will eventually be operating on the job. Only when these more important matters have been addressed should attention be paid to new buildings.

References

Ammon, A., and Robertson, L. "Emerging Technologies in the Workplace." *AACJC Journal,* Mar. 1985, pp. 22–27.

Barker, R. "Bringing Science into Industry from Universities." *Research Management,* Nov.–Dec. 1985, pp. 22–24.

Beder, H. "Principles for Successful Collaboration." In H. Beder (ed.), *Realizing the Potential of Interorganizational Cooperation.* New Directions for Continuing Education, no. 23. San Francisco: Jossey-Bass, 1984.

Blumenthel, D., and others. "University-Industry Research Relationships in Biotechnology: Implications for the University." *Science,* 1986, *232,* 1361–1366.

Budnick, F. S., and Mojena, R. "University-Industry Cooperative Research Centers: The Rhode Island Experience." In D. M. S. Lee (ed.), *Management of Technological Innovation: Facing the Challenges of the 1980s.* Worcester, Mass.: Worcester Polytechnic Institute, 1983.

Craig, R. L., and Evers, C. J. "Employers as Educators: The 'Shadow Education System.'" In G. G. Gold (ed.), *Business and Higher Education: Toward New Alliances.* New Directions for Experiential Learning, no. 13. San Francisco: Jossey-Bass, 1981.

Deegan, W. L., and Drisko, R. "Contract Training—Progress and Policy Issues." *AACJC Journal,* Mar. 1985, pp. 14–17.

Eveslage, S. A. "Retooling for Tomorrow's Economy with Corporate Outreach Programs." *Educational Record,* Spring–Summer 1986, pp. 48–53.

Fingeret, A. "Who's in Control? A Case Study of University-Industry Collaboration." In H. Beder (ed.), *Realizing the Potential of Interorganizational Cooperation.* New Directions for Continuing Education, no. 23. San Francisco: Jossey-Bass, 1984.

Friedman, R. S., and Friedman, R. C. "Managing the Organized Research Unit." *Educational Record,* Winter 1984, pp. 27–30.

Frye, A. L. "Communicating the Value of University Research to Industry." In *Industry-University Research Relations: A Workshop for Faculty.* Washington, D.C.: National Science Foundation, 1983.

Gerstenfeld, A. "University-Industry Cooperation: WPI—A One-Hundred-Year History." In D. M. S. Lee (ed.), *Management of Technological Innovation: Facing the Challenge of the 1980s.* Worcester, Mass.: Worcester Polytechnic Institute, 1983.

Hall, K. R. "Industry-University Interaction Case Study: A Faculty Perspective." In *Industry-University Research Relations: A Workshop for Faculty.* Washington, D.C.: National Science Foundation, 1983.

Jaschik, S. "Community Colleges Are Changing Their Roles to Meet Demands for New Types of Job Training." *Chronicle of Higher Education,* Apr. 2, 1986, pp. 13–15.

Johnson, E. C., and Tornatzky, L. G. "Academia and Industrial Innovation." In G. G. Gold (ed.), *Business and Higher Education: Toward New Alliances.* New Directions for Experiential Learning, no. 13. San Francisco: Jossey-Bass, 1981.

Kaplan, D. J. "Components of Successful Training Programs." In R. J. Kopecek and R. G. Clarke (eds.), *Customized Job Training for Business and Industry.* New Directions for Community Colleges, no. 48. San Francisco: Jossey-Bass, 1984.

Kopecek, R. J., and Clarke, R. G. (eds.). *Customized Job Training for Business and Industry.* New Directions for Community Colleges, no. 48. San Francisco: Jossey-Bass, 1984.

Linnell, R. H. (ed.). *Dollars and Scholars.* Los Angeles: University of Southern California Press, 1982.

Luther, D. B. "Partnerships for Employee Training: Implications for Education, Business, and Industry." In R. J. Kopecek and R. G. Clarke (eds.), *Customized Job Training for Business and Industry.* New Directions for Community Colleges, no. 48. San Francisco: Jossey-Bass, 1984.

Lynton, E. A. "Colleges, Universities, and Corporate Training." In G. G. Gold (ed.), *Business and Higher Education: Toward New Alliances.* New Directions for Experiential Learning, no. 13. San Francisco: Jossey-Bass, 1981.

Matthews, J. B., and Norgaard, R. *Managing the Partnerships Between Higher Education and Industry.* Boulder, Colo.: National Center for Higher Education Management Systems, 1984.

Paris, K. "Employers as Evaluators." *AACJC Journal,* Mar. 1985, pp. 28–30.

Peters, L. S., and Fusfeld, H. I. "Current U.S. University-

Industry Research Connections.'' In National Science Foundation, *University-Industry Research Relationships: Selected Studies.* Washington, D.C.: National Science Foundation, 1983.

Ploch, M. ''Industry Invests in Research Centers.'' *High Technology,* May 1983, pp. 15–18.

Powers, D. R., and Powers, M. F. *Making Participatory Management Work: Leadership of Consultive Decision-Making in Academic Administration.* San Francisco: Jossey-Bass, 1983.

Roberts, G. ''Industry-University Interaction Case History: An Industrial Perspective.'' In *Industry-University Research Relations: A Workshop for Faculty.* Washington, D.C.: National Science Foundation, 1983.

Rosenbloom, R. S., and Kantrow, A. M. ''The Nurturing of Corporate Research.'' *Harvard Business Review,* Jan.–Feb. 1982, pp. 115–123.

Roy, R. ''University-Industry Coupling: Philosophical Underpinnings and Empirical Leanings.'' In *Industry-University Cooperative Programs.* Washington, D.C.: Council of Graduate Schools, 1980.

Salsbury, J. M. ''Entrepreneurship or Seeking Industry Sponsorship of University Research.'' In *Industry-University Research Relations: A Workshop for Faculty.* Washington, D.C.: National Science Foundation, 1983.

Sparks, J. D. ''The Creative Connection: University-Industry Relations.'' *Research Management,* Nov.–Dec. 1985, pp. 19–21.

SRI International. *The Higher Education–Economic Development Connection.* T. Chimura, principal author. Washington, D.C.: American Association of State Colleges and Universities, 1986.

Tornatzky, A., and others. *University-Industry Cooperative Research Centers: A Practice Manual.* Washington, D.C.: National Science Foundation, 1982.

Weiss, M. A., and White, D. C. ''The MIT Energy Laboratory and the Role of Industry-University Interaction.'' Address at ''The Industry-University Connection,'' the 1980 ASM Materials and Process Show and Congress, Cleveland, Ohio, Oct. 30, 1980.

Whitburn, M. D. ''Freedom in the Research and Teaching of Rhetoric: University-Industry Cooperation.'' *ADE Bulletin,* Winter 1984, *79,* 34–39.

5

Reconciling Differing Needs
of Academe and Industry

The goals and values of business and higher education differ considerably, and the range of problems that can occur in business–higher education cooperative relationships is impressive. As in any endeavor, being able to distinguish the more serious potential conflicts from the merely irritating is an important skill.

Previous chapters have argued that businesses want education and training programs that emphasize basic skills, teamwork, practical experience, and problem solving. They want teachers to be up to date and familiar with real-world applications of the theories they teach. Businesses want to be consulted in program design. They also want course scheduling made more convenient and bureaucratic procedures streamlined. These needs are related to the goals of business, which are short term and profit oriented. Training usually is expected to impart immediately usable skills that will improve profitability or productivity.

By contrast, university training emphasizes individual achievement and theoretical underpinnings of practical applications, allowing professional updating through the course of each graduate's career. At the same time, however, most professors would be pleased if their students acquired certain of the skills desired by industry, as most students will eventually use them.

Indeed, higher education generally does not find the needs of businesses so outlandish that they are unwilling or unable to accommodate them in program design. In fact, a long tradition of meeting industrial training needs may be traced through the histories of land-grant and community colleges. When businesses specify their needs so narrowly that further accommodation through adjustments in curriculum would not be feasible without fundamental changes in institutional mission, noncredit courses and workshops provide a mutually satisfactory alternative. Other business and industry needs regarding teacher qualifications, consultation during program design, and reduced bureaucratic requirements can be met by changes in administrative styles or by relatively simple modifications in policy and practice. Universities are not—and should not be—willing to sacrifice their traditions or theoretical approach to learning in order to open "hamburger colleges" on their campuses, but short of that extreme example of a narrow-range, applied curriculum, many opportunities exist for colleges and universities to offer appropriate training and education services to companies.

In cooperative research, differences in values and goals between business and higher education sometimes give rise to conflicting needs and to problems that can seem more difficult to reconcile. Conflict avoidance and problem resolution may be undertaken in five provinces: (1) project management; (2) institutional policies and practices, often organized into guidelines to aid in conducting specified kinds of projects or activities; (3) contractual agreements; (4) administrative oversight; and (5) personal integrity and professional responsibility. Project management and organization of institutional policies and practices will be discussed in this chapter. The next chapter will present information on contractual agreements, administrative oversight, and personal integrity and professional responsibility.

Project Management

MacCordy (1983, p. 18) described "umbrella" research agreements:

The most prevalent type of research agreement is one which covers a single project conducted either by a lone investigator or by a small set of collaborating investigators. Recently, increased use of umbrella type agreements has become apparent, agreements which establish a company sponsored research program involving multiple independent projects in a particular field, such as research on hybridomas, computer applications, or materials science. Normally such an umbrella research program extends over several years and is continuously open to new research proposals from any faculty member doing research in the field of interest. The program is administered by a small group of scientists drawn from both the company and the university. The group performs the peer review function, selecting the most promising proposals, and providing financial support from a fund set up by the sponsoring company. The umbrella concept appears to be an especially productive way for a company to continuously tap a wide variety of faculty ideas in broad areas of applied science and technology, under an operating concept which assures effective communications and close cooperation between university and company scientists.

As the description of umbrella agreements indicates, the range of duties of a project manager can be extremely broad, depending on factors such as scale of the project in terms of research horizon being explored, funding and industrial participants, and location of the project in the university structure—that is, within a department versus in a research center that is not under departmental control. Duties and challenges include day-to-day management of work flow, paperwork, decisions regarding personnel and equipment, and other routine matters necessary to move projects ahead; they also include fostering survival in the university jungle, where projects rarely are killed mercifully but may die slow deaths from starvation—unless the directors are fund-raising or media stars, or the programs are readily identifiable as integral to the university's mission or of service to the personal ambitions of the president, key trustees or legislators, or other influential personages. Maintaining professional standards; initiating and nurturing contacts with businesses that are fruitful in terms of project definition and support; and leveraging maximum funding through contacts not only with businesses and industries, but with the university president and foundation, national associations, private foundations, state government, and federal agencies are other key aspects of project management.

Many of the duties and problems encountered by a cooperative research project manager need not be discussed here because they are similar to those of managers of other units throughout an institution. However, certain sources of problems a project manager must confront routinely occur because the project is located at the interface between higher education and industry. Three sources of considerable importance are cultural differences; responsibility to promote technology transfer; and responsibility to define, select, monitor, and evaluate projects.

Cultural Differences. Dubinskas (1985) has written about cultural differences between managers and scientists in genetic engineering companies. A number of his observations reflect problems faced by entrepreneurial faculty members who have created startup companies. They also parallel differences that can exist between university researchers and company representatives in cooperative research projects and, ironically, between professors and campus administrators.

As Dubinskas explained (p. 24), cultural conflicts in genetic engineering companies occur, basically, because of their mix of personnel: "Emerging companies in older technologies such as aerospace and microelectronics have generally groomed their managers on the inside, promoting scientists and engineers to management posts. By contrast, the new biotechnology firms have a high proportion of non-scientists as managers. The main expertise of these managers, who are trained in traditional business schools such as Stanford and Harvard, is in dealing with the outside financial world of investors rather than with the internal world of research and development. In addition, the companies' scientific staffs are recruited fresh from academic labs. Unlike scientists in, say, microelectronics firms, they have no industrial experience."

"Because of these differences," Dubinskas continued, "start-up biotechnology companies often show two public faces—one of academic science and the other of financial entrepreneurship. And like the Janus of Roman mythology, the two faces frequently look in opposite directions. Bench scientists and executives clash over what goals the company's researchers should pursue, whether the firm's direction should change, and how the choices should be made. Such conflicts can portend problems for either the short-term products that guarantee cash flow or the long-term research projects that offer hope for a future big success." An example that has been cited frequently is Nobel laureate and former Harvard professor Walter Gilbert's 1984 resignation as chairman and CEO of Biogen. Gilbert reportedly resigned because he wanted to pursue research that interested him personally but that seemed to offer little chance of short-term payoff.

Sources of conflict between managers and bench scientists noted by Dubinskas (pp. 26–30) included the following:

1. Differences in style of dress, surroundings, and work can exacerbate more important differences between the groups.
2. Managers and researchers work in different time frames, with managers under constant pressure to meet deadlines, reach goals, and produce satisfactory financial reports. Scientists, by contrast, "set their sights on distant and perhaps indistinct goals," according to Dubinskas. Each group thus can accuse the other of being "unrealistic."
3. Differences in designations of personal development also can create gulfs between the two groups, with managers valuing financial returns to their companies and themselves, and researchers valuing intellectual growth. According to Dubinskas, managers may regard scientists as juvenile, and scientists may regard managers as in a state of "arrested or frozen development."
4. Scientists are trained to seek problems the boundaries of which are unknown and which therefore promise opportunities for discovery, whereas managers are taught in busi-

ness schools to work within the framework of problems with definite boundaries.

To overcome these cultural differences, Dubinskas recommended that leaders on both sides involve themselves in producing solutions, that flow of intergroup communications be improved, that physical space be redesigned to encourage interactions, that each side learn about the other's work, and that all join together in setting and revising goals.

A related problem encountered by cooperative research project managers that can be traced to cultural differences, in part, is stereotyping. When one contingent of a university-industry research team criticizes the other, the spokespersons may focus on cultural traits of the other group that irritate them, exaggerating or overgeneralizing from these cultural traits to explain behavior. Examples of such stereotyping are

- Industry scientists are second rate, because they will sacrifice anything, including scientific rigor, for profit.
- University researchers are too theoretical to be of much use in finding solutions to real-world problems.

Persons wedded to stereotypes can ignore much evidence to the contrary. An industrial manager who is convinced that university researchers are "unfit" to help his firm, for example, may be slow to recognize good ideas in a report written by a university research team. To give another example, stereotyping may interfere with clear thinking when a company sponsor criticizes the slow progress that is being made in a university-based research project. The university administrator responsible for responding to such a complaint should not automatically assume that the company is merely exhibiting a "typical" obsession with speed based on an underlying obsession with profit. In fact, the project may be progressing at a rate unacceptable by any standards. Judging individuals on their merits is the best way to avoid stereotyping.

Whether or not stereotyping is occurring, cultural differences between businesses and institutions of higher education can seem so great that perhaps only patience and good faith can bridge the gap. An example was given by Pittman (1986, p. 10D): "There's a lot of fine tuning that needs to be done in university-corporate relationships. There's a fundamental cultural difference between industry and the academic world. When industry talks about long-range, they're referring to this afternoon. Academics talk of 20, 30, 40 years from now."

An important step in the "fine tuning" Pittman recommended requires both groups to try to use mutually understandable language. Familiarity with "academic jargon" and "business boilerplate" grows as each partner learns about the other's policies and practices that will affect a proposed joint project. Language equally clear to both sides can be used in drafting contracts. During key interchanges, as during project planning, progress reports, and project reviews, the project manager must assume responsibility for making certain that each party fully understands the other. By taking time to clarify terms at the beginning of projects, many problems can be avoided later.

Since project managers may be required to deal on a daily basis with problems that arise out of university-business cultural differences, understanding the range and nature of such differences can be useful. The SRI/AASCU study (SRI International, 1986, pp. 50–52) referred to the "three cultures" model developed by Szanton (1981, p. 64), which listed ten major attributes that differ among academic, public, and private institutions: (1) driving interest, (2) time horizon, (3) mode of thought, (4) mode of work, (5) mode of expression, (6) desired outcome, (7) preferred form of conclusion, (8) concern about feasibility, (9) stability of interest in topic, and (10) confidentiality interests. It is interesting to note that the cultures of public and private institutions differ from academic institutions on all measures, but public and private institutions are similar to each other on only six of the ten measures (2, 3, 4, 5, 8, 9). With many cultural differences affecting university-industry partnerships in addition to problems directly related to the project itself, effective research managers frequently are busy people.

Promoting Technology Transfer. Peters and Fusfeld (1983, p. 17) stated: "All the mechanisms identified as cooperative research interactions require an element of collaboration, even if only at the initial negotiation phase. However, the collaboration is usually only in general terms. One scientist [interviewed] suggested that the only true collaborative research projects occurred when the principal investigator at the university was also on the board, or was an executive of the company, as in the German model of interaction. He said that only in this way could the scientist ensure that the development and design work be truly integrated with the evolution of the feasibility of a concept, developed within the university. This appears to be an extreme statement, but does characterize a difficulty in designing truly cooperative research interactions between university and industry."

This passage implies that close relations between a business and a university (collaboration) are important for promoting transfer of technology. Participation in a major decision-making capacity on both sides of a relationship, as in the German model, however, might be construed as conflict of interest at many universities in the United States. Frequent interaction with industrial representatives, including design and development personnel, as appropriate, might be both an effective and an acceptable alternative way for a project manager to discharge his or her responsibility to promote project-related technology transfer. Peters and Fusfeld noted (p. 41): "On occasion, the faculty member [project manager] will also have a consulting arrangement with the company to help manage or give advice regarding the company programs related to the university sponsored research. This is particularly true in the case of programs that involve very sizable funding levels."

Although extensive transorganizational contacts may promote technology transfer, some of the researchers interviewed by Peters and Fusfeld expressed concern that extremely close or long-term interactions might be unhealthy for both sides. Industrial scientists worried about losing "sight of practical solutions and research designs" if exposed too long to the university's environment of basic research. Regarding university scientists, Peters and Fusfeld stated: "There is a fear that with extensive collaboration, a university professor will be 'bought,' and directed away from pursuing new avenues of research. One physicist [interviewed] warned that industry is only interested in supporting a knowledge base which is already formally conceptualized. University scientists, he said, must be allowed to explore so they can provide the technical base of the future."

In Chapters Ten and Eleven of this book, Frederick Betz provides further discussion of technology transfer.

Responsibility for Project Selection. A principal investigator and colleagues may ask company sponsors to suggest—perhaps annually—"areas of emphasis" to be used as the basis for designing a research program. Or an advisory board consisting of university scientists and company representatives may be formed to assist in project selection (Peters and Fusfeld, 1983). In any case, prime responsibility for program design, project selection, and allocation of resources frequently falls on the shoulders of directors of cooperative research projects and university research centers. Concern has been expressed repeatedly in the academic community that industry-funded research proposals do not have to undergo the peer-review process that federal agencies require. If carefully composed, an advisory board seems a reasonable alternative, capable of providing adequate critical assessment. Experts from other institutions sometimes are included on such boards.

Complaints expressed regarding the mode of project selection in industry-sponsored research reflect underlying concern not only for project quality but for the goals or direction of such projects. Zinser (1986, p. 8) identified research direction as one of eight elements of academic freedom, and she defined the concept as both a right and an obligation:

Research Direction:

- The *right* of scholars to choose their research topic and direction of inquiry.
- The *obligation* of scholars to promote and conduct research centered upon the pursuit of knowledge in their field/s of inquiry, as opposed to that which is driven by nonacademic self interests.

This analysis addresses an easily overlooked distinction regarding industry funding of university research projects. The *right* to choose research direction is not interfered with when industries have authority to decide what projects they will fund, because university researchers are free to seek funding elsewhere for projects of their choice. Some interpretations of the *obligation* regarding research direction, as Zinser defined it, are more stringent than others. Some do not see the two conditions (scientific interest versus nonacademic self-interest) expressed in the statement as necessarily mutually exclusive; that is, certain projects conceivably may satisfy both academic and nonacademic interests simultaneously. Many pragmatic scholars who take care to define their research interests within the limited realm of interests for which funding is likely to be available may not think it important to question whether the interests of their sponsors are being served while they carry out industry-funded projects. Such an attitude is not a new phenomenon.

Institutional Policies and Practices

The literature contains frequent mention of concerns regarding university-industry partnerships. For example, researchers surveyed by Peters and Fusfeld (1983, pp. 112–116) mentioned nine concerns: (1) academic freedom, (2) conflict of commitment, (3) openness of the university, (4) commingling of funds, (5) objectivity and credibility, (6) choice of research topics and type of research activity, (7) exploratory research and seed money, (8) gaps in communication, and (9) equity. Barber (1985, p. 24) listed seven risks that arise out of differences in characters and missions of universities and industries: (1) reduced university autonomy, (2) intermingling of public and private funds, (3) appropriateness of the research, (4) openness and publication, (5) patents and licenses, (6) conflict of interest, and (7) conflict of commitment. McHenry (1985, p. 42) expressed concern for (1) academic necessity to avoid secrecy and to publish, (2) patents and exclusive versus nonexclusive licenses, (3) conflicts of interest, (4) antitrust violations, (5) product liability suits against the university, and (6) adverse public reaction to the involvement of universities in proprietary research. McHenry noted that big companies will provide the necessary response regarding possible antitrust violations (point 4), and that universities should avoid research that may lead to product liability suits (point 5). Regarding possible adverse public reaction (point 6), McHenry warned universities: "Don't get involved in proprietary research unless you are ready to take the risk of public backlash."

A number of universities have written guidelines for conduct regarding university-industry partnerships that contain both restatements of existing policies and practices and additions written in response to emerging needs. Barber (1985, pp. 25–28) reported, for example, on the *Interim Guidelines for University-Industry Relations* issued by the University of California in 1982. These guidelines contained statements related to faculty responsibilities, openness and freedom to publish, faculty–graduate student relationships, and use of university facilities.

Colleges and universities writing guidelines find it natural to vary content according to the kinds of cooperative relationships with industry in which they are or plan to be engaged. In addition, according to Zinser (1986, p. 12), four goals should be expressed in any set of guidelines for cooperative projects:

- Aim primarily to educate for effective self-regulation
- Be liberating as well as restricting
- Protect academic freedom while providing incentive to innovation
- Promote variety and experimentation in university-industry relationships

The following ten management guidelines developed by Varrin and Kukich (1985, pp. 385–388) to promote successful interactions with industry also provide specific recommendations to colleges and universities. These should be included in institutional guidelines when the nature of the projects being undertaken warrants them:

1. Retain publication rights;
2. Retain ownership of all patents;
3. Establish copyright policies for software;
4. Minimize the use of proprietary information in research and do not require graduate students to sign confidentiality agreements;
5. Create research units with faculty and students, and hire full-time researchers to staff such units if necessary;
6. Faculty should not be permitted to consult with sponsors in the sponsored research area;
7. A faculty entrepreneur's company should not be permitted to sponsor his or her research on campus;
8. Beware of international agreements;
9. Share personnel and equipment with industry;
10. Prepare a model research agreement for potential industrial sponsors.

From this diverse information, several characteristics of guidelines emerge: They should address issues of general concern to the academic community; at the same time, they should be tailored to the specific needs of the institution; as Zinser emphasized, their goals should be both practical and liberating; and they should contain both specific recommendations where experience by the university community has been sufficient to identify clear and present dangers, and general statements to guide efforts in areas not so well explored or in which professional responsibility must be relied upon and initiative encouraged.

In drafting guidelines, most universities and many colleges would wish to address the central issues of academic freedom, freedom to disseminate research findings, conflict of interest, patents and licenses, and contracts. Following are summaries of major concerns regarding the first four issues, along with additional information regarding the content and focus of guidelines; contracts will be discussed in the next chapter.

1. *Academic freedom.* Academic freedom is the umbrella concept that encompasses and permeates all deliberations regarding university-industry partnerships, their success, and their long-term effects on higher education. The concept includes, according to Peters and Fusfeld (1983, p. 112), "freedom to explore new subjects, to publish without delay or political constraint, and to allocate one's resources and time to what the principal investigator sees as most productive for his research." Research contracts may include clauses designed specifically to protect these freedoms. In so doing, however, limits may be specified to guarantee arenas within which particular freedoms may be exercised, whereas prior to the contracts no such limits had existed. Some faculty members do not realize that contracts that guarantee some freedoms may limit others.

Imagine, for example, a contract that specifies that faculty members affiliated with a program agree to devote approximately one-third of their research efforts to basic research and two-thirds to applied projects. Is the academic freedom of researchers who accepted such terms of their own free will undermined? Cynics might claim that as a result of shrewd bargaining, they had succeeded in reducing their freedom from 100 percent to one-third.

Imagine a horse that, for all anybody knows, feels as free in a twenty-acre back pasture as its ancestors did on the open range two centuries ago. The cost of recovering open range is incalculable, and the modern horse leads a useful life in terms of meeting its owners' needs. If the pasture fence breaks, the horse may stay in the pasture, near a sure source of feed and in familiar surroundings, rather than break for freedom. All is well—except that much has been lost. Fencing the open range of academic freedom had best be done carefully.

Zinser (1986, pp. 7–8) included eight rights and obligations in her analysis of the concept of academic freedom: exchange of information, publication, teaching, selection and promotion of faculty, research direction, governance, collaboration, and neutrality. This description of each element of academic freedom simultaneously as a right to be exercised *and* as an obligation to be assumed parallels George Bernard Shaw's statement, "Liberty means responsibility." Faculty members who agitate to exercise in full the rights of academic freedom while choosing to ignore obligations paired with those rights do not nourish the tradition or promote its survival.

2. *Freedom to disseminate research findings.* As Brown (1985, p. 14) pointed out, "The continued rapid development of basic research rests upon rapid dissemination of new findings which in turn inform the next set of experiments." The importance of publication of research findings was further described by Coberly (1985, p. 321): "Research results must be freely and completely published if they are to be valuable in updating educational material. Freedom of publication is also necessary if the research is to be subjected to critical analysis by others knowledgeable in the field. Failure to publish research can result in duplicate programs and waste of time and other resources. It can delay solutions to important problems and inhibit the advancement of technical knowledge. Most research colleges involve students. If students work on projects that cannot be freely discussed, their education is of value only to the research sponsor. The research may also be of little value to the professor, because it cannot be used in teaching or discussed with colleagues."

Tatel and Guthrie (1983, p. 23) gave a concise description of concerns expressed by academics regarding limits that may be placed on information exchange by industry sponsors of university-based research:

> Firms often want to benefit from research results before they become generally known. Hence, the firms may want to impose proprietary conditions on the research they sponsor. For example, they may want to delay publication excessively, have the university keep research results confidential to protect the firms' competitive position, or require the university to protect as trade secrets any capability resulting from the research. Freedom to publish is a basic tenet of any university policy. One problem, however, is that patenting and licensing research products for manufacture may depend on maintaining some degree of secrecy.

Firms have recognized, perhaps reluctantly, that openness is important to scientific progress. Accordingly, contractual agreements provide that university scientists are free to publish research results. However, universities have allowed delaying publication for a limited time period to permit filing of patent applications or to enable the industrial sponsor to comment.

Many universities have developed institutional policies on the subject of delay of publication. The Association of American Universities' report *University Policies on Conflict of Interest and Delay of Publication* (1985), revealed that thirty-two of forty-nine institutions had written policies regarding freedom to publish results of sponsored projects. Most policies permit delay that is not unreasonable, as determined on a case-by-case basis for legitimate purposes, such as allowing sponsors to file for patent rights.

Institutional policies commonly are reflected in the publication agreement included in the contract that is signed by a university and a corporation launching a cooperative research program. A sample publication agreement from the *Practice Manual* published by the National Science Foundation (Tornatzky and others, 1982, Appendix A) reads "[NSF-sponsored] Center personnel reserve the right to publish in scientific journals the results of research conducted in the Center. The member companies, however, shall have the opportunity to review any paper containing any of the results of the research program prior to submission of the paper for publication and shall have the right to request a delay in publication for a period not to exceed one (1) year from the date of submission to the member companies, provided that the company makes a written request for such delay within ninety (90) days from the date the proposed publication is mailed to the company. Publication of information shall be permitted at any time, however, following the use of this information by a sponsoring company in any patent application or product."

This kind of agreement, which authorizes delay in publication under specified conditions, has become common. As Tolbert stated (1985, p. 52), however, "The overriding consideration is that both parties keep in mind the importance of intellectual exchange among investigators in furthering progress, and that both consider the ultimate right of the university investigator to publish as unchallengeable.'' Tolbert is advocating a principle of informed decision making also emphasized by Zinser (1986); that is, understanding which points are nonnegotiable.

The fact that publication agreements seem straightforward does not imply that the arena of information exchange and publication is problem free. Brown (1985, p. 15), for example, made an important observation regarding trade secrets: ''The general area of 'trade secrets' is perhaps most troublesome in terms of the potential for conflict with the University's norms for publication and dissemination of research results. Trade secrets involve research results, techniques, specialized equipment, and so on, which are in themselves not patentable, but which may have considerable commercial importance. Such material has proprietary value only when its confidential nature is maintained.'' Brown noted that because maintaining the confidential nature of trade secrets would preclude dissemination of information concerning them, universities may make it a practice simply to avoid entering agreements that may involve violation of trade secrets.

Other problems are not easily avoided, nor are they easy to correct once identified. Garrett noted (1985, p. 96): ''It is difficult to know when a faculty member's attendance to seminars is limited for proprietary reasons, when cell samples and machinery are not shared between entrepreneurially rival laboratories on campus, when students are told to keep their mouths shut or when faculty members self-censor their discussions and papers because they believe they may be onto something patentable.'' It is also difficult to know when scientists postpone or neglect to disclose potential or actual negative effects revealed by their research because to do so would be good reason for sponsoring industries to withdraw support of the programs. Garrett recommended (p. 97) appointment of broadly representative oversight committees to watch for violations of campus guidelines regarding conduct of university-industry cooperative research.

As noted earlier, Zinser (1986, pp. 7–8) listed exchange of information and publication as two of the eight elements of her concept of academic freedom. These she defined as follows:

Exchange of information:

- The *right* of scholars, students and the public to have access to information, resources, research property, laboratories, and expertise of the academy.
- The *obligation* for scholars and students to share ideas and information freely and openly, and to promote collegial exchange of resources.

Publication:

- The *right* of scholars and students to communicate, disseminate, and publish freely and openly, without censorship or delay.
- The *obligation* of scholars and students to report, publish, and disseminate new knowledge in a timely manner.

Is open exchange of information at risk because of the success of some university-industry partnerships? Zinser's definition mode again is useful in revealing where the greatest danger may lie. Even when contracts do not specify nor industries request that information not be exchanged or published, university researchers who foresee chances to make money through commercialization of their discoveries may decide to keep information secret until satisfactory deals have been struck. Less timely dissemination of research results, therefore, may occur not only because industries wish to keep secret potentially profitable information, but because some university researchers may feel the same way. Such researchers are violating the obligation to disseminate information and failing, thereby, to uphold adequately a principle of academic freedom.

3. *Conflict of interest.* A conflict of interest question that once stimulated fiery debates was whether faculty members should refrain from requiring students enrolled in their courses to purchase textbooks they had written. Some recent questions involve situations in which potential rewards could make textbook royalties seem unworthy of the fuss. Examples include

whether a professor may also be president of a biotechnology firm or own a sizeable block of stock in the computer company that is sponsoring his or her research or conduct research for a corporation that is providing venture capital for the computer software company he or she is forming.

A statement by Linnell (1982, p. 135), taken out of context, would have struck some pre-1960s faculty members as funny: "The very special privileges bestowed by society on academic institutions were never intended to provide an opportunity for energetic and creative people to become wealthy." It is to be hoped that many professors of the day, regardless of their lack of wealth, would have agreed with Linnell's proposed response to the problem, which White (1984, p. 241) summarized as "Prohibit the practice!" Traditionally, professors have chosen their profession for rewards other than money, and today many continue to believe that their achievement through service to their students, their institutions, their disciplines, and their avocation generates satisfactions that the private sector does not provide, although salaries are higher there.

Linnell wished to control abuses involving use of position to gain wealth either by adding conflict-of-interest policies—he proposed eleven in all (1982, pp. 117–123)—at the institutional level, or by changing the way outside activities are conducted. To accomplish the latter, he advocated a new kind of full-time, full-year academic employment. Orleans (1984, p. 271) described the new relationship as follows: "All paid professional activities by faculty will be undertaken on behalf of the institution, which will own their intellectual products and the revenues deriving from such activities." Proceeds would be divided according to faculty interests and institutional needs. Orleans called the plan "simplicity itself." It enhances whatever rewards faculty members seek from the academic life, and diminishes potential conflicts that might negatively affect faculty members and their institutions. Linnell's proposals, however, seem unsuitable for the academic environment, because many professors dislike rules and treasure their freedom to identify interesting outside activities.

Not all conflicts of interest involve financial gain. Mac-Cordy (1983, p. 17) found conflicts in a range of situations in which a faculty member could be influenced by personal interests to use his university position improperly or fail to meet his professional obligations responsibly. Realizing that many people are not resolute enough to resist temptation in the absence of guidelines and, in fact, may not be able to recognize a potential conflict of interest when such a situation arises, MacCordy recommended that "clear, comprehensive and specific criteria" be developed by institutions to judge potential conflicts. After noting that prohibiting certain activities, keeping formal records, and reexamining long-term commitments at regular intervals can help achieve desired results, MacCordy made an important observation (p. 17): "If called upon, the burden of demonstrating that planned or continuing personal activities should pose no threat to any university interest should rest with the individual."

Boyer and Lewis (1986) urged colleges and universities to develop more explicit policies governing consulting work by their faculty members. Four-year colleges and universities need somewhat different policies, because universities are likely to have higher-ranked, higher-paid personnel involved in consulting. Schools and departments within a single institution may need to develop variations on the central policy, depending on external activities of faculty members. Policies should specify what constitutes consulting—a neglected element in most policies currently in effect—and should include guidelines for regulation of such activity. Guidelines should not discriminate against the most motivated and productive faculty members. For example, an arbitrary limit of allowing one day per week for consulting may penalize, to no purpose, faculty members who are able to contribute more while continuing to discharge their regular teaching and research obligations.

The *Chronicle of Higher Education* ("Policy Governing . . . ," 1985, p. 7) reported that forty-six of fifty-one institutions responding to a survey conducted by the Association of American Universities stated that they had written institutional policies to help avoid conflict of interest problems associated with outside sponsors paying consulting fees to faculty members or supporting their research. Most institutions with written policies had revised them within the past five years. Nineteen of the institutions leave disclosure of possible conflict to the discretion of faculty members participating in sponsored projects, and twenty-six require disclosures as a precondition of participation.

Written policies probably are consulted more frequently in some fields than others. As early as 1983, Bouton reported (p. 63): "So many academics have been hired as part-time consultants to industry that, a year or two ago, an investment company looking for an unaffiliated molecular biologist reportedly approached 20 researchers before it found one without a commercial tie. Today, scientists agree, it would be difficult to find even that one among top researchers, so rapid and comprehensive has the entanglement with industry been."

The *Self-Regulation Initiatives* issued by the American Council on Education (ACE) (1986) addressed potential ethical issues that may confront faculty members and institutions involved in corporate-funded research. The document remarked on the difficulty of offering "detailed prescriptions for good institutional practice" (p. 1) because faculty members involved in consulting, externally funded research, and management of private firms are affiliated with colleges and universities of varying types, experiences, and resources and are engaged in projects in a broad variety of research areas.

Institutional conflict of interest was defined by the ACE document (p. 1) as occurring when "corporate or governmental arrangements . . . place faculty and research activities in conflict with . . . primary academic privileges and values." A university should not own firms that develop or sell products or services based on discoveries made at the university, nor should it endorse corporate products or services. Such alliances cast doubt on the institution's objectivity.

Examination of individual conflict of interest, the ACE document noted (p. 2), has centered on potential conflict of interest and conflicts of commitment, the latter often being treated as a species of the former. Guideline formulation by institutions should include consultation with all interested parties and legal counsel. The resource document pointed out that "the potential for conflict of interest is present when an agent (one acting for another) has a private and personal interest and a potential private and personal benefit in a transaction'' (p. 2). As the document stated, this potential is not new. ''But the degree to which basic research itself can now lead to the creation of private advantage, the erosion in some fields of the very difference between basic and applied research, and the much greater sums of money at stake—these factors are relatively new.'' In addition, the commercialization process can move more quickly.

According to the ACE document, temptations for faculty members involving conflict of interest include profit and sequestering. The document noted that ''a common arrangement is for royalties to be distributed to the principal investigator, his or her department, and the college or institution—after institutional expenses associated with securing the patent and license are subtracted'' (p. 2). Sequestering occurs when concern for profit leads faculty members to keep research findings secret. This impedes testing by peers and advancement of knowledge.

To allow informed decision making, disclosure policies may be designed by institutions. Faculty usually must report management responsibilities, stock ownership, and regular consulting arrangements. If involvement in a firm occurs, a faculty member should take temporary or permanent leave from the university to discharge the duty. Universities also bear responsibility for making knowledge generally available. An example of a practice that may conflict with that responsibility is granting of exclusive licenses.

Conflicts of commitment include competing demands on time and energy of faculty members, which may result in neglect of teaching duties or associated responsibilities. Consulting can be worthwhile for the company served and the consultant. The company benefits from the consultant's expertise, and the consultant gains experience. Faculty members must confine such work to approved discretionary time and make clear to clients that they are not agents of the university.

The resource document recommended periodic review of consulting activities by individuals, particularly if an institution has not developed standardized procedures. Reports of intent to consult, accomplishments, and ongoing activities—including time commitments, use of university resources, and potential conflicts of interest—help demonstrate public accountability, prevent abuse, and help keep the institution informed. The document made a fundamental point: "As with other higher education activities, self-regulation is always to be preferred over government regulation" (p. 2).

4. *Patents and licenses*. The statement of patent rights that follows and the comments that accompany it were taken from a report on *Emerging Biotechnologies in Agriculture* issued by the National Association of State Universities and Land-Grant Colleges (1983, pp. 61–62).

Patent Rights

The University shall maintain title to all patents which are derived from this research project. The Sponsor shall receive a right of first refusal to a license in such patents in return for a reasonable royalty based on the gross receipts from products manufactured under such patents. The Sponsor is obliged to exercise all reasonable diligence to create and promote a public and commercial demand for products which are developed under license granted by this agreement. In the event the Sponsor does not fulfill its obligation to exploit patent rights, such patent rights shall revert to the University to be used in accordance with its policies. In any event, the right to use the patents for scientific pursuit and education shall remain in the University. All rights of researchers to any patents shall be governed by the internal policy of the University.

Comments

The section of the contract concerning patent rights will vary significantly depending on the policies of the University and the Sponsor. Traditionally license terms would be negotiated only after both parties know exactly what is being licensed. However, such terms may be included as an inducement for private sponsors to engage in collaborative research efforts with the University. Generally, the University will wish to retain title to the patent. Since it is important to the University's function to maintain maximum utilization and availability of the patent to the public, a clause must be inserted that requires the Sponsor to exercise due diligence in exploiting and marketing the patent. The University may wish to obtain some degree of control over licensing and sublicensing by the Sponsor in order to protect the public purpose of the University.

Many University/Industry agreements grant generous patent rights to the Sponsor in order to receive substantial funding. Often the Sponsor is granted "all substantial rights" in project patents. This is quite useful in the utilization of capital gains tax provisions.

The University may be required by policy to retain all substantial rights in the patents and issue exclusive and/ or non-exclusive licenses to the Sponsor. Also, the income that the University receives may take on various forms, such as, a percentage of the selling price, a fixed commission, a percentage of net sales, a set assignment fee, etc.

Contract might call for a distribution of patent rights between the Sponsor and the University. In that case, each party would receive an undivided interest in all substantial rights to the patent.

Patents have been particularly important to universities since the United States Supreme Court ruled that a discovery that is the result of human invention, including living organisms (*Diamond* v. *Chakrabarty*, 447 U.S. 303, 1980), is patentable. A patent that produces significant income is as important to a university as a source of research funding. If an agreement specified, for example, that 30 percent of proceeds would go to the inventor and 10 percent would go to expenses and lawyers' fees, the remaining 60 percent may be divided between the inventor's department and the institution or between the institution and the state system.

A report issued by the Office of the General Counsel of the National Science Foundation (National Science Foundation, 1983, p. 263) outlined the basic rights secured by a patent.

1. The right to exclude others from practicing (making, using, or selling) the invention (this is a basic legal right secured by a patent, and is enforced by prosecuting infringers),
2. The right to practice the invention (without being prosecuted for infringement),
3. The right to license others to practice the invention,
4. The right to license the right to exclude others, and
5. The right to receive royalties from those licenses.

The report commented: "Universities have three primary interests in patents. Primarily, they (and particularly their patent administrators) want to share in the income generated by university inventions. Second, they wish to protect themselves against charges that they have conspired to suppress or impede a new technology by ensuring that such inventions are commercialized. Finally, they wish to minimize the legal complications of commingling research support. To satisfy these interests, universities would prefer to 'own' all five basic patent rights."

Problems that universities encounter with "exclusive-strategy" firms and "nonexclusive-strategy" firms also were described by the NSF report (pp. 263–265). Exclusive-strategy firms, like universities, prefer to have total control of patent rights because ownership of title, control of exclusivity, and royalties all can greatly affect profits. Nonexclusive-strategy firms allow universities to keep patent rights, if they are allowed to apply the invention. The report pointed out, however, that nonexclusive-strategy firms forgo exclusive rights not out of altruism but because they operate in an area of fast-moving technology in which inventions can become obsolete or are "invented around" before patents can be issued; they produce complex products, involving many patents, which inclines the firms toward cross licensing; and (3) they are market dominating and, as such, would more likely be harmed by limitations on the spread of technology.

In reporting on the survey of researchers they conducted for the National Science Board, Peters and Fusfeld (1983, p. 38) stated that although patent and licensing agreements were cited as potential problems, researchers experienced in working with industry viewed them as "not real problems." Negotiations between corporate and university lawyers were, however, acknowledged as a problem that could delay or even prevent a corporate relationship from being established. Peters and Fusfeld also reported (p. 23) that average processing time for a biotechnology patent was thirty-one months, and the average for all patents was twenty-two months.

Many diverse questions arise regarding patents. Protecting inventions will be a problem in biotechnology, for example, until newly created organisms can be reliably indentified. Also, to patent monoclonal antibodies, which differ from each other in very slight—but crucial—ways, methods of precisely describing the differences must be developed. A further consideration was posed by the *Wall Street Journal* (Stipp, 1986, p. 33): "If secrecy regarding research is not increased—as many university scientists hope it will not be—more than one company may commercialize a product. The result must be an increase in extended and complicated court battles over patent rights. Not only patent rights and earnings but credit for inventions and scientific reputations are at stake."

In another *Wall Street Journal* article, McMahon (1986, p. 30) commented on some occurrences of the first half of the decade, during which companies in the United States increased R&D spending by more than 86 percent:

> Since 1980, Congress has strengthened the patent laws, created a new form of protection for semiconductor chips, established the copyright/ability of computer programs, extended the term of drug-related patents to offset delays in Food and Drug Administration approval, reduced the antitrust risks associated with cooperative research ventures among competitors, and established a new federal appeals court for patent-infringement cases.
>
> In the same period the attitude of the Antitrust Division of the Justice Department toward intellectual property has about-faced. Ten years ago the division was busily proclaiming many common patent-licensing practices to be per-se antitrust violations, and fighting against new laws strengthening intellectual property protection. The division sought to promote competition by permitting free copying of successful products and considered intellectual property to be inherently in conflict with the antitrust laws.
>
> Today the division realizes that the copying of existing inventions by "free riders" discourages investment in efforts to develop new products and technologies in the first place. It strongly advocates increased intellectual property protection and points to results of studies showing that companies that invest heavily in research and development have about three times the growth rate, twice the productivity rate, one-sixth the price increases and nine times the emloyment growth of companies with low R&D investment.

The way these and other matters develop will affect research universities, which must protect their basic mission of advancing knowledge by avoiding curbs on information exchange, but which must also be sufficiently secure financially to support the research necessary to sustain such a mission.

References

American Council on Education. "Higher Education and Research Entrepreneurship: Conflicts Among Interests." In *Self-Regulation Initiatives: Resource Documents for Colleges and Universities*, no. 4. Washington, D.C.: American Council on Education, 1986.

Association of American Universities. *University Policies on Conflict of Interest and Delay of Publication*. Washington, D.C.: Clearinghouse on University-Industry Relations of the Association of American Universities, 1985.

Barber, A. A. "University-Industry Research Cooperation." *Journal of the Society of Research Administrators*, Fall 1985, pp. 25–28.

Bouton, K. "Academic Research and Big Business: A Delicate Balance." *New York Times Magazine*, Sept. 11, 1983, pp. 62–64, 118–126, 151–153.

Boyer, C. M. and Lewis, D. R. *And on the Seventh Day: Faculty Consulting and Supplemental Income*. Washington, D.C.: Association for the Study of Higher Education, 1986.

Brown, T. L. "University-Industry Research Relations: Is There a Conflict?" *Journal of the Society of Research Administrators*, 1985, *17* (2), 7–17.

Coberly, C. A. "Conflicts in University-Industry Interactions." *Engineering Education*, Mar. 1985, pp. 320–323.

Dubinskas, F. A. "The Culture Chasm: Scientists and Managers in Genetic-Engineering Firms." *Technology Review*, May–June 1985, pp. 24–30, 77–84.

Garrett, L. "There Are Problems." *Journal of the Society of Research Administrators*, Fall 1985, pp. 91–97.

Linnell, R. H. (ed.). *Dollars and Scholars*. Los Angeles: University of Southern California Press, 1982.

MacCordy, E. L. "Industry-University Research Relations: A University Perspective." In *Industry-University Research Relations: A Workshop for Faculty.* Washington, D.C.: National Science Foundation, 1983.

McHenry, K. W. "University-Industry Cooperation: An Industrial View." *Journal of the Society of Research Administrators,* 1985, *17* (2), 31–43.

McMahon, K. "Patents Better Protected, but Look Who's Getting Them." *Wall Street Journal,* Mar. 4, 1986, p. 30.

National Association of State Universities and Land-Grant Colleges, Division of Agriculture, Committee on Biotechnology. *Emerging Biotechnologies in Agriculture: Issues and Policies, Progress Report II.* Washington, D.C.: National Association of State Universities and Land-Grant Colleges, 1983.

National Science Board. *University-Industry Research Relationships: Selected Studies.* Washington, D.C.: National Science Foundation, 1983.

Orleans, J. H. Book reviews of *Partners in the Research Enterprise* and *Dollars and Scholars.* In *Journal of College and University Law,* 1984, *11* (2), 257–273.

Peters, L. S., and Fusfeld, H. I. "Current U.S University-Industry Research Connections." In National Science Foundation, *University-Industry Research Relationships: Selected Studies.* Washington, D.C.: National Science Foundation, 1983.

Pittman, G. F. "The Old College Tie." In "A Special Report: Technology in the Workplace." *Wall Street Journal,* sec. 4, Nov. 10, 1986, pp. 10–11D.

"Policy Governing Faculty Conflicts of Interest Found in Effect at Most Research Universities." *Chronicle of Higher Education,* Mar. 6, 1985, p. 7.

SRI International. *The Higher Education–Economic Development Connection.* T. Chimura, principal author. Washington, D.C.: American Association of State Colleges and Universities, 1986.

Stipp, D. "Biotech Firms Face Host of Thorny Issues in Seeking to Secure Commercial Rights." *Wall Street Journal,* Feb. 25, 1986, p. 33.

Szanton, P. *Not Well Advised*. New York: Russell Sage Foundation, 1981.

Tatel, D. S., and Guthrie, R. C. "The Legal Ins and Outs of University-Industry Collaborations." *Educational Record*, Spring 1983, pp. 19–25.

Tolbert, T. L. "Industry-University Research Cooperation: Convenience or Necessity—The Industrial View." *Journal of the Society of Research Administrators*, Fall 1985, pp. 45–52.

Tornatzky, A., and others. *University-Industry Cooperative Research Centers: A Practice Manual*. Washington, D.C.: National Science Foundation, 1982.

Varrin, R., and Kukich, D. "Guidelines for Industry-Sponsored Research at Universities." *Science*, 1985, *227*, 385–388.

White, L. Book reviews of *Partners in the Research Enterprise* and *Dollars and Scholars*. In *Journal of College and University Law*, 1984, *11* (2), 237–255.

Zinser, E. "Building Informed Relationships Between Academia and Industry." Address to State Higher Education Academic Officers, Tenth Annual Inservice Education Program Seminar, Asheville, N.C., Oct. 19–22, 1986.

6

Establishing Sound Contracts
and Oversight Procedures

Some problems that arise in the course of a higher education-
business partnership can be dealt with on the spot by a program manager and others can be resolved in accordance with
institutional policies and practices or in conformance with guidelines developed for the purpose. Still others may be avoided al-
together because both parties are proceeding according to the
terms of a contract governing their relationship. The chances
of drafting a sound contract are greatly improved if both the
university and the firm are aware of what commonly can go
wrong in research partnerships, develop appropriate guidelines
on key issues, and understand what safeguards can be placed
in contracts to avoid such problems.

Contractual Agreements

Smith (1984, p. 25) listed five areas in which problems
often occur in cooperative programs:

1. *The relevance of a proposed line of inquiry to the essential missions of the university and the industry*—how to design a
   collaboration program that maintains balance between
   the university's pursuit of research as an integral part
   of the educational process, and industry's search for
   useful knowledge to be applied in the development of
   products, processes and services.

197

2. *Time frame for research efforts*—how to organize a pro-
    gram that accommodates to different time constraints
    of industry and the university.
3. *The issue of proprietary rights versus openness*—how to
    assure the protection of proprietary information pro-
    vided by industry while meeting the statutory and
    ethical requirements of the university, which demand
    that research serve a broad public good, that it be con-
    ducted in an atmosphere of openness and free ex-
    change and that results be available for distribution
    on a non-confidential basis.
4. *The issue of patents and copyrights*—how to determine
    methods of licensing that will promote the progress
    of science and technology, assure that discoveries and
    inventions are used in ways most likely to benefit the
    public and provide both adequate recognition of the
    inventors and appropriate financial support to the
    universities.
5. *The issue of conflict of commitment*—how to assure that
    the primary allegiance of the faculty member remains
    with the university.

Smith (1984, p. 26) cited the first two problems as the
most common and the first to be mentioned by prospective sponsors and described the last three problems as important because
they can affect basic university values. Smith's discussion of all
five problems will be summarized because his description of how
the Massachusetts Institute of Technology handles these problems provides good examples of issues discussed not only in this,
but in previous sections.

Smith pointed out that MIT is a land-grant institution,
and, as such, is experienced in providing services to and nurturing close ties with industry. The institute had "a very substantial involvement" with the chemical and petroleum industries
in the 1930s and 1940s and with the electronics and semicon-
ductors industries in the 1950s and 1960s during their periods
of rapid development. Furthermore, each department is reviewed
each year by a Visiting Committee, composed largely of persons from industry, which reports on progress to the MIT Corporation, the institute's governing body. The institute also
operates strong industrial-liaison and continuing education pro-

grams and views consulting (one day per week) as part of a faculty member's professional obligations. The institute's policies regarding the five problems of research contracts that Smith defined have been refined through experience, and they make good sense.

The first and second issues, relevance of a proposed line of inquiry to the university and the industry and the time frame for research efforts, were discussed by Smith (p. 29) using MIT's Exxon-sponsored program in combustion as an example. In the program, projects were selected by a committee consisting of two Exxon representatives and the MIT principal investigators. The MIT investigators suggested topics and the committee selected those to be funded according to four criteria:

- Potential for significant contribution to science and technology.
- Breadth of applicability.
- Relevance to long-term Exxon and national interests.
- Potential for interaction between MIT and Exxon researchers.

Once topics were selected, support was pledged for them until the students involved had completed their investigations, whether or not Exxon lost interest in the topics. The committee met about twice a year and sent minutes of meetings to the Office of Sponsored Programs.

The third issue, proprietary rights versus openness, can be dealt with effectively, according to Smith, by appropriate guidelines:

1. MIT does not engage in proprietary research, and all results may be freely disseminated.
2. MIT students may discuss their research freely.
3. Because a principal investigator may have to have access to proprietary information to continue productive research, MIT grants to sponsors a thirty-day delay in submitting publications to allow sponsors to check their contents for inadvertent disclosure of proprietary information, with a possible sixty-day extension if information has been included that is relevant to a patent.

Solutions to the fourth issue, patents and copyrights, are more fluid because the duty to facilitate technology transfer must be balanced against the sponsor's claim to benefit from discoveries resulting from company-backed research. MIT retains ownership of all patents, and it often grants nonexclusive worldwide licenses to sponsors. Sometimes, to encourage corporate investment in commercialization of discoveries, limited-term, royalty-bearing, exclusive patent rights are granted to sponsors— but "always with march-in rights and performance milestones so that the company cannot simply sequester the technology and do nothing with it" (Smith, 1984, p. 27). According to Smith, royalty rates and duration of license often have been negotiated after a patent has been issued—a practice that works well if good faith exists on both sides. Sponsors are granted a thirty-day review period prior to publication of results, with the possibility of a sixty-day extension if a manuscript reveals information that should be or is being submitted for patents.

Solutions to the fifth issue, conflict of commitment, Smith stated (p. 28), rest on "rules governing faculty behavior and good citizenship":

1. Each faculty member must annually disclose all outside activity, including whether compensation for work was in the form of fees or equity interest. Department heads refer questionable cases to the provost for further review.
2. No faculty member is permitted to hold line responsibility in an outside firm. Faculty members may take leaves of absence for up to two years for managerial service with firms, but then must either change the relationship or leave the institute.
3. No arrangements are permitted that allow a sponsor special access to the institution; that is, no sponsor is granted the right of first refusal regarding continuing work or allowed to become the sole industrial sponsor of a laboratory because the potential for conflict of interest is too great.

These solutions form a sensible model because they invoke rules where rules are needed and allow flexibility where it is appropriate. The issue of the relevance of projects to both participants must be dealt with repeatedly throughout the life of an umbrella program that funds a succession of projects. Both sides have considerable influence in the negotiations: The sponsor can withdraw financial support, and the research team can withdraw expertise, if satisfactory terms cannot be maintained. At institutions where faculty strength is not so remarkable that the threat of withdrawal is a telling pawn in the balance between the partners, however, concessions must be avoided that would interfere with fulfillment of the institution's mission, even if granting them would guarantee continued project funding.

Matthews and Norgaard (1984, pp. 181-192) compiled a number of additional useful points relevant to contracts. First, they reminded negotiators that contracts must address not only the needs of researchers and administrators involved in projects but the broader needs of the university and the corporation entering into the contract. Second, the authors noted that because researchers commit so much to projects, they may not be willing to allow them to come to an end at the proper time. "For this reason, a contract should clearly specify what will have been accomplished by the end of the project or what events will signal its conclusion" (p. 189). A contract also should specify the conditions under which each partner may withdraw from the agreement, and it should specify when various duties switch from university scientists to company engineers during the course of a project.

MacCordy (1983, pp. 18-20) recommended ten kinds of provisions to be included in the agreement governing any single- or multiple-project program to create "unequivocal understanding":

1. *Scope of Work Provisions*—to define what research is to be done; state whether the university actually agrees to do it or only to give the task its best effort; and establish that the only university personnel on whom the agreement places obligations are the actual project participants.
2. *Key Personnel*—to identify university participants, their duties and any pertinent restrictions that will apply; for example, consulting for other companies.

3. *Reports*—to establish routines for providing written reports and oral briefings, which are essential to productive relationships.
4. *The Term, or Project Period*—to define the project period, the terms under which it can be terminated (the university wants a period of support long enough to provide a fair chance of achieving success and to attract researchers and graduate students to the project, and the company wants to be able to terminate funding if progress is unsatisfactory), and the schedule of support (lump sum, year by year).
5. *Funding Arrangements*—to satisfy particular sponsors' requirements, which tend to be less stringent than those of federal agencies.
6. *Publication*—to reaffirm the university scientist's need to publish and to specify acceptable delay period to allow filing for patents.
7. *Confidentiality of Information*—to specify that the company must have personnel sign confidentiality agreements who have access to proprietary information and that the company agrees to protect university proprietary information from inquisitive competitors.
8. *Agreement Clauses*—to assign responsibility for patenting resulting inventions, preferably to the company, for then they must defend them, as necessary.
9. *Licensing of Inventions*—to establish provisions for licensing of inventions that result from research, often an exclusive, royalty-bearing license, which requires the company to pursue commercialization diligently.
10. *Disputes Clause*—to identify means by which disputes are to be settled; omission indicates parties may resort to litigation or binding arbitration, means that are sure to destroy the effectiveness of the relationship.

Grounds (in Reams, 1986a, pp. 108–109) also identified major issues to be considered in designing an agreement:

Checklist Areas to Consider in Designing an Agreement

1. *Description of the Work*
2. *The Principal University Investigator*
3. *The Cost of the Research*
4. *Confidentiality*

5. *The Right to Publish*

    This is unequivocal, and it should be so stated. To satisfy both parties' concerns about disclosure of patentable information, a pre-publication review period is usually considered reasonable if that period is short, but allows for preparation of a sound patent application prior to publication. Note that publication may include an oral presentation, particularly if made before a recognized scientific meeting and preceded by an abstract.

6. *Patent Rights and Licensing*

    An agreement leading to the sharing of rights to potential revenues should consider:

    a. *Filing*

        Who files in what counties and who funds filing, prosecution, and maintenance can be handled in different ways but needs to be addressed. Again, it should be noted that the absolute requirement of many foreign countries requires filing before any publication is made.

    b. *Commercialization*

        The sharing of rights leading to the sharing of potential revenues according to the contributions of both parties and the constraints of the market is to be diligently sought. The framework for such sharing can be established without specific details which frequently cannot be supplied until such time as an invention is made (if indeed that occurs) and its value assessed. Such a framework can take the following form:

        Patent Assignment—Determined according to the policy of the university.

        License—Option for either exclusive or non-exclusive rights to the sponsor with royalties or other payments to be negotiated. Royalties may depend upon a number of factors which cannot be determined initially; they may depend upon the type of license, whether or not there is joint inventorship that includes both university and industry personnel, and other considerations. Any period of exclusivity should be sufficient to encourage commercialization.

        Diligence—Provisions to encourage diligent commercialization can take the form of reasonable pre-

paid royalties, although a "best efforts" clause
with a stated date for commercialization may be
sufficient.

Caldart (in Reams, 1986a, p. 109) advised all universities
to note in contracts that they "retain control over all internal
decisions" and to be aware that agreements that allow industry
representatives a presence on campus may call into question
the integrity of the institution.

MacCordy (1983, p. 15) recommended that research administrators and university attorneys be contacted when advice
is needed on certain matters, such as these:

1. The functioning of companies: how companies' internal
    decisions are made, especially as they relate to R&D in-
    vestments and new product commitments, and how to de-
    termine which companies might be interested in a proposed
    project.
2. The protection of intellectual property by patents, copy-
    rights, and trade-secret laws.
3. The drafting and negotiation of contract agreements for
    research services and licensing of intellectual property.
4. The interpretation of government regulations and those of
    other research sponsors as they relate to patentable inven-
    tions, copyrights, software, and technical data.
5. The interpretation of university policies and practices related
    to the ownership and licensing of intellectual property, the
    sharing of royalty income, faculty consulting, conflicts of
    interest, academic freedom, proprietary and classified re-
    search, and associated matters.

Fowler (1982–83) identified fifteen categories of legal
issues to note when drafting research agreements between universities and sponsoring industries. Reams (1986, pp. 50–94)
used these categories as an organizational structure to discuss
many of the most important such legal issues. Fowler's categories are given here as an additional checklist to use in drafting research agreements:

1. The scope of the research project
2. Nature and extent of the sponsor's commitment to the project
3. Nature and extent of the university's undertaking pursuant to the agreement
4. Control over the conduct of the funded research program
5. Exclusive right of the industrial sponsor to fund research in the area involved in the agreement
6. The extent and terms of actual technical or scientific collaboration by the industry participants
7. Reporting requirements
8. Funding
9. Competing interests in the use of research results
10. Receipt of proprietary information from industrial sponsor
11. Patent rights
12. The licensing of "know-how"
13. Indemnification and hold harmless agreements
14. Use of university's name
15. Potential conflicts of interest on the part of the university researchers

Each of the lists of issues and provisions regarding drafting of research agreements that have been presented in this chapter has included some repetition of important matters, yet each has also revealed more detail of the complex range of potential situations that must be addressed in such contracts. Reams's analyses and summaries of precedents in case law, business law, and statutory law that pertain to each point in Fowler's checklist are recommended reading. The following summary briefly states some of Reams's key observations and cautions.

Regarding category 1, scope of the research project, both Reams (1986a, p. 51) and Fowler (1982–83) emphasized the importance of defining the scope of the project carefully, including project control and terms regarding exclusive or nonexclusive funding, so that if unexpected results occur, disputes over patent rights can be avoided. The nature and extent of the sponsor's commitment (category 2) are especially important to a university that has invested in new buildings and equipment for a project. Outstanding progress does not guarantee continued support, but it may give a company reason to think seriously of making even greater investments in the project—independent of the university. An agreement should guarantee funding so long as research continues to meet prespecified targets, or until negotiated project time or funding has expired. Unfortunately, many projects do not lend themselves to specification of intermediate targets.

Statements of the nature and extent of the university's commitment (category 3) cannot guarantee specific results of industry-sponsored projects or commit funds of the university (a nonprofit, charitable, tax-exempt corporation) to a speculative, proprietary, research enterprise. A "best-effort" basis should be specified for conduct of research, with no penalty for default. Regarding category 4, control over conduct of the program, contracts should specify that providing funding for research does not imply any control of the project by the sponsor.

The exclusive right of the industrial sponsor to fund research in the area involved in the agreement (category 5) may be granted by a university, since the sponsor is interested in commercialization (although not of an invention with rights invested in others, including other industrial sponsors or the federal government.) The extent and terms of scientific collaboration by industrial participants (category 6) must be specified in a contract to avoid problems during the project, particularly because the sponsor's nonfinancial contribution in source material or equipment may be essential to its success. Reporting requirements (category 7) should be specified that are reasonable to carry out and meet the needs of both parties. Since institutions are accustomed to complying with federal requirements, some industrial sponsors may wish to adopt the same procedures.

Funding (category 8) can be provided through a variety of options, although three are common: advance funding, periodic funding according to a predetermined schedule, and reimbursement. A combination approach may be most useful. Reams recommended that this section of a contract address the issues of overhead costs, ownership of equipment purchased with research funds, a cost index to offset inflation, internal distribution of funds, and construction and remodeling costs essential to the project.

Category 9, competing interests in use of research results, is one of the most important on the list, as its negotiation rests on bridging the differences between higher education's mission of disseminating knowledge and businesses' goal of keeping knowledge secret if doing so may be profitable. Delay in publication to examine manuscripts and file patent applications should be negotiated on a case-by-case basis. Reams (1986a, p. 67) reminded universities: "The sponsor should not be permitted any control or editorial leeway in textual matters, analysis of scientific results, or statements of conclusions."

Category 10, receipt of proprietary information, can pose a quandary in that secrets are difficult to keep on campus, yet proprietary information may be essential to contracted research. Limits may be set in a contract regarding what constitutes confidential information, or how long the university is required to keep such information confidential. Reams noted (pp. 68–69) that "the use of contracts to impose restrictions on the use of sponsor developed computer software can also present confidentiality problems and directly limit the research effort. . . . Trade-secret protection . . . may be the best option to prohibit unauthorized use of software. If a program is properly treated as a trade secret, the rewriting of the program does not prohibit legal action for violation of trade secrecy."

Category 11, patent rights, is important because it involves reconciliation of the interests of the investigator, the university, and the sponsor. Licenses give sponsors the right to commercialize products of research while retaining ownership of property. Reams recommended (pp. 74–75): "A university's patent policy should clarify the source of the institution's interest in an invention; identify the rights of the institution, the inventor(s), and the research sponsors; create a method of royalty distribution among interested parties; and establish dispute resolution procedures among the interested parties. Implementation of the patent policy should be carried out by administrators on recommendation of a patent committee composed of faculty members from the arts, as well as science and engineering." Reams emphasized (pp. 76–79) the administrative regulations pursuant to the Uniform Patent Legislation Act, which is important to colleges and universities because it granted nonprofit organizations and small business "a right of first refusal to title in inventions they have made in performance of government grants and contracts."

Reams's discussion of licensing know-how (category 12) focused on several issues. First, since negotiating contractual provisions to cover patents of projects not yet invented can be very difficult, specification of licensing terms to be in effect once invention has been accomplished and patents have been secured may be preferable. Second, the sponsor's access to intellectual property—that is, technology developed with the sponsor's funds—must be protected, perhaps by giving the sponsor a royalty-free, nonexclusive license to use such technology internally. Reams (pp. 84–89) provided a useful analysis of tax aspects of university-industry research.

Indemnification clauses (category 13) in contracts indicate agreement between the parties as to which will assume the risk of liability. Liability risks should be assumed by the profit-oriented partner. Reams warned that "construction of indemnity contracts appears to be the source of considerable litigation" (p. 62).

Use of the university's name (category 14), logo, or seal by a sponsor should be prohibited under the terms of a research agreement to prevent the appearance of product endorsement.

Conflict of interest (category 15) has already been discussed in other sections. Reams (p. 69) divided this topic into "unjust enrichment" and "conflict in commitment" and noted that since such conflict is an ethical issue that must be decided on each university campus, it generally is not a proper subject for inclusion in a contract. The exception (Fowler, 1983,) is "a provision whereby the industrial sponsor agrees that no faculty member, staff member (and perhaps student) from the college or university has or will have any interest in, or will participate as an officer, director or consultant in or to, the organization during the course of the agreement." Reams noted (1986a, p. 71) that no conflict of interest problem may exist vis-à-vis faculty consulting, if consulting is defined not as "outside" work, but as an "aspect of traditional academic inquiry." Faculty holdings in sponsor companies are not perceived by Reams generally to constitute a conflict-of-interest problem. In fact, requiring disclosure might constitute attempted invasion of privacy.

Dispute-resolution mechanisms may not be thought necessary, but researchers sometimes do behave unprofessionally. Thus, Reams listed several such mechanisms: a panel of fact finders, arbitration, settlement by "minitrial" (use of a neutral third party as arbitrator or mediator), a summary jury trial, review through a settlement conference, and referral to private dispute-resolution organizations (Coolley, 1983, p. 164).

Reams (1986a, p. 92) also noted that Marsh (1983, p. 183) had identified several reasons technology agreements fail. Licensing agreements and many contractual agreements may fail because the technology was improperly evaluated, partners were improperly selected, negotiations were improperly conducted, or licenses were improperly implemented and serviced.

Near the end of his book, Reams (1986a, pp. 110–158) examines four major contracts: the Massachusetts General Hospital–Hoechst, A.G., contract of 1980; the Washington University–Mallinckrodt, Inc., agreement of 1981; the Washington University–Monsanto Biomedical Research agreement of 1982; and the Washington University–Anheuser-Busch Companies, Inc., micromixing agreement of 1983. Table 10 compares sixty-five contractual provisions, terms, and clauses for three of these major contracts: the Massachusetts General Hospital–Hoechst, A.G., contract of 1980; the Washington University–Mallinckrodt, Inc., agreement of 1981; and the Washington University–Monsanto Biomedical Research agreement of 1982. This table is presented to allow comparison of the terms of three well-known contracts involving large corporate project support and to provide another even more extensive checklist of items to be considered when drafting contracts.

Reams interviewed representatives of various partners to determine the success and present status of the agreements, noting that the Mallinckrodt and Monsanto hybridoma contracts might not be renewed. He concluded (p. 158): "The rules of contracting have made for successful research ventures between industry and institutions of higher education. No serious legal or cooperative issues appear to have manifested themselves.

Table 10. Comparative Summary of Contractual Provisions.

CONTRACTUAL PROVISIONS, TERMS AND CLAUSES	Hoechst	Mallinckrodt	Monsanto
1. NUMBER OF PROJECTS	multiple but specific	multiple but specific	multiple and to be specifically identified in the future
2. ADMINISTRATIVE STRUCTURE OF PROJECTS	Scientific Advisory Board of Department; membership consists of two members from Massachusetts General Hospital; two from Hoechst and two independent	Advisory Committee; membership consists of four university members and one Mallinckrodt member	Advisory Committee membership consists of four Monsanto members and four University members
3. TIME PERIOD OF AGREEMENT	April 14, 1981, through September 30, 1990	September 1, 1981, through August 31, 1984	July 1, 1982, through June 30, 1987
4. PROVISION FOR CONTINUATION OF AGREEMENT	automatic extension in five years unless written notice given	extended in three years by negotiated agreement	extension by mutual agreement at three anniversary
5. EXTENSION OF PROJECTS IF CONTRACTS ARE NOT CONTINUED	no statement	negotiable at Mallinckrodt's request for one year	negotiable at Monsanto request for one year
6. METHOD OF SELECTION AND APPROVAL OF PROJECTS	selected by each Senior Investigator and approved by Director	selected and approved by majority of members of the Advisory Committee	selected and approved by five out of eight members of the Advisory Committee

CONTRACTUAL PROVISIONS, TERMS AND CLAUSES	Hoechst	Mallinckrodt	Monsanto
RATIO OF BASIC RESEARCH TO APPLIED RESEARCH	no statement	no statement	30% basic/70% applied
PROVISIONS FOR INTERACTION BETWEEN SCIENTISTS	sponsor may send up to four representatives per year	no statement	sponsor may send unspecified number of representatives plus have access to university office space
INDEPENDENT REVIEW OF RESEARCH PROJECTS	presented for comment at annual symposium	no statement	review permitted after two years
FORMULA FOR ADJUSTMENT OF CORPORATE FUNDING FOR INFLATION OR DEFLATION	1981 dollars adjusted by formula—see §2.2 C	no statement	GNP Defeator Index used as part of formula—see §8.2(a)
TITLE TO EQUIPMENT PURCHASED WITH SPONSOR'S FUNDS	title to MGH but for Department use only	title to university	title to university at time of purchase
PUBLICATION RESTRICTIONS ON UNIVERSITY RESEARCHER	review by sponsor required but no control over manuscript	review by Advisory Committee with sponsor allowed to request a three month delay	review by sponsor for patentability at least one month prior to publication; sponsor may request delay of submission for a reasonable time to establish patent rights

CONTRACTUAL PROVISIONS, TERMS AND CLAUSES	Hoechst	Mallinckrodt	Monsanto
13. OWNERSHIP OF PATENTS AND TECHNICAL DEVELOPMENTS	MGH with assignment to sponsor if MGH has no interest in title	to the university with exclusive license to sponsor	to the university w exclusive license t sponsor
14. PROTECTION PROVIDED FOR UNIVERSITY PROPRIETARY INFORMATION	no statement	sponsor to take all reasonable precautions for ten years	sponsor to take reasonable precaut
15. PROTECTION PROVIDED FOR SPONSOR'S PROPRIETARY INFORMATION	no statement	personal commitments to be made by researchers	personal commitme of confidentiality b individual participa
16. OBLIGATION OF SPONSOR TO COMMERCIALIZE RESEARCH RESULTS	if not commercialized by sponsor, license reverts to non-exclusive status	no statement	no statement
17. SPONSOR TO MONITOR RESEARCH FOR PATENTABLE AND NOVEL INVENTIONS	yes	yes	yes
18. PROMPT REPORTING AND FILING FOR PATENT-ABILITY BY SPONSOR	yes	yes	yes
19. PROMPT REPORTING OF POSSIBLE RESULTS BY UNIVERSITY TO SPONSOR	yes	yes	yes

CONTRACTUAL PROVISIONS, TERMS AND CLAUSES	Hoechst	Mallinckrodt	Monsanto
WHO FILES FOR PATENT	sponsor	sponsor	sponsor
WHO FILES FOR FOREIGN PATENTS	sponsor	sponsor	sponsor
WHO PAYS COST OF PATENT FILINGS AND PROSECUTION	sponsor	sponsor	sponsor
IS PROSECUTION BEYOND PATENT OFFICE REJECTION REQUIRED	no statement	no	no
MAY UNIVERSITY UTILIZE INDEPENDENT PATENT COUNSEL	no statement	yes, for review only	yes, for review only
ROYALTY TO UNIVERSITY ADJUSTED BASED ON CONTRIBUTION OF SPONSOR	yes	no statement	yes
UNIVERSITY TO PROVIDE RECORDS FOR PATENT APPLICATION	yes	yes	yes

CONTRACTUAL PROVISIONS, TERMS AND CLAUSES	Hoechst	Mallinckrodt	Monsanto
27. UNIVERSITY TO ASSURE TITLE TO ALL TECHNICAL DEVELOPMENTS	yes	yes	yes
28. UNIVERSITY WAIVER OF PATENT CLAIM AGAINST SPONSOR	no statement	no statement	yes
29. INDIVIDUAL INVENTOR WAIVER OF PATENT CLAIM AGAINST SPONSOR	no statement	no statement	yes
30. INDEMNIFICATION CLAUSE FOR CLAIMS ARISING FROM PATENT CLAIMS	no statement	no statement	yes; patent filed and prosecuted by Comp on University behalf
31. UNIVERSITY AGREES TO GRANT LICENSES TO SPONSOR	yes	sponsor has right of first refusal to license	sponsor must elect to accept license within two years of filing
32. EXCLUSIVE LICENSE ON PATENTABLE INVENTIONS TO SPONSOR	yes, if not on collaborative research	yes	yes
33. LICENSES ON NON-PATENTABLE TECHNICAL DEVELOPMENTS TO SPONSOR	no statement	exclusive for ten years	non-exclusive and non-revocable

CONTRACTUAL PROVISIONS, TERMS AND CLAUSES	Hoechst	Mallinckrodt	Monsanto
LICENSING OF NON-PROGRAM PATENTS BY UNIVERSITY TO SPONSOR	right to best possible license	no statement	yes, to best extent possible
LICENSING REQUIREMENTS SPECIFIED IN AGREEMENT	yes	yes	yes
REASONABLE ATTEMPT TO BE MADE BY SPONSOR TO MARKET RESEARCH RESULTS	indirectly	yes	yes
IF REASONABLE EFFORT NOT MADE BY SPONSOR TO MARKET RESULTS, THE NON-EXCLUSIVE SUBLICENSE RESULTS	yes, after three years	no statement	yes
INDUSTRY SPONSOR REQUIRED TO SUBMIT MARKETABILITY SCHEDULE DURING PERIOD OF EXCLUSIVE LICENSE	no statement	yes	yes
SPONSOR PERMITTED TO SUBLICENSE	no statement	yes	yes, with notification by university
ROYALTY PAYMENTS BY SPONSOR TO UNIVERSITY	not to exceed 50% of the fair commercial royalty rate for such license (6.4)	royalty schedule based on Net Selling Price with a rate scale (8.14d)	royalty rate to be negotiated at licensing

CONTRACTUAL PROVISIONS, TERMS AND CLAUSES	Hoechst	Mallinckrodt	Monsanto
41. IF NO ROYALTY RATE AGREEMENT, ARBITRATION IS PROVIDED	yes	no statement	yes
42. LAW TO BE APPLIED TO AGREEMENT	Massachusetts	Missouri	Missouri
43. ACTION TO BE TAKEN IN EVENT OF INFRINGEMENT	no statement	no statement	sponsor to obtain discontinuance or bring suit (11.18.1(1))
44. WHO MAY SUE INFRINGER?	no statement	no statement	Sponsor may sue in its name or university's name; university may sue in its name if sponsor does not sue
45. INFRINGEMENT SUIT COST RECOVERY	no statement	no statement	Settlement or recovery shall first be used to pe expenses of the party bringing the suit; balan to be distributed 2/3 to party bringing suit and 1/3 to other party.
46. HAS UNIVERSITY RIGHT OF APPROVAL PRIOR TO SPONSOR BRINGING SUIT?	no statement	no statement	yes
47. UNIVERSITY MAY ASSIGN TITLE TO SPONSOR BRINGING SUIT	no statement	no statement	yes

CONTRACTUAL PROVISIONS, TERMS AND CLAUSES	Hoechst	Mallinckrodt	Monsanto
RIGHT OF UNIVERSITY TO LICENSE ELSEWHERE IF SPONSOR DOES NOT ELECT TO LICENSE	no statement	yes, with sponsor receiving 50% of royalties	yes, but no license permitted to sponsor's competitors
TERMINATION OF AGREEMENT FOR BREACH OR DEFAULT	no statement	90 day written notice unless breach is cured	90 day written notice
TERMINATION FOR INSOLVENCY OF A PARTY	no statement	30 day written notice	30 day written notice
PATENT AND LICENSE RIGHTS SURVIVE TERMINATION OF AGREEMENT	no statement	yes	yes
INDEMNIFICATION OF UNIVERSITY BY SPONSOR FOR LIABILITY ARISING FROM USE OF PRODUCTS	no statement	yes	yes
UNIVERSITY WARRANTS SUFFICIENT INSURANCE AND WORKMEN'S COMPENSATION FOR ITS EMPLOYEES	no statement	no statement	yes
SPONSOR TO HOLD UNIVERSITY HARMLESS FOR SPONSOR'S EMPLOYEES INJURED AT UNIVERSITY	no statement	no statement	yes, if no negligence by university

CONTRACTUAL PROVISIONS, TERMS AND CLAUSES	Hoechst	Mallinckrodt	Monsanto
55. ASSIGNMENT OF RIGHTS AND OBLIGATIONS BY EITHER PARTY	yes, if to a corporation controlled by one of the parties and with a guarantee from the party of the performance of its assignee	no	no
56. MAY UNIVERSITY SUBCONTRACT	no statement	no statement	only with approval of sponsor
57. USE OF UNIVERSITY OR SPONSOR'S NAME WITH PUBLICITY	no statement	may use other party's name only with permission	use of other party's nam only with permission
58. RESEARCH PARTICIPANT NON-DISCLOSURE AGREEMENT	yes required	yes	yes
59. DISTRIBUTION OF PRODUCT BY UNIVERSITY FOR RESEARCH ONLY	no statement	yes	no statement
60. THIRD PARTY COMPETITOR DISTRIBUTES SIMILAR PRODUCT SIGNIFICANTLY AFFECTING SPONSOR'S BUSINESS, THEN ROYALTY PAYMENT TO UNIVERSITY MAY CEASE	no statement	yes	no statement
61. REPAYMENT OF SPONSOR'S COSTS REQUIRED AT TERMINATION OF AGREEMENT	fair market value of equipment and furniture plus half of cost of construction of building to be repaid	no	no

NTRACTUAL OVISIONS, RMS AND CLAUSES	Hoechst	Mallinckrodt	Monsanto
PROVISION FOR ALTERNATIVE FUNDING TO UNIVERSITY	sponsor has exclusive right to fund research unless sponsor declines	no statement	no statement
CONTRACT FUNDING STATED	$67.3 million over 10 years	$3,881,250 over three years	$23.5 million over five years
DESIGNATED DIRECTOR OF RESEARCH OR PRINCIPAL INVESTIGATOR	MGH to appoint with consultation of sponsor; Dr. H. Goodman initially designated	Dr. Joseph M. Davie	appointed by university— Dr. D. Kipnis
PROVISION FOR RESOLUTION OF DISPUTES	none; Joint Committee of three trustee members of MGH and three senior executives of Hoechst serve to oversee agreement and forum for communicaton	no statement	Royalty rate disputes may be submitted to binding arbitration under rules of American Arbitration Association

Source: Reams, 1986a, pp. 132–141. Used by permission.

Mutual respect between the parties and good communication appear to have avoided any legal difficulties. Contract law, state and federal statutes, and self-regulatory guidelines appear to be successful in that no evidence appears that any draconian measures or law suits have been employed by the parties. The major reason for the potential non-renewal has resulted from the shift in corporate research interests, not from dissatisfaction with the research results or perceived failure of either party to perform according to its contractual commitments."

Peters and Fusfeld (1983, p. 71) stated that "Over 50 percent of industrially supported research at universities is by way of contracted research. Such industrial support in the past has generally been for small amounts ($20,000–$50,000) on a project-by-project and year-by-year basis." In contrast, in an article in the *Wall Street Journal* (1986, p. 32) Reams described the $70 million, ten-year research contract in molecular biology signed in 1980 by Massachusetts General Hospital, an affiliate of Harvard Medical School, and Hoechst, A.G., a West German chemical corporation, and the $62 million, twenty-year research contract to study brain functioning signed in 1985 by Georgetown University and FIDIA Pharmaceutical, an Italian firm. Reams urged U.S. firms to begin to support long-term R&D projects in the academic sector. He stated, "Advances in high technology are coming at a rapid pace. . . . Corporate America is going to find itself contractually shut out of the action. Many European countries, Japan, and such industrialized countries as Brazil, South Korea, Taiwan, Singapore and others are developing significant competitive high-technology industries that require continued access to basic resources. They will come looking to U.S. universities if companies here do not."

The Role of the Administrator

If a problem occurs that cannot or should not be handled by a project manager, perhaps because a situation has arisen that is, or threatens to be, in violation of institutional policies or practices or certain terms of the research contract, the problem may be called to the attention of a senior administrator.

Administration of research agreements varies widely, with authority in some schools resting with the provost, in others with the dean of the graduate school. Large institutions may have a vice-president for research, under whom may be consolidated responsibility for negotiating research agreements, applying for patents, and other legal affairs; keeping financial accounts (including identifying sources and determining the amount of payments and determining whether contracting companies are paying the university to do research for which they received payment from the federal government); approving overhead and fringe-benefit rates; approving major equipment purchases; and performing other bureaucratic functions. The vice-president for research may also be responsible for management of university-owned research laboratories, industrial parks, or incubators.

Offices of research have assumed the task of actively seeking out opportunities for contracts by identifying innovations or potential innovations and calling them to the attention of appropriate businesses, by providing support services to entrepreneurial faculty members, and by forming interdisciplinary groups of faculty members that extend beyond the boundaries of a single department to meet particular industrial needs. Oversight of individual contracts and research centers or institutes often rests with department chairs, the dean of the faculty, or the dean of the graduate school. Procedures vary widely, but on some major projects, operation of the research facility and conduct of research are supervised through the chair-dean-provost chain, whereas financial approvals rest with the vice-president for research or finance. Projects that cut across disciplines or schools may be monitored by interdepartmental or interschool oversight or advisory committees. Such committees may be chaired by the vice-president for research or a designee who possesses appropriate technical expertise. Leveraging research funds with state or private money and identifying venture capital for startup companies, which sometimes are the brainchildren of entrepreneurial faculty members and may be located in university incubators, also may be among the duties of some vice-presidents for research.

A vice-president for research is responsible, it is to be hoped, to a president who is willing to champion the idea of university-industry cooperative projects, attend meals and meetings with businesspeople, legislators, and trustees to elicit support for such projects, and make sure that his or her support of cooperative programs is generally known on campus. Without a presidential champion, much still can be accomplished, but it will take longer. It is also to be hoped that a vice-president for research oversees project managers who have initiative, common sense, persistence, and the ability to inspire people to achieve their best, and who also are excellent researchers and fund raisers. Again, with less talent available, much still can be accomplished, but it will take longer. Authority and responsibility are, by necessity, markedly decentralized in university-industry cooperative relationships. As a result, leadership on all levels is essential for partnerships to function effectively and be most productive.

Matthews and Norgaard (1984, pp. 173–180) made a number of excellent points regarding administration of university-industry partnerships. They agreed that champions are needed, preferably at the presidential level. "Championing the cause, however, is not enough. Educators and executives must understand how to translate their strategic vision of the partnership into concrete activities" (p. 173). Success depends on being able to coordinate different organizational cultures and tap the creativity and initiative of independent-natured scientists on both sides. It depends on meeting the often diverse expectations of both parties, as well as those of the many individuals involved.

In addition, Matthews and Norgaard stated, "Managing the partnership between industry and higher education requires not only diplomatic skill but a deep commitment to the strategic importance of alliances. . . . It involves convincing others within one's own organization and a willingness and ability to negotiate with outside parties. Bringing a partnership to life requires a rare combination of vision fortitude, and patience. . . . Developing linkages on an organizational level is perhaps the greatest challenge to the management of partnerships" (pp. 175–176). Not only must boundary-spanning units be designed to bridge the gap between organizations, such units must acquire an identity by being depended on by both the academic and industrial communities to provide services needed to support cooperative ventures, command resources to support their activities, establish their own policies and procedures, and maintain high visibility.

Administrators in a hierarchical organization who believe that the essence of being a good administrator is giving orders and making sure others obey them will be dissatisfied with the consultation and patient construction of interdependent relationships that characterize successful university-industry collaboration. Rarely does a single administrator on a joint project have authority to order all individuals or units from all sectors either to cooperate or perform their assigned duties. Rarely does an advisory board have the authority to order a participant to change research agendas, buy equipment, expend funds for any purpose, or employ particular indiviuals. Persuasion, influence based on expertise, and ability to influence resource allocation by one of the participating organizations—a company, university, or state economic development agency—are the most reliable methods of producing desired changes in behavior.

Usually, board members, administrators, or other personnel who are successful at initiating or overseeing university-industry cooperative projects tend to be entrepreneurial and willing to pursue dreams, to invest, and to take risks. As has been stated, vice-presidents for research have duties of great variety. Success comes easier in such a role if the administrator is knowledgeable beyond narrow technological competence; that is, if he or she understands the fundamentals of economic development, how other sectors make decisions, and other general principles that influence the undertakings for which he or she is responsible.

Since no single individual can know all that is required to make a university-industry partnership succeed, a team should be assembled that captures most of the important skills or knowledge required for success. In technological research and development projects, for example, experts in the disciplines involved must be included in decision making from the earliest stages. In addition, administrators, laywers, and accountants involved in the enterprise must be generally educated and, if not experienced in the particular kind of project to which they have been assigned, must dedicate themselves to becoming informed laypersons regarding that science or technology. Administrators' and bureaucrats' lack of familiarity with vocabulary, concepts, research goals, and resource requirements can be fatal to an effort.

Research is the responsibility of project scientists—but administrators and bureaucrats must appreciate its implications in terms of facilities, time and effort of faculty members and graduate students, and other campus-related concerns; and its results in terms of products, patents, manufacturing processes, and other market-related issues. Information about the marketplace, competition, patent rights, federal requirements for use of human subjects or animals, federal accounting regulations and patent rights, the needs of venture capitalists and investors, and any number of other matters should be accessible to some if not all members of an administrative team. A good science or engineering background always is helpful, as is social sciences training that contributes to management skills and the understanding of varied organizational cultures.

Understanding how institutional policy is made, how programs are approved, what policies and programs may have to be modified to give new partnerships a fair chance of success, and how to change policies or programs and who can do so is valuable information. This is not to say that traditions or elements of the cultures of organizations that are involved in collaborative relationships must be discarded. To the contrary, full appreciation and guardianship of traditions and cultures are essential to avoiding insurmountable opposition to collaborative relationships at campus, corporate, or governmental levels.

Traditional campus governance structures can be utilized to achieve the broad consultation that is important in designing guidelines and in developing large university-industry projects in which local, state, and federal government and multiple companies and universities may be involved (Powers and Powers, 1983, pp. 103–109). When consultation with external constituencies as well as with units throughout a university is required to allow a project to proceed expeditiously, an effective approach is to appoint representatives of influential councils and committees internal and external to the institution to a central advisory, coordinating, or planning council. Drafts of policies produced by this council may be carried by representatives to their parent committees or organizations for deliberation and endorsement. When consensus is reached, recommendations should be forwarded by the committees back to the central council.

Task forces may be organized to report to the coordinating council. Chairs should be selected on the basis of knowledge and experience in the subject to be addressed by the task force. Adjournment to allow members to consult with their parent organizations should be an important part of the process. By bringing into the open perceived points of conflict regarding a new endeavor such as a research park, plans may be made that avoid or resolve the issues. The process can be lengthy and difficult, but well worth the effort if the alternative is to discontinue the project because behind the scenes various constituencies, alarmed at perceived losses to be suffered, sidetrack every good beginning until leaders grow too frustrated to proceed.

Personal and Professional Responsibility

Oversight by program managers, deans, and vice-presidents; development of institutional policies, practices, and guidelines; and design of contracts all help research partnerships to proceed smoothly. As in all human endeavors, organizational structures and routines, lines of authority, and rules are only aids; following them will not guarantee optimal decision making all the time.

The saying in business, "To have good work done, hire good people," is equally true in university-industry cooperative projects, however. If enough individuals in leadership positions, from project managers to presidents, have the fortitude and perceptiveness to make sound professional judgments, events tend to make progress toward long-range goals—although the passage may not be smooth. Researchers and administrators in both organizations may be anxious to reach agreements on contracts and project design at the expense of institutional traditions and values. Some well-intentioned people are not perceptive regarding the implications and effects of new relationships or changes in policies and practices. Sometimes causing a flurry of displeasure over a cooperative project may be necessary to rouse attention to the fact that the project could have unacceptable consequences for the institution if allowed to proceed as planned by its backers. Successful projects meet the needs of both partners, not only the actual participants in the projects but also their employer institutions.

In some situations, conditions are so perfect for an effort that it will flourish regardless of the quality of leadership. Even under optimal conditions, however, if the president of a university or some other leader of a partnership effort tells the truth only as he or she wishes it to be, supports projects not on the basis of quality but on the basis of favoritism, creates good press coverage by taking credit for the ideas and achievements of others, or in other ways does not display the high standards of professional behavior that an institution should expect from its leaders, project funds from industries and support provided by state government will not be sustained over time nor spent as wisely as possible. Throughout the institution, people may become lethargic, attempting to withdraw from the situation, or they may adopt the president's standards and begin working primarily for self-aggrandizement instead of directing their best efforts to projects at hand for the good of their institution. Waste of resources will result, and the long-term development of the institution may be stunted, even though current projects seem to be flourishing in every way.

Linnell (1982, pp. 124–125) identified three important ethical issues generated by faculty involvement in corporate projects. First, conflict may arise between time devoted to corporate projects and time devoted to basic academic work. Time pressures may cause neglect of students, interfere with collegial interactions, and eliminate time to reflect. Linnell made the extremely important observation that devoting time to reflection may be the most important duty of any professor.

A second ethical issue identified by Linnell was described as cognitive dissonance between the concept of intellectual inquiry and inhibitions to communication caused by control of information when outside interests influence earnings. A third concern was loss of public credibility when apparent conflicts of interest generate suspicions that self-interest governs faculty members' actions. Losses of credibility could, over time, threaten public support for higher education and greatly reduce the public's confidence in the objectivity and expertise of faculty members.

When such problems occur within a university, they manifest themselves in particular acts of colleagues, superiors, and persons in the unit for which a faculty member is responsible or in his or her own behavior. Criticizing colleagues can upset a department, criticizing a superior carries the threat of being fired or transferred, criticizing persons in the unit for which one is responsible causes stress, and nobody cares to admit to improper behavior. If criticism can be offered gently, in a modest spirit and for the sake of a project, it will be less likely to arouse wrath and stands some chance of being effective.

A better approach is to try to keep such problems from arising in the first place. Unfortunately, this requires time, that commodity that too many faculty members and administrators lack above all else. Still, if individuals throughout a university make an effort to gather accurate information about developing situations that may threaten academic traditions and values, learn about precedents elsewhere, refer to accepted guidelines, discuss matters with colleagues and administrators (who may have encountered similar incidents and circumstances before), and then have the courage to express their observations in proper quarters, events are more likely to turn out for the best. Whether projects succeed or fail, pride can be taken in the knowledge that best efforts were made.

References

Coolley, R. B. "Alternatives to Litigation." *Les Nouvelles,* 1983, *18,* 163–167.

Fowler, D. R. "University-Industry Research Relationships: The Research Agreement." *Journal of College and University Law,* 1982–83, *9,* 515–532.

Grounds, P. W. "University-Industry Interaction: Guide to Developing Fundamental Research Agreements." Allentown, Pa.: Council for Chemical Research, 1983.

Linnell, R. H. (ed.). *Dollars and Scholars.* Los Angeles: University of Southern California Press, 1982.

MacCordy, E. L. "Industry-University Research Relations: A University Prespective." In *Industry-University Research Relations: A Workshop for Faculty.* Washington, D.C.: National Science Foundation, 1983.

Marsh, C. "Where Agreements Fail." *Les Nouvelles,* 1983, *18,* 183–187.

Matthews, J. B., and Norgaard, R. *Managing the Partnerships Between Higher Education and Industry.* Boulder, Colo.: National Center for Higher Education Management Systems, 1984.

Peters, L. S., and Fusfeld, H. I. "Current U.S. University-Industry Research Connections." In National Science Foundation, *University-Industry Research Relationships: Selected Studies.* Washington D.C.: National Science Foundation, 1983.

Powers, D. R., and Powers, M. F. *Making Participatory Management Work: Leadership of Consultive Decision Making in Academic Administration.* San Francisco: Jossey-Bass, 1983.

Reams, B. D., Jr. *University-Industry Partnerships: The Major Legal Issues in Research and Development Agreements.* Westport, Conn.: Quorum Books, 1986a.

Reams, B. D., Jr. "U.S. Companies Neglect Academic Research." *Wall Street Journal,* Feb. 11, 1986b, p. 32.

Smith, K. A. "Industry-University Research Programs." *Physics Today,* Feb. 1984, pp. 24–29.

7

Future Challenges
and Opportunities
for Educational Alliances

Partnerships between higher education and business have pro-
voked considerable concern about their negative effects on colleges and universities. The glacial slowness with which change
occurs in institutions of higher education can be frustrating, but
also reassuring when potential threats to academic traditions
arise. As in China, the Middle Kingdom, revolutions come—
and go—in higher education.

Even so, in watching money pass to universities from
industry, all sorts of questions about the implications of such
activity have occurred to onlookers. Will researchers become
secretive about their work, with profit for themselves and their
backers at stake? Will increased contact with higher education
provide industry with opportunities to lure away the most gifted
from faculties across the country? Industry support tends to come
in small, short-term allotments, which may be withdrawn as
corporate interests change. Industrial support of university research may cause faculty members to drift into more applied
and less basic research; will this short-term pattern of funding
also cause them unconsciously to restrict the scope of their research designs? How will contractual restrictions and demands
affect distribution of faculty members among disciplines? Are

universities about to become laden with engineers and biochemists but suffer a lack of philosophers? Will perversion of mission and loss of quality result from offering training programs for industry—turning colleges into "tinker-techs"? Will presidents increasingly be hired more for good looks and diplomacy in dealing with legislators, CEOs, and the press than for more substantial leadership skills? Will public relations offices increasingly be asked to stage "events" for presidents with these parties so that the public receives favorable impressions of business–higher education alliances?

Muller (Desruisseaux, 1985, p. 26) warned that research partnerships can lead to lack of cohesion within universities. Many advances in knowledge in science and technology cut across departments, as do new centers, institutes, and projects, many of which are quite large. Faculty members spend less time working within their departments, which suffer as a result, and more with various superstructures, which suffer because they cannot hire faculty members of their own. This can lead to lack of cohesion, which is made all the worse by the fact that research grants are made to individual faculty members who retain only loose ties to their departments. Muller also pointed out that some internal restructuring is essential for institutions involved in cooperative research. Projects that cut across traditional departmental boundaries find resistance that sometimes cannot be overcome without internal restructuring to accommodate new relationships. How will the university of the future be structured to accommodate interdepartmental projects and loosely moored faculty members? Dealing with this issue effectively is particularly important because it involves maintaining faculty reward systems and control over program quality.

Questions also arise regarding non-tenure-track faculty members who are of great utility in both cooperative education and research programs. They can be paid with contract monies and released when a need no longer exists for their courses or when the research interests of corporations change or short-term investigations are completed. This practice can exploit non-tenured personnel, whose response sometimes has been to unionize—independent of tenure-track faculty—causing a host of other problems. It also may fuel growth of a ''second level'' of faculty on campuses, who often are unfairly presumed to be second rate—being untenured—regardless of their abilities and the quality of service they may be providing to the institution, students, and business clients. Roemer and Schnitz pointed out (1982, p. 527): ''Perhaps the most disturbing prospect occasioned by a dual labor market in higher education is that of introducing into the academic world a basis for permanent discrimination.'' Some evidence exists that what the authors called ''academic day labor'' is quite common. Examples include part-time English faculty, faculty in continuing education programs, and business faculty lacking doctorates who are assigned adjunct rank. In spite of departmental review procedures, will program quality inevitably suffer because some itinerant scholars, even though they are competent teachers and knowledgeable specialists, may not invest themselves in programs as heavily as do resident scholars, and will this effect be more marked as even more part-time faculty are hired to work on training and research contracts with industry?

Still other questions that arise concern self-regulation. Scientists have always practiced self-regulation, but as more academic scientists and engineers become associated with industries, fewer may be sufficiently disinterested to speculate on the directions in which research is turning and on the potential uses of results and their effects on society. The general public tends to be matter-of-fact regarding many inventions, perhaps because the range of potential problems seems too vast or the knowledge required to understand them seems too great. Broome noted (1986, p. D3): ''Until now, engineers would have been judged wicked or demented if they were discovered blatantly ignoring the philosopher Cicero's 2,000-year-old imperative: In whatever you build, 'the safety of the public shall be the highest law.' Today, however, the Ford Pinto, Three-Mile Island, Bhopal, the Challenger, Chernobyl and other technological horror stories tell of a cancer growing on our values. They are judged to be *ordinary*.'' For engineers and scientists, is fulfilling the specifications of legal contracts sufficient discharge of professional responsibility? Can serving business and government interest be defined as serving the public interest? Martin and Schinzinger were correct in their 1983 book *Ethics in Engineering* in concluding that "engineering is an experiment involving the public as human subjects." Will increased ties with industry diminish the instinct of faculty members to rebel against such positions?

The problem of ties to industry prejudicing self-regulation is compounded by another problem. Neufeld (Cowen, 1987, p. 19) noted that modern research has changed in a way that threatens its integrity. Reproducibility has become impractical because so much expensive, specialized equipment and training are required. Neufeld added that scientists may feel they have no time to test another's work. The result is that increasingly, scientists must assume without reproducing experiments that the results are valid, even when those results are about to serve as the foundation of additional experiments. What future lies ahead for science—and for the public that receives results, sound and flawed, of scientific inquiries—if opportunities for scientists to check one another are limited?

Dickey (1984, p. 96) also commented on the changing requirements of research: "Science has become dependent upon complex expensive research facilities, for which few universities have sufficient human or financial resources. One consequence is that universities must now band together, or join with non-academic institutions, in regional or disciplinary consortiums. A second is that as the cost of research facilities rises, government supervision, if not control, becomes more direct. A third consequence, with even more troubling implications for academic institutions, is that the role of the individual researcher must diminish."

Dickey emphasized (p. 96) the "supreme" freedoms that "make the university an unsurpassed environment for basic research." These include "the freedom to be peripatetic, the freedom to act independently, the freedom to learn, the freedom to teach, the freedom to ignore the 'real world,' and the freedom to fail." The freedom to fail is not, perhaps, a freedom that some would think of immediately as fundamental to freedom of inquiry, yet if a scientist feels constrained to pursue only inquiries that seem to have a fair chance of success (and defining success may mean defining "acceptable" results of investigations), then freedom of inquiry may, in fact, have been abrogated. Likewise, closer ties with industry may affect other freedoms Dickey listed, particularly if the scope of projects is limited by industrial sponsors when contracts are negotiated.

Many of the questions posed in this chapter cannot be answered until university-industry relationships mature and the range of their effects becomes better known. The picture is further complicated by reported developments in the business world. According to the *New York Times* (Prokesch, 1987, sec. 3, p. 1), management of corporations is changing radically. Corporations are reviving from the early 1980s slump, but at extreme cost. The *Times* stated: "Today, in an age of global competition, rapid technological change and too much productive capacity, chief executives are beginning to march to a set of standards they never dreamed of embracing in the past. The new order eschews loyalty to workers, products, corporate structure, businesses, factories, communities, even the nation. All such allegiances are viewed as expendable under the new rules. With survival at stake, only market leadership, strong profits, and a high stock price can be allowed to matter. With this mind set, chief executives are losing interest in maintaining a favorable American trade balance, or even manufacturing in America." If a part of a company isn't making money, it is sold. If a good idea requires extended investment to give a market a chance to develop, chances are it will not be pursued. Few managers, according to the article, view it as their responsibility to create or preserve jobs. Big investments with distant payoff may depress stock prices and make the company vulnerable to a takeover.

Further, the vertically integrated corporation seems to be coming to an end. No longer will monolithic factories be owned by single corporations. Instead, federations of companies will own networks of small plants, each of which will make components that are shipped for assembly to the markets where final products will be sold (Prokesch, 1987). New chief executives are not civic leaders but are submerged in operating their businesses. They are not visionaries but cost cutters, not builders and preservers of businesses, but are quite willing to sell off a firm if the move would increase the umbrella corporation's stock price. Lack of emotional involvement in businesses and single-minded focus on profits, because profits mean survival, is the name of the game, now that U.S. companies are competing in the international marketplace.

What would be the effects on universities of working in cooperative relationships with the "new corporation," as described in the *New York Times*? How would increased attention to profits affect interest in research? How would lack of interest in nurturing companies affect inclination to invest in updating and upgrading programs for employees? These questions are less disturbing to contemplate than the effects on society such corporate changes could produce.

The "new corporation" may be viewed as one response to the changing current economy, which often is described as undergoing a natural progression as jobs have been lost in manufacturing and gained in service industries. Cohen and Zysman (1987a) disagreed with this view. Writing in *Technology Review,* Cohen and Zysman stated (p. 54): "Manufacturing matters mightily to the wealth and power of the United States and our ability to sustain the open society we have come to take for granted. But this contention is a distinctly minority view in the United States today."

The authors noted that manufacturing employment has declined from 50 percent of all jobs in 1950 to 20 percent now, and that service jobs have increased until they now provide about 70 percent of all employment. The authors claimed that according to the mainstream view, economic development involves continual evolution from older, less profitable undertakings to new, more profitable ones. Having shifted from farming to industry, the United States now is shifting from industry to high technology and services. In the mainstream view, reindustrialization is not the path to pursue; in fact, abandoning so-called sunset industries seems to be regarded as a natural adjunct to developing services and high-technology enterprises. Supposedly everybody benefits from such change, which is "part of an ever-evolving international division of labor" (p. 56).

Cohen and Zysman continued: "This view is soothing in its message, calm in tone, confident in style, and readily buttressed by traditional economic theory. We believe it is also quite possibly wrong. At the heart of our argument is a notion we call 'direct linkage': many service jobs are tightly tied to manufacturing. Lose manufacturing and you will lose—not develop—those high-wage services. Nor is the relationship between high tech and manufacturing, like that between services and manufacturing, a simple case of evolutionary succession. High tech is intimately tied to manufacturing, not a free-floating laboratory activity."

The authors' point is that the post-industrial economy is a myth. They state (p. 56): "If the United States wants to stay on top—or even high up—we can't just shift out of manufacturing and into services. Nor can we establish a long-term preserve around traditional blue-collar jobs and outmoded plants. If the United States is to remain a wealthy and powerful economy, American manufacturing must automate, not emigrate. Moreover, it must automate in ways that build flexibility through the imaginative use of skilled labor. In a world in which technology migrates rapidly and financial services are global, the skill of our workforce and the talents of our managers together will be our central resource."

As Cohen and Zysman point out, labor shifted out of agriculture, but production in agriculture did not decline; in fact, it continues at all-time highs. As a result of automating agriculture, great numbers of high-salary jobs were created in related industries and services such as agricultural chemicals and machinery. The authors estimated that in addition to the three million jobs actually involved in agriculture, an additional three to six million jobs exist that are directly linked to agriculture. In industry, likewise, which directly provides twenty-one million jobs, another forty to sixty million jobs in service industries directly depend on manufacturing production. If manufacturing production is lost, the problem is that the directly linked, high-paying service jobs will also migrate offshore. Wholesaling, retailing, and advertising won't be affected; foreign-made products will be addressed instead. The authors gave as examples of jobs that would be affected (p. 59) "design and engineering services; payroll, inventory, and accounting services; finance and insurance; repair and maintenance of plant and machinery; training and recruitment; testing services and labs; industrial waste disposal; and the accountants, designers, publicists, payroll, transportation, and communications firms that design and service production equipment." Truckers who ship raw materials and semifinished goods also would be affected.

What is to be done? Cohen and Zysman concluded (p. 62): "The key generator of wealth . . . remains production. The United States is shifting not out of industry into services but from one kind of industrial economy to another. . . . Instead of ceding production, public policy should actively aim to convert low-productivity, low-wage, low-skill production processes into high-technology, high-skill, high-wage activities—whether they are included in the manufacturing unit itself or counted largely as service firms."

Some authors would disagree with Cohen and Zysman that such a conversion is likely. Levin and Rumberger (1983, p. 10), for example, claim that jobs of the future will be available in low-skill occupations; that use of computers "de-skills" the work force because using a terminal is simple and one does not have to understand how it works to use it. Are workers, therefore, being overtrained? In the Levin and Rumberger model, higher education would play little role in worker training, which would more likely be accomplished in vocational education institutions. The Cohen and Zysman (1987a) recommendations imply a more central role for higher education in training high-skill workers. Increases in adult enrollments across the country show that more education rather than less is being adopted by many as the prudent response to the changes that are occurring in the economy of the United States as a result of its entry into the international marketplace.

In addition, in most states, the central role played by education in economic development already is recognized, and funds are being allocated by state governments to improve both public school systems and state colleges and universities. This emphasis on improving education reflects a basic change in the means by which states are promoting economic development. That is, as the *Wall Street Journal* noted (Kotlowitz and Buss, 1986, p. 1), ''the tide is starting to turn'' in localities' giveaways to lure corporations. Bids have become excessive in terms of the numbers of jobs received. Tax breaks to companies reduce tax revenues so that public services can't be provided. ''And after years of chasing handouts, some businesses now admit that such subsidies don't make or break their location decisions.'' Quality of the labor force, natural resource base, and ''quality of life'' factors are being cited in locational decisions instead. As a result, improving quality of education is being emphasized.

Business–higher education partnerships are a sign that the entrepreneurial spirit is very much alive and well in the United States. Whether or not such partnerships survive and become a part of the service missions of great numbers of colleges and universities remains to be seen. In any case, at a time of economic change and stress, a commendable effort is being made to use resources available to respond positively to change.

Two points may be made in closing. First, educators working in depressed localities, trying to do with virtually nothing what other states are able to spend millions to accomplish, may wish to remember that while negative responses to suggestions that higher education may be of assistance in helping businesses improve productivity can be discouraging, nevertheless, they are a sign of some degree of interest: They are responses. Far more serious—and more common in areas that most need help—is complete unresponsiveness. It can take an educator down a peg or two to realize that people think his ideas are silly. Yet in a depressed region any business that has managed to survive has the right to feel proud of that accomplishment. A sense that somebody must have been doing something right is natural when all around one, other businesses are failing with regularity. How could outsiders know better what to do?

At the same time, if anything is needed in such areas, it is instillation of a spirit of entrepreneurism, with its intrinsic openness to new ideas and change and its eagerness to take advantage of opportunities. The story goes that when Edison invented the light bulb, lamp makers responded by producing improved wicks. This unfortunately depicts the kind of behavior too often encountered in depressed areas; that is, continuing to put the resources one does have into an outmoded activity because it at least has the virtue of being familiar. Colleges and universities can and ought to teach skills and attitudes crucial to entrepreneurism—such as analytic and synthetic skills, faith in one's abilities, and the value of persistence—in addition to the technical and business knowledge necessary for success.

The second closing point is a reminder to colleges and universities that state money, including economic development funds, always comes tangled in strings. Ironically, in states with less need and more money to allocate, fewer strings may be attached, whereas in states with great need and less money, concern about waste can be so great that too many strings may be attached to allow the money to be spent as wisely as it might be.

The *Chronicle of Higher Education* (Jaschik, 1986, p. 15) noted, as one of six problems associated with cooperative projects, that "research has been hindered by politicians who are more concerned about their constituents' interests than about their states' economic development goals." It is not surprising that politicians protect the interests of their supporters. The only game to be played in some state capitols is to become one of those whose interests are protected. Attitudes toward pork-barreling may depend on whether constituents feel they are receiving their fair shares.

Politicians often do not understand how institutions of higher education operate and suggest approaches that strike university leaders as highly unsatisfactory. Politicians also are prone to making anything a media event. They may take it upon themselves to promise on behalf of a university more than it feels it can deliver, and then charge it later with failure and false promises.

There is a saying among state systems' officers that in times of stress, the institutions in a system circle their wagons—and then turn their rifles inward and fire at each other. As difficult as cooperation may be, especially when funding is at stake, working together to draft plans for equitable distribution always is preferable to allowing politicians to dominate decision-making processes.

In all facets of higher education–business partnerships, cooperation is a sound approach. Relations with industry are themselves cooperative. In addition, colleges and universities that individually do not have sufficient resources to mount a particular technical assistance program may be able to do so cooperatively. Banding together to share the costs of laboratory equipment in some cases may be the only way to purchase it. Sharing the salary costs of distinguished—and expensive—researchers also may be cost effective. Going as a group to the legislature to request funds for research and training packages designed to promote economic development may bring success where multiple visits by individual institutions would fail.

The opportunities open to universities through cooperation with industry are extensive. Paths can be found to take advantage of the benefits of partnerships without sacrificing traditions or departing from professional, ethical conduct. The public sector, the private sector, and education have previously strived to remain sharply separated from one another. In a world increasingly oriented toward science and technology, the challenge of the twenty-first century will be to make the boundaries among the sectors sufficiently permeable that all groups can work together for common advantage.

References

Broome, T. H., Jr. "The Slippery Ethics of Engineering." *Washington Post,* Dec. 28, 1986, p. D3.

Cohen, S. S., and Zysman, J. "The Myth of a Post-Industrial Economy." *Technology Review,* Feb.–Mar. 1987a, pp. 54–62.

Cohen, S. S., and Zysman, J. *The Myth of a Post-Industrial Economy.* New York: Basic Books, 1987b.

Cowen, R. "Critics Find Flaws in Some Scientific Research Studies." *Christian Science Monitor,* Jan. 27, 1987, p. 19.

Desruisseaux, P. "Academe and Business Tighten Ties: Corporate Giving Nears $1.5 Billion." *Chronicle of Higher Education,* Nov. 6, 1985, pp. 1, 26.

Dickey, J. S., Jr. "Basic Research, Money, and the Academic Environment." *Chronicle of Higher Education,* Oct. 24, 1984, p. 96.

Jaschik, S. "Universities' High-Technology Pacts with Industry Are Marred by Politics, Poor Planning, and Hype." *Chronicle of Higher Education,* Mar. 12, 1986, p. 15.

Kotlowitz, A., and Buss, D. D. "Localities' Giveaways to Lure Corporations Are Causing Outcry." *Wall Street Journal,* Sept. 24, 1986, pp. 1, 23.

Levin, H. M., and Rumberger, R. W. "The Educational Implications of High Technology." Unpublished paper, Institute for Research on Educational Finance and Governance, School of Education, Stanford University, Palo Alto, Calif., 1983.

Martin, M., and Schinzinger, R. *Ethics in Engineering.* New York: McGraw-Hill, 1983.

Prokesch, S. "Remaking the American C.E.O." *New York Times,* Jan. 25, 1987, sec. 3, pp. 1, 8.

Roemer, R. E., and Schnitz, J. E. "Academic Employment as Day Labor." *Journal of Higher Education,* 1982, pp. 514–531.

PART TWO

Partnerships for Training: Putting Principles into Action

Carol B. Aslanian

8

Providing Contract Training
to Organizations

The presence of successful businesses and other public and private organizations in a community is important to the economic health of the community and the stability of the colleges located there. Education and training are critical components in building corporate strength, which leads to more jobs and more residents. Throughout their lives, not only workers but other family members increasingly are turning to institutions of higher education for new knowledge and new skills. Serving this new clientele provides colleges with opportunities to strengthen their curricula in terms of programs and quality and, in turn, supports the economic growth of the community.

Contract training refers to an arrangement in which an organization, whether a business, a government agency, or a voluntary association, contracts directly with a college (a postsecondary institution, public or private, two-year or four-year) for instruction of its employees, its clients, or its members (College Board, 1983, p. vii). Because an organization is no more effective than the people who make it up, the organization itself, in a sense, learns as a result of the education or training of its own members. In short, the organization is the student. The organization can be thought of as becoming more aware, analytical, responsive, adaptable, and survival prone as the people it comprises develop such traits and skills.

Why Is Contract Training Needed?

The amount of money spent on business and industrial training each year is staggering. According to Eurich (1985, p. 6), estimates of corporate expenditure on education "range from a relatively conservative low of $40 billion spent annually by private sector employers only to an apparently extravagant high of $100 billion spent by both public and private sector employers. . . . Even when the salaries and wages paid during training are omitted for purposes of comparison with higher education costs, it appears that private corporations may be approaching the total amount spent annually by our nation's universities and other four-year colleges, both public and private. That figure for 1981–82 . . . was just over $60 billion." When one considers, for example, that in 1977, American Telephone and Telegraph spent $700 million on training as compared to Massachusetts Institute of Technology's budget of $222 million, the implications are sobering (Eurich, 1985, p. 8).

Furthermore, the demand for training is predicted to increase. Economists tell us that the United States is undergoing reindustrialization—that the older, large-scale automobile, steel, and textile industries will decrease in total employment size, while the new communications industries will continue to grow. Demographers predict that in the 1990s, the United States will face a shortage of entry-level workers in new areas of technology and an oversupply of middle-level workers with outmoded skills. Automation of work and other changes in technology, intensified foreign competition, economic pressures of inflation and unemployment, changing attitudes and expectations toward work and careers, and continuing government regulation of employment practices force businesses to seek new and creative ways to respond to these problems to ensure their own survival. Since demands for retraining can be expected to increase, contractual arrangements with employers will provide an even more fruitful area of development for colleges.

Through the College Board's Community Assessment Program (CAP), recent market research has shown that employers did, indeed, want services from their nearby colleges

(Brickell, 1985). (During the course of the research, more than 30 colleges were studied and more than 300 companies were visited for the purpose of locating training demands for credit and noncredit courses, degrees, certificates, and diploma programs on a wide variety of topics, including management, computer literacy, technical writing, supervision, and interpersonal relations.) In fact, demand for these educational services far exceeded the colleges' abilities to supply them.

Although some colleges have responded to this demand, many have not. Lack of collegiate response has led some major corporations to develop costly, complex, in-house training departments; to seek private-sector training companies or outside consultants to provide nonacademic training for their employees; or even to create corporate colleges—fully accredited, degree-awarding institutions. These colleges are money-making entities that recruit, train, and educate students much like traditional colleges. Since 1970, the Rand Corporation has offered a Ph.D. in policy analysis. The Wang Institute of Graduate Studies, established in 1979 by the Wang Corporation, offers a master's degree in software engineering. The College of Insurance, established in 1947 by the Insurance Society of New York, offers an M.B.A. and B.B.A. with a major in insurance, a B.S. in actuarial science, and an associate of arts degree in occupational studies. The Arthur D. Little Management Education Institute, established in 1964, offers an M.S. in administration and management (Eurich, 1985, Table 3). At least eighteen organizations have established accredited degree programs, which they offer to employees as well as to the public at large.

This state of affairs has two important implications. First, colleges will find an expanding market for their services if they choose to provide learning where learning is most critically needed. Second, and more ominous, needs will not exist forever. Organizations, in increasing numbers, are creating programs themselves to meet their needs, as economic pressures dictate training, retraining, or updating of their work forces. Since their survival may depend on training services, employers cannot afford to rely on colleges to develop them, unless the colleges are able to move fairly quickly to provide cost-effective programs.

Reasons Adults Pursue Learning. Incredible change has occurred in the United States throughout the twentieth century and is continuing to occur in broad-sweeping strokes. In increasing numbers, workers are learning throughout their lives merely to keep up with change. Learning must occur in response to changes in employment and lifestyle and advances in technology. A nationwide study of 2,000 Americans (Aslanian and Brickell, 1980, p. 43) demonstrated that more than half of those twenty-five years old and older had studied in the past year, and that 83 percent of that group said they had learned in order to cope with particular changes in their lives.

For example, moving from one status in life to another requires learning new information, skills, attitudes, or values. Becoming a foreman, an executive, or a lieutenant involves learning how to maintain new relationships as well as mastering new technical knowledge or skills. So does getting married, becoming a mother or a widow, or joining a political party or fraternal organization (Aslanian, 1985, p. 56).

Identifiable events trigger an adult's decision to learn. Taking a job or losing a job, marrying or divorcing, becoming sick, being elected to office, or moving to a new city are the kinds of events that the Office of Adult Learning Services has discovered trigger adult learning (Aslanian and Brickell, 1980, p. 55). For example, changes in current jobs trigger some adults to learn just to keep those jobs: "I graduated with a degree in teaching, decided against teaching, and got a job in business. When I was going through four years of college, learning how to teach students American history, I missed a lot of math courses and other subjects I now use daily on the job. I'm taking a U.S. Department of Commerce course in advanced export administration. I am in the export business, and my job has grown by leaps and bounds—more commodities and more countries to deal with. I need to improve my administrative skills so I can keep up with my job" (Aslanian and Brickell, 1980, p. 69).

"Running faster just to stay in the same place" requires continual learning. Fields involving changing technologies, government-mandated updating, or intense competition also demand it. Adults, for example, who hold professional and technical jobs (an increasing slice of our technological economy) are twice as likely to enroll in courses as are adults in mining and construction. In addition to adapting to changing job requirements, moving into a new job, being promoted, or being fired can trigger adult career learning.

The Aslanian and Brickell study showed that 83 percent of adult learners wanted to see some reward for their learning. For the 83 percent who learned in order to cope with changes, learning was utilitarian, and for the other 17 percent, the process of learning was its own reward.

The 83 percent of adult learners for whom learning was a means to an end may be classified according to seven life-change areas: career, family, leisure, art, health, religion, and citizenship. Such a classification reveals that more adults learn in order to make career transitions (56 percent) than for all other reasons combined, with family and leisure transitions competing for a distant second place (Aslanian and Brickell, 1980, p. 54).

These findings help to explain why at present at least 40 percent of college students are twenty-five or older and why one out of two college students studies part time and works part time (*Higher Education Daily,* 1985, p. 6). Between 1970 and 1980, the median age of the population shifted from twenty-eight to thirty, and it continues to shift in this direction. As a result, the profile of the traditional student is changing dramatically. Smaller families and a decline in the number of high school students are forcing colleges to place greater emphasis on part-time adult learners. Eighty percent of the adult learners who studied in the past year were educated, urban, white-collar workers, who spent most of their time with their careers and families; thus their studies were in topics related to work and home. Adults have more leisure time than ever before, in addition to increasing discretionary incomes, of which they can be expected to invest significant amounts in education.

For some time now, however, up to 60 percent of all adult learning has taken place *outside* institutions of higher education (Aslanian and Brickell, 1980, p. 155). Employers provide most of that learning in the workplace, and churches, libraries, museums, and the military account for the rest.

Reasons Organizations Support Adult Education. Colleges examine the kinds of training organizations need in order to survive and grow. By maintaining ties with colleges, organizations can help ensure their continued productivity. For example, when the Monsanto Company recognized that the technical and engineering skills of some of its engineering staff had become obsolete, the company took steps to update and upgrade staff members' working knowledge of current practices. The program they pursued, in collaboration with the University of St. Louis, was designed to update engineering, chemical, and computer skills for a group of eighteen engineers selected from a nationwide pool. For Monsanto, making sure management staff kept abreast of current trends in fields critical to performance was crucial to its status among domestic competitors (College Board, 1983, p. 16).

Responding to foreign competition, General Motors decided to introduce a new line of cars in an effort to recapture a lost market segment. Employees consequently needed to be retrained in new repair and servicing methods. A change in marketing strategy forced GM to learn how to implement this new plan, and the organization as student rechanneled its learning efforts into a new area (College Board, 1983, p. 29).

Why is it to the advantage of organizations to look outward rather than inward for the kinds of training and education assistance, support, and skills they need for their employees? First, the particular kind of expertise required may not be available internally. Second, duplication of services and facilities usually is not cost effective. College campuses can provide facilities at minimal charge to companies. Hiring teachers to form large training departments within companies is a costly venture that bites into profits. In addition, top managers frequently prefer to use the expertise of colleges from which they have graduated. Although most colleges cannot compete with some companies, such as the Jet Propulsion Laboratory and Digital Research, in providing expertise in certain high-technology fields, higher education still prevails as the seat of learning and innovation in many areas.

College Board Study of Contract Training

In 1982, the Office of Adult Learning Services of the College Board conducted a nationwide survey of training by contract to understand the phenomenon better (College Board, 1983, p. viii). The purpose of the study was twofold: to assist colleges that were considering or had begun to develop such training arrangements with local organizations and to assist organizations that were considering contracting with colleges to see how this new method of "working together" could be most beneficial to them. Results showed that types and scope of arrangements between business, government agencies, and voluntary associations and colleges are as varied as the entities themselves.

Patterns of Arrangements. Results of the College Board study revealed that contract-education arrangements form certain patterns:

1. Every type of college has the capacity to teach and has been involved in training by contract—from Harvard University to Piedmont Technical College in South Carolina, St. Mary's University in Texas, Seattle Central Community College, and the University of Georgia.

2. Every type of organization has the capacity to learn and has been involved in contract training—from Monsanto Textiles Company to the Catholic Diocese of Corpus Christi, the Wood County Welfare Department in Ohio, and the Insurance Company of North American (CIGNA).

3. Every organization that has contracted for training with a college has been large enough to supply a class and pay for its tuition.

4. Every kind of subject matter has been taught, from peptic ulcer therapy to financial management, computer training for managers, conversational French, letter writing, economics, and other standard or specially designed courses.

5. Contracts for single courses have been far more common than contracts for degrees, and courses that offer occupational enhancement have been sought far more often than those that do not.

6. The duration of courses varies widely—from one day to one week, to six months, to three years.

7. The length of courses has usually been determined by what has needed to be learned, rather than by what could be taught in a standard semester course.

8. Methods of instruction have varied, including lectures, discussion groups, video presentations, role playing, case studies, and computer-assisted teaching. A pattern that became apparent across all forms of instruction was that learners were confronted with real-life problems and were given assistance in learning how to solve them.

9. All kinds of instructors have been employed—from college faculty or adjunct faculty to instructors from the organizations themselves to outside consultants. Most teachers were members of college faculties, however.

10. Every kind of location has been used—not only college campuses, but offices, labs, training facilities, and factories owned by organizations. Class location tends to be an either/or situation—at the college or at the organization, but not at both. Typically, an organizational site has been chosen.

11. Services provided by colleges have varied enormously, from teaching to academic counseling, tutoring, course design, and career-development seminars. Colleges also have provided access to classrooms, libraries, and supplies. In other words, colleges provide organizations with the same services they provide traditional students.

12. Similarly, services contributed by organizations may include providing classroom space, time off from work for employees to enroll in courses, travel expenses for faculty members, instructors, tuition payments, computers, or job placement services. Most organizations recruit and select employees who will undergo training, give them full pay throughout the training, and provide facilities and administrative assistance.

13. Contractual charges vary according to the courses to be taught. Organizations usually pay for training, but in some cases, government or private agencies meet some of the expenses. Usually standard tuition charges form the basis of the contractual fee, with adjustment to reflect the extra costs to the college in treating an organization as a student.

14. Certification has been awarded in a broad spectrum of ways, including academic credits, degrees, occupational certification, continuing education units, or documentation of satisfactory performance. Most commonly credit has been awarded for standard academic credit hours.

15. Evaluations have been as varied as the programs. Approaches have included questionnaires about course content, instructors, and facilities; on-the-job observation; analyses of job placement records; and followup studies to determine promotions and salary increases. The colleges, the organizations, the students, and third-party evaluators have all carried out evaluations. The most common method of evaluation is the questionnaire, completed by students during and after training, accompanied by followup studies conducted by the organization on subsequent job performance.

Types of Arrangements. An example of a training-by-contract arrangement between businesses and colleges is that between Data General Corporation and the University of New Hampshire and the School for Lifelong Learning, institutions in the New Hampshire university system. Approximately 100 employees, whose primary work responsibility was assembling computer circuit boards, worked toward associate degrees in general studies. All had high school diplomas or GEDs, and some had taken college courses. The University of New Hampshire provided computer courses that offered an introduction to statistics and such computer languages as BASIC, COBAL, Pascal and FORTRAN. In addition to technical courses, students studied mathematics, English, history, and other general studies courses. Three 15-week sessions were offered each year. The computer courses were taught in five-member groups and emphasized computer programming and software exercises. Lectures and group discussions were the primary methods used in teaching the general courses.

Approximately half the faculty were from the University of New Hampshire's departments of computer science, mathematics, and English. The others were adjunct faculty members from the School for Lifelong Learning. The School for Lifelong Learning printed all course materials, assessed students' prior learning, and provided on-site academic counseling, study-skills sessions, and career-development workshops. Data General provided classroom facilities and computer equipment for the courses, released students for academic counseling, and promoted courses within the company. Data General paid the university a total of approximately $165,000: $185 per student per four-credit course, which included the university system's standard off-campus fee of $45 per credit hour, plus a service fee. The program was evaluated through student ratings, student grades, and job performance ratings (College Board, 1983, p. 6).

A second type of arrangement between colleges and government agencies is typified by one at Bowling Green State University in Ohio. The university contracted with the Ohio Department of Welfare and the Wood County Welfare Department to provide classrooms, library facilities, office space, administrative services, and a noncredit course in work readiness for 500 trainees. The trainees were receiving Aid to Families with Dependent Children (AFDC). More than half the participants had been successfully employed but had lost their jobs as a result of the declining economy. Others were long-term welfare recipients. Participants' educational preparation ranged from attending some high school to completing high school diplomas, to enrolling in some college courses. Their average age was thirty.

Classes met four days a week for four weeks, from 9:00 A.M. to 4:30 P.M. Speakers, group activities, self-assessment, and role playing were among the instructional methods used. Four coordinators conducted programs in résumé preparation, interviewing, and job maintenance, which totaled 120 hours of training in work readiness. An additional twenty adjunct faculty members were hired from throughout the state to teach specialized topics. The county and state welfare departments determined the eligibility of participants, administered the grant, and made referrals for interviews. Seventy-five percent of the participants were placed in community-work jobs, and the remaining 25 percent found unsubsidized employment. All students were awarded certificates of completion (College Board, 1983, p. 50).

Still a third type of arrangement is that between a college and a voluntary organization. For example, Azusa Pacific University in Azusa, California, contracted with the Salvation Army School for Officer Training in Palos Verdes, California. All Azusa Pacific University courses were based on videotaped lectures, accompanied by a textbook and a study guide. A Salvation Army instructor conducted each course, answered questions, monitored assignments, and administered examinations. Each instructor or proctor from the Salvation Army was approved by the dean of Azusa Pacific University. Sixty-four students from western states, in training to assume assignments as officers in the Salvation Army, participated in the degree program. All had completed high school, and about half had taken some college courses.

Nine videotaped courses (twenty-seven units) were offered, including psychology, philosophy, sociology, history of religion in America, world civilization, communications, and the fine arts. The videotapes were produced between 1976 and 1982 through a national consortium of colleges. Azusa Pacific also provided tests and study guides, registration, and financial aid (through a Basic Educational Opportunity Grant) for those pursuing an associate of arts degree, and academic counseling for students planning to transfer to a bachelor's degree program.

Tuition was $180 per course. Contracted cost for sixty-four students for one year was approximately $48,000. Evaluations were conducted by the students, who evaluated the instructors, the course materials, and the library. The Salvation Army education director also evaluated the course material. Students who completed the program were awarded an associate of arts degree in general education by Azusa Pacific University.

The College Board study of contract training revealed that whether courses are credit or noncredit; arranged for a business, a government agency, or a voluntary organization; faculty-taught or videotaped, contract training requires determining the need for training and tailoring a program to fit those specific needs. Every variable should be selected to serve the needs or convenience of the organization, including facilities, methods, materials, instructors, and participants.

Stress Points. Not unlike any two individuals who are try-ing to establish a working relationship, stress points arise when a college and an organization try to establish a contract train-ing arrangement.

For a college, difficulties in establishing a relationship with an organization are varied and diverse. Some administrative concerns include how to manage the paperwork, how to accredit the courses being offered, what standards for course prepara-tion and grading to use, and how to evaluate courses and train-ees. From an academic perspective, complaints heard repeatedly involve the difficulty of maintaining educational impartiality and integrity; that is, how to avoid narrowing the focus of courses in response to overly specific requirements by the organization, or how to maintain academic standards when the organization is determining what will be learned and for how long. Colleges also experience some measure of frustration because the tradi-tional philosophy of higher education has emphasized theory and methodology, whereas organizations emphasize practical applications and results.

Another difficulty is that an organization can be a very unruly student. Colleges are often faced with impossible demands from the private sector—which is used to quick decisions and fast results—to prepare courses and proposals, sometimes over-night. This comes as a shock to academicians, who are accus-tomed to deliberating at length over curriculum content.

Colleges also may balk at the narrowness of focus for students, believing that students receiving tailored training have fewer opportunities to consider a variety of career and academic possibilities. They also argue that the narrow social contacts fostered by contract training limit students and hamper not only their immediate development, but, ultimately, their career mobil-ity and flexibility. Close employer supervision of course material and evaluations also may inhibit the freedom of colleges to main-tain stringent academic standards. Failure of the trainees may imply that the college has failed. Colleges also experience dif-ficulty in finding the right talent to teach the courses they offer. This is an important issue, since often the success of a course rests heavily on the abilities of the instructor.

Contract training also presents difficulties from the organization's point of view. First, colleges are organized to serve traditional students. Trainees from organizations demand first-class facilities, unlike traditional students, who are more willing to study in less than optimal conditions. Second, whereas traditional students may ask for relevance in their curricula, organizations demand it. Colleges cannot always adapt their curriculum accordingly because to do so may contradict their mission, violate their standards, or strain their resources. Third, an organization wants the power to choose the faculty assigned to it and to select the instructors for particular courses. Many colleges resist this procedure because faculty traditionally control such matters. Fourth, organizations often are suspicious of liberal arts courses. Some hold that liberal arts courses raise worker expectations by making them think too much. "Thinking too much has little to do with the bottom line results orientation of organizations" ("Business and Universities," 1982, p. 61). Fifth, organizations commonly demand that training be conducted on their premises, not on campus. They also demand that classes be taught during evenings and weekends, which leads to staffing problems for the college (Brickell, 1985).

Organizations face some other pressing questions when initiating a contract training agreement. How can they make a training program profitable? Should they attempt to subsidize the program? Should they count it as a loss and hope for long-term benefits to the institution? Should they seek government scholarships and loans for students and accept the controls these may bring? Should they maintain only accredited programs, or should they accept nonstandard faculty training and nontraditional programs?

The fact bears repeating that demand for training by organizations far exceeds the supply. Although colleges and organizations may view one another as being very different entities, increasingly colleges are becoming more like businesses, and businesses are taking on more responsibilities that traditionally belonged to colleges. Each can learn from the other. Colleges, like businesses, must look at their markets, evaluate them, and service them to the best of their abilities. Colleges and businesses pursuing contract training share similar objectives, overlapping functions, similar personnel, and similar organizational structures. The proliferation of academic corporations and corporate colleges is proof of that fact.

Advantages of Contract Training

The advantages of contract training cannot be denied. Compared to traditional education, it gives students more convenient times and places to study, less worry about finances, clearer understanding of the connections between theory and applications, greater contact with other students who have similar career objectives, more chances to practice classroom skills on the job, less concern about jobs after graduation, greater ease in updating skills throughout their careers, and greater access to instructors who are current in their fields.

Further, fostering good ties with organizations can benefit a college in other ways through financial support, talent, and opportunities for teachers to put their theories into practice using real-life conditions. In fact, any or all of the types of possible alliances between colleges and organizations could develop out of a training-by-contract relationship, including research and development projects; sharing of facilities or staff; and internships, apprenticeships, and opportunities for work-study programs. Unless colleges choose actively to seek contracts from their new prospective students (organizations) and to recruit them as zealously as they recruit traditional students, however, the opportunity to do so may disappear. Once organizations have invested heavily in setting up their own programs, they will be unlikely to abandon that investment.

What should be done? Overall, colleges will have to be aggressive in seeking out businesses and organizations, studying company needs, adjusting the content of their curricula, modifying their time schedules, and teaching exceedingly well to show job-related results. They will have to find those instructors who are best qualified to teach, not drawn necessarily from the faculty or with the usual academic credentials. They will have to recruit from the military, the government, professional associations, consulting firms, research and development labs, companies, the retired, and other nations (Brickell and Aslanian, 1981, p. 26).

This can be done. In fact, the College Board's study of contract training revealed that sound partnerships have been established nationwide. Who can doubt that contract training will play a key role in the responsibility of colleges in preparing the United States to meet the future? As the College Board states (1983, p. ix): "Colleges are taking organizations into the twenty-first century. All kinds of institutions of higher education—two- and four-year, public and private, large and small—are helping to lead all kinds of businesses, industries, government agencies and voluntary associations into the future, a future that will encompass declining productivity, persistent inflation, rising international competition, aging industrial plants, and ever-increasing technology. Organizations have to be ready in order to survive. Those that will survive will be those that invest in creative thinking, in new methods in training, and in engaging their employees in new experiences. Survival will mean flexibility, change and learning."

References

Aslanian, C. B. "The Causes and Timing of Adult Learning." In *Adults and the Changing Workplace.* Washington, D.C.: American Vocational Association, 1985.

Aslanian, C. B., and Brickell, H. M. *Americans in Transition: Life Changes as Reasons for Adult Learning.* New York: College Entrance Examination Board, 1980.

Brickell, H. M. "The Organization as Unruly Student." Paper presented to Governor's Conference on Adult Learning, Jackson, Miss., Mar. 1985.

Brickell, H. M., and Aslanian, C. B. "The Colleges and Businesses Competition." *New York Times,* Aug. 30, 1981, p. 26.

"Business and Universities: A New Partnership." *Business Week,* Dec. 20, 1982, pp. 58–62.

College Board. *Training by Contract: College-Employer Profiles.* New York: College Board, 1983.

Eurich, N. P. *Corporate Classrooms*. Princeton, N.J.: Carnegie Foundation for the Advancement of Teaching, 1985.

Higher Education Daily, 1985, *13* (65), 6 (citing U.S. Department of Education, National Center for Education Statistics).

National Center for Education Statistics. *Participation in Adult Education: 1981*. Washington, D.C.: National Center for Education Statistics, 1982.

9

Identifying Clients
and Developing Program Contracts

Locating potential client organizations has been a problem for many colleges that wish to undertake contract training. Until recently, colleges have invested little in assessing the marketplace for adult students, having focused instead on the traditional eighteen-to-twenty-two-year-old student population. Current priorities may be just the reverse. As numbers of traditional-age students have declined, many colleges have become eager to recruit adult students, whose numbers and demands for continuing education are growing.

The National Center for Education Statistics projects that by the early 1990s, college enrollments will be split equally between students twenty-four years of age and under and students twenty-five years of age and older. Similarly, the National Center estimates that about half of all college students will be enrolled full time and half part time. During the ten-year period from 1982 to 1992, National Center data show, the traditional college-age population will decrease by 20 percent, and the adult student population will increase by roughly the same amount (National Center for Education Statistics, 1985, p. 6).

In recent years, colleges have begun to turn to faculty members who specialize in marketing, to private consultants, and to various agencies for assistance in assessing the adult student market. One approach, developed by the College Board, is described here as an illustration of the steps involved in a comprehensive and effective assessment of the adult student market (Aslanian, 1985).

Community Assessment Program

The Community Assessment Program (CAP) is a new but well-tested approach to analyzing supply and demand (not need) for adult learning, which has been developed by the Office of Adult Learning Services of the College Board. It is designed to assist college administrators in improving and expanding their services to the adult student. The program consists of a five-part analysis of a college's markets.

1. *Analysis of the Community.* During the first stage of a Community Assessment Program, demographic and socioeconomic characteristics of the region served by a college are determined. Data assembled from U.S. Census statistics and from state, regional, and local sources reveal who lives in the area, how the population is changing, how the workplace is changing, which segments of the population are seeking further education, and how these conditions are affecting the educational environment. This analysis of the community provides the college with a "learning map" of its service area that identifies specific "neighborhoods" or tracts of high, medium, and low demand for learning among adults. The analysis further delineates the potential market for the college by pinpointing specific census tracts containing households most likely to produce adult learners. (This is done through comparison of sociodemographic variables of the households to sociodemographic variables that have been shown to correlate with adult participation in higher education.) Recommendations concerning where the college should concentrate its marketing efforts are made based on this analysis.

2. *Survey of Adults.* Next, adults' study plans are identified through in-depth telephone interviews. Based on the College Board's experience that the best indicator of future study is past formal learning, adults interviewed are those who have studied in the recent past. They are asked to describe in detail the types of courses (both credit and noncredit) or degree programs in

which they enrolled; the institutions they attended; and the times, places, and costs of their coursework. The survey also asks them to rate both the college that is sponsoring the College Board survey and other colleges in the region. In addition, it assesses their understanding of key features of the sponsoring college and the importance of these features in their decisions regarding enrollment.

This part of the Community Assessment Program provides experience-tested data on which decisions about how to attract adult students to a college may be based. These data replace speculation with evidence about the adult learning market for the college, including information about how large the market is and what the college must do to increase its current market share. Results can be used to design, schedule, locate, and price courses and to select geographical areas containing concentrations of adults likely to attend the college so that recruiting efforts can be focused on those high-probability areas. They can also be used to design and write effective advertisements and place them in media to which the greatest proportion of the market is exposed. Finally, they can indicate whether a college is competitive with other colleges in its appeal to adults and what it might do to improve its appeal (Aslanian, 1985, pp. 39-45).

3. Analysis of Other Providers. Offerings of other providers of adult education and training—including secondary and postsecondary, public and private institutions—then are studied, whether providing education is an essential or a peripheral mission for them. The college sponsoring the College Board assessment must judge which of these other providers has a share of the adult learning market large enough to influence enrollment in programs and courses it might offer in the future. The College Board analyzes all data and reports on current status, recent trends, and future plans for adult courses and programs for all other providers examined in the service area of the sponsoring college. This information helps the college to decide rationally whether to enter the adult market, withdraw from it, or extend activities. It also provides the data necessary to enable the college to shape an effective marketing strategy for its programs, determine a distinctive place for itself in the current marketplace, and acquire new or complementary ways to serve adults (Aslanian, 1985, pp. 39–45).

4. *Survey of Faculty and Administration.* The number and variety of adult education courses and programs that a college can provide to meet demands of individuals and organizations depend on the qualifications and attitudes of its faculty members and administration. Many colleges believe themselves capable of providing only very limited adult education opportunities. Limits arise not from administration and faculty uncertainty about how to increase adult enrollment, but from their ambivalence about whether they want to increase it.

Each college has a distinctive character, a particular image, and a traditional mission, especially in the minds of its faculty members and administrators. Central to a college's character are the kinds of students who attend it. Thus, the CAP assessment asks faculty members and administrators to consider the size of future adult enrollment in relation to the number of younger students who can be expected to enroll.

Other significant issues also are examined, including administration of adult-oriented programs, admission standards, academic standards, curriculum, and related faculty matters. Questions asked include these: How should the college organize itself to deal with adult students—by creating a separate administrative unit or by "mainstreaming" adults into regular units? Should admissions criteria for adults be identical to those for younger students? Should performance standards be identical for adults and younger students? Do adults need special curricula? Should regular faculty members be required to share the teaching load, or should adjunct faculty members be employed to teach adults? Other topics surveyed include faculty compensation, contracts with organizations, fiscal policy, and the interest of individual faculty members in teaching adults. In short, the values and views of the administration and faculty, which are key factors in shaping college policies, are examined.

A short questionnaire is used to collect opinions from faculty members and administrators. A set of tables then is produced displaying opinions about how adult education should be conducted at the college. The tables show any differences of opinion in the faculty and among various units of the college and any discrepancies between faculty opinion and administrative opinion.

5. *Survey of Organizations.* During the CAP assessment, a survey of business and industry, government agencies, and voluntary associations is carried out to find out what education and training these groups want and need for their employees, clients, or members. The survey specifically identifies contract training opportunities for the college; that is, opportunities wherein organizations would contract directly with the college to supply instruction. The survey does not address any arrangement in which individuals enroll in one or more college courses at their own initiative and pay tuition charges and other expenses, with employer organizations subsequently reimbursing tuition fees or other expenses. Contract training, in contrast, refers to arrangements in which the organization itself is "learning" by arranging for the education or training of the individuals whom it employs.

The survey of organizations is essentially a demand analysis of the training courses or programs that organizations actually will support. (Specific steps to ensure that actual demand is identified are described later in this chapter.) It is a search for courses or programs that organizations insist on having immediately and for which they can supply and pay for sufficient enrollment to make the projects financially rewarding to the college that would provide them. It is not a study of what organizations may need in the future, might be able to encourage employees to attend, and perhaps could justify in their budgets. It is a search for contracts that can be signed immediately, with courses to be undertaken within three to six months. If such courses are successful, additional contracts often follow.

An important step in this stage of the CAP assessment is to identify the organizations to be approached through face-to-face interviews with top executives. Written profiles that describe the education and training demands of the organizations that are interviewed, accompanied by a list of recommended "next steps," are the final products of this segment of the CAP process. Each profile is sufficiently detailed to guide the drafting of a training contract.

How to Survey Organizations

Nine essential steps must be carried out in conducting a survey of organizations within the community a college serves. The steps are

1. Determine types, sizes, and geographical areas of organizations to contact.
2. Obtain lists of eligible organizations (that is, organizations of the type, size, and location that the college can serve).
3. Select organizations for the survey.
4. Prepare interview guides.
5. Select interview staff.
6. Schedule appointments for interviews.
7. Conduct interviews and collect data.
8. Prepare profiles of demand.
9. Respond to demand appropriately.

Brief discussion of each of these steps may be helpful.

1. Determine Types, Sizes, and Geographical Areas of Organizations to Contact. The types of organizations a college should consider in surveying the market for adult education include businesses and industries, government agencies, and voluntary associations.

Businesses and industries include manufacturers, retailers, utilities, and service organizations, as well as companies dealing in finance, real estate, insurance, transportation, distribution, communications, construction, mining, and petroleum. Companies in areas related to health, agriculture, or high technology also should be examined. Examples of the broad variety of businesses and industries that have contracted with colleges for training include Goodyear Corporation, AT&T, Hazleton Laboratories, State Mutual Life Insurance Company of America, Foss Launch and Tug Company, General Motors Corporation, Miller Brewing Company, and American Fletcher National Bank.

Government agencies include municipal, county, state, and federal agencies. Examples of government agencies that have contracted with colleges for training are City of Atlanta (Georgia), Elkhart School District (Elkhart, Kansas), California Work-Site Education and Training Act (CWETA) project, United States Army, United States Air Force, the New York State Division of Alcoholism and Alcohol Abuse, and the Ohio Department of Welfare.

Voluntary associations include professional groups and labor unions, as well as religious, social service, cultural and artistic, political, educational, health, and leisure groups that people join voluntarily. Examples of voluntary associations that have contracted with colleges for training are Bank Personnel Managers Association, YMCA Camp Kern, Brotherhood of Carpenters and Joiners, House Administration Committee (United States Congress), Catholic Diocese of Corpus Christi, and the Association of City Clerks and Secretaries of Texas.

The size of the organizations the college chooses to interview is an important consideration. Should a college choose to service a company with more than 300 employees, staff, members, or clients? Organizations of this size or larger would be most likely to have the resources needed to sign a contract training agreement and to have funds earmarked for training and tuition. Extended programs have natural attrition as employees travel, transfer, and leave the organization. Surprisingly, companies that have established in-house training programs are often most receptive to the kinds of educational opportunities colleges can offer. Having established systems for training, they understand the importance of learning and have identified what they need and how to obtain it.

An organization with fewer than 300 employees, on the other hand, might be less complicated and easier to service. Small companies should be targeted for shorter, less expensive programs (such as a one-day seminar on time management) applicable to the total company population.

The location of organizations poses important questions, particularly if the college's faculty members are unaccustomed to traveling off campus to offer courses. Should the college choose organizations within or outside its immediate service area? Many colleges provide services across county and state lines and must be capable of accommodating distant clients. Others are bound by agreements to teach only in specified areas and cannot teach out of state. Indeed, many public colleges and two-year community colleges have service-area limitations of some kind. Even so, an organization that wants a particular college to offer courses at branch offices in various locations could be accommodated even if a service agreement were in effect granting other colleges exclusive rights to offer courses in those areas. The college must, however, take the initiative to obtain all necessary waivers quickly.

2. *Obtain Lists of Eligible Organizations.* Lists of eligible organizations—those that meet the criteria set for type, size, and location—can be obtained through a variety of sources. College staff members, trustees, members of advisory councils, and other college-related groups that involve people from the community can be excellent sources of suggestions regarding organizations to interview. Most college libraries and placement offices have directories and other reference documents of local organizations. Further, directories of local organizations can be found through agencies such as chambers of commerce, manufacturers associations, regional planning commissions, county and municipal offices, and the Board of Trade. State agencies, particularly those that deal with professional associations, licensing, and labor and economic development, can also be a rich source for nomination of organizations. Finally, the local Yellow Pages can be used to identify special categories of organizations, such as those in the government and voluntary sectors.

3. *Select Organizations to Interview.* Several points are essential in determining which organizations should be contacted initially.

First and most important, no assumption whatsoever should be made regarding which organizations will or will not want to discuss contract training. Experience has shown that few, if any, generalizations can be made regarding which organizations will contract with which colleges for training. The most direct and effective route to follow is simply to contact each organization to determine whether it is interested. For example, a college may assume that because certain organizations have already established good working relations with other providers, they would not be interested in the services of another college. This is not necessarily true. Most organizations are wise consumers, and if they have already contracted with a competitor, they may be particularly eager to receive competing offers to be sure they are receiving the best services for their investment.

Second, a range of organizations to be interviewed must be determined. A selection drawn from all possibilities should be considered, including businesses and industries, government agencies, and voluntary associations. Choosing a variety of different types of organizations to survey allows a college to generalize conclusions for the entire market with some degree of confidence. On the other hand, predictions of who will request services are unreliable; a bank on one corner may request services, whereas the bank on the opposite corner may not.

Third, a college should determine the number of organizations to interview on the basis of the number it can service well. The College Board's experience in helping more than thirty colleges locate contract clients among organizations indicates that demand for education among organizations exceeds supply from colleges. If a college is just beginning to initiate contacts, ten or so companies would be sufficient for an initial survey. Experience has shown that once a college begins the survey process, it often finds an overwhelming demand for its services. Even when a college interviews only ten organizations, it may find that each one has some demand. The college ultimately may only be able to supply training for two or three of the organizations it interviewed.

Finally, choices of organizations to interview must be discussed with other college staff members. The possibility must be eliminated of contacting an organization that already has a similar training contract with the college or a conflicting demand on college resources. Simultaneously, the college should identify individuals within the target organization who should be contacted first because of some current or prior association with the college. Representatives from the alumni office, development office, and career or placement center of the college must be included in this review, along with the office of academic affairs and continuing education personnel.

4. *Prepare Interview Guides.* Several instruments are necessary in conducting organization interviews: an appointment questionnaire, an organization questionnaire, and a course and program questionnaire.

An appointment questionnaire should be used to collect several key pieces of information during initial telephone interviews with company officials to determine whether a meeting to discuss contract training should be scheduled. Names, titles, and locations of all persons within the organization contacted must be described individually on separate appointment questionnaires. If an organization did not want to schedule an interview with the college to discuss contract training, the appointment questionnaire should state the reasons for the company's decision. Reasons range from claims that the company does its own training or contracts for training with another college to claims that the company hires only people who are trained for their jobs or is not ready at the present time to undertake a training program. Names of organizations that refused interviews should be kept on file to avoid calling them again in the near future—or to be sure to call them again in the near future, if they so requested.

When an organization agrees to be interviewed, information about the interview, including the exact day, time, and location of the meeting, must be recorded on individual appointment questionnaires. Names and titles of organization officials who are expected to attend must be noted, as well as such information as the names of other providers the company has used in the recent past, particular courses or programs the company currently needs, and any association the company may already have with the college.

Organizations frequently ask colleges what they have to offer. The college must have a menu of services at hand so that it is ready to answer such a question. The college should not initiate discussion of what it can supply, but should focus instead on the needs of the organization that it has been able to identify. The company must not be misled into thinking that the college will offer only courses of its own choosing. Colleges that are successful in gaining and fulfilling training contracts owe their success in part to their willingness to become more demand oriented; that is, more responsive to what the organization thinks it wants or knows it needs.

Finally, in scheduling appointments with organizations, a question always arises regarding who from the organization should be invited to attend. The most important persons from the organization to attend such meetings always are those who are responsible for contracting for training and development activities.

An organization questionnaire should be used to ask questions of organizations at the beginning of an interview (usually scheduled for two hours). Such questions include

1. What other organizations, colleges, or outside vendors has this organization contracted with recently?
2. How much did these contracts cost the organization?
3. What types of employees does the organization have and how many employees are there of each type? (Solicit broad occupational groupings, such as secretaries, technicians, engineers, middle-level managers, and so forth.)
4. What kinds of training, if any, are already available to these groups?
5. For which of these groups does the organization want training from the college?

A course and program questionnaire should be prepared for each group of employees for whom the organization wants training and development and for each course or program requested. Answers to the following questions must be obtained:

1. What course or program does the employer have in mind?
2. What specific topics do the employers wish to have emphasized in this course or program?
3. How many employees would be trained in this course or program?
4. Where would the training take place?

5. During what season of the year would the training course or program be offered?
6. How long (in weeks) would the course or program be?
7. On what days of the week would classes be conducted?
8. During what hours of the day would classes be scheduled?
9. How many total clock hours would be allotted for the training?
10. Does the organization want the college to offer credit for the course or program?
11. Would training take place on organization time or on the employee's time?
12. Would the organization require or merely encourage employees to attend the training sessions?
13. Would the organization advertise and promote the training program?
14. Would the organization offer incentives to employees to complete the program?
15. Would the organization supply the space and materials required to conduct the training program?
16. How would the organization prefer to compensate the college for the services provided?

5. Select Interview Staff. A college must select its best representatives for the first meeting with an organization. The representatives who are sent will influence the organization's perception of how well the college is able to assess and meet its needs. Therefore, representatives should possess the following qualities:

1. *Broad knowledge of the college rather than familiarity with only one field or area.* Since the organization may not limit itself to courses in only one field, representatives should be present who can discuss a range of services, including program options and faculty expertise.
2. *Attractive personality.* Staff members who are personable are better salespersons for their colleges.
3. *Familiarity with various types of organizational structures.* Staff who are familiar with various types of organizational struc-

tures will be able to satisfy company needs more readily because they will understand the accommodations that must be made.

4. *Availability and energy.* Staff members who have the time to undertake interviews and the energy to carry through on the outcomes are essential to the success of contract training programs. Faculty members often must be given release time to devote to such programs to guarantee their success and raise the probability of obtaining future contracts. Lacking release time, faculty members may be too overburdened with their regular work to be good salespersons.

6. Schedule Appointments for Interviews. When beginning an interview process, appointments should be made within a six-week period to track and make decisions about the ten or so organizations being contacted, rather than spreading out the appointments over a period of months. When initiating a call to an organization, the college staff member should start at the top; that is, the president's office should be contacted first if no other course is obvious. If the president cannot respond to an inquiry directly, the call will likely be transferred to the person in charge of purchasing or training.

The person calling an organization must be very specific regarding the reason for the call. He or she should state that the college wants to meet with appropriate organization officials to discuss training needs that the college can fulfill. Ceremonial visits to discuss one another's histories or futures should be avoided, as should multiple-purpose meetings that add the subject of initiating training contracts to a chain of other subjects (for example, organization gift-giving interests, faculty exchanges, or equipment donations).

The spokesperson for the organization should be asked to name three representatives to attend the meeting. The college likewise should indicate that it will bring three representatives. The organization should be asked to try to bring a person from the training department, a person of vice-presidential rank, and a person who operates a unit within the organization. Having these three functional areas represented will make available to the college broad-based information about the organization's training requirements.

Having scheduled an interview with an organization, a letter of confirmation should be sent restating who will be at the meeting, as well as the time and place.

7. *Conduct Interviews and Collect Data.* An interview should be focused on the organization's demands for courses and programs. Time should not be wasted extolling the virtues of the college. About 10 percent of the discussion should be devoted to questions from the college staff, and about 90 percent of the discussion should focus on the organization's training requirements. In some cases, the organization may want to know what the college has to offer. The college's response should emphasize what it does best. Marketable centers of strength within the college should be identified before the interviews begin. Experience (if any) in serving other organizations also should be stated.

College staff members should be responsive during interviews but avoid making definite commitments. An interview is a fact-finding exercise. Information is to be collected and taken back to the college so that sound decisions can be made regarding the services that the college is ready, willing, and able to supply. Before a meeting ends, organization officials should be told when they will next hear from the college.

8. *Prepare Profiles.* Documentation of an interview is necessary if information gathered is to be shared with colleagues. A profile for each organization should be prepared, recording responses given to questions posed in the organization questionnaire and the course and program questionnaire. The interview staff should compare specific demands made by the organizations interviewed to their college's ability to supply the requisite training. Additional fact finding should be conducted by telephone or through additional interviews, if required. For example, the college can call on experts to discuss ways of meeting specific needs of organizations or collect more exact demand information from the organizations before responses or proposals are submitted.

9. *Respond to Demand.* As profiles of demand from the organizations that have been interviewed are reviewed, several factors must be considered as decisions are made regarding ap-

propriate responses. First, which organizations are the best prospects as clients for the college? That is, given the information gathered from the profiles and personal insights, which organizations are asking for training and development assistance in areas that are consistent with the priorities of the college? Further, can the college provide expertise in those areas? The college staff members responsible for a survey often can determine accurately whether the college has the expertise to provide the desired training. On the other hand, whether faculty members are willing to provide needed training is a question that may require administrative judgment at various levels, as well as review of the responses to a survey of faculty and administration.

Colleges need not wait, however, for the results of a faculty and administration survey to determine whether contract training should be sought and what contract training can or should be conducted. A college should not be limited by preconceived notions of faculty members or administrators; to do so would prevent the college from obtaining from organizations a comprehensive view of demand. Once demand has been defined and explained, faculty and administration attitudes often change. Furthermore, in order to meet demand from organizations, colleges may have to turn to faculty members from other institutions because their regular full-time faculty members may be too busy or too committed to other institutional duties to provide contract courses. Some faculty members are not sufficiently flexible or skilled in teaching to offer high-quality contract training. If such faculty members show little interest in cooperating, their wishes should be respected.

Most important, in responding to the organizations that have been surveyed, colleges must act in a responsible and timely fashion. Immediately after an interview, a letter of appreciation should be sent to company officials, accompanied by a brief review of the next steps the college proposes to take in responding to the organization. Followup telephone conversations or short meetings could be scheduled with the organization if more data are necessary to make a constructive response. Within weeks, a detailed plan and required contracts should be developed for consideration by the organization.

Sample Profile of an Organization-
University Contractual Agreement for Training

A brief profile of a contractual agreement between Advanced Technology, Inc., of Reston, Virginia, and American University in Washington, D.C., is shown in Figure 5.* This profile provides information about the details of a successful contract.

Figure 5. Profile of a Contractual Agreement for Training.

Advanced Technology, Inc.
Reston, Virginia
Graduate Certificate in Management Information Systems

Students	Open to full-time Information Technology Group (ITG) employees with bachelor's degrees.
Content	A graduate certificate program of fifteen hours of coursework from the Center for Technology and Administration at American University. This program provides the foundation for understanding computer applications and management information systems. Courses may be transferred into a master's degree program in Management Information Systems.
Schedule	Five 3-credit courses meet once a week each for three and a half hours for ten weeks, during evenings.
Methods	Instructors meet with Advanced Technology, Inc., employees and supervisors to decide how to enhance course syllabi to meet corporate educational needs.
Faculty	All courses are taught by American University faculty members of the Center for Technology and Administration.
Location	All courses are held at Advanced Technology, Inc., facilities in Reston, Virginia, and Woodlawn, Maryland.
College services	American University provides on-site registration, advisement, and book delivery to coordinate with the schedule of classes at Advanced Technology, Inc.
Organization services	Advanced Technology, Inc., provides classrooms and facilities, as well as in-house liaison.
Contract charges	Advanced Technology, Inc., pays a fixed price per student for a minimum number of enrollments per course.
Evaluation	Students evaluate the program according to regular university procedures.

*Figures 5 through 8 were all provided by Kathryn Mannes, Director of Contract Programs, The American University.

Certification   Upon completion of the program of five courses, students will be awarded a Graduate Certificate in Management Information Systems at a certificate ceremony.

Contact   Kathryn Mannes
Director, Contract Programs
American University
4400 Massachusetts Ave., N.W.
Washington, D.C. 20016

The contractual agreement with Advanced Technology, Inc., originated with a call to the company by a member of the American University staff. The client had been selected because it appeared to be a large, growing company that might have a need for contract training that the university could provide.

Over a number of months, university representatives worked closely with personnel from the human resources and training departments of Advanced Technology, to develop a program and a program rationale that could be presented to top management. The program rationale addressed two company priorities: (1) to recruit and retain employees in a competitive field and (2) to provide all employees with a common knowledge bases.

Representatives of American University brought together deans and directors of appropriate academic units with the vice-president of Advanced Technology who would be instrumental in deciding whether or not the training program would be undertaken. Later, representatives from Advanced Technology and American University met to design a curriculum, select courses, approve textbooks, and so forth.

In the contract Advanced Technology agreed to provide enrollment for a minimum number of courses each year. The contract was negotiated to accommodate the structure of Advanced Technology's benefits program, with payment for courses based on individual student rates collected in one total sum from the organization. The university also agreed to award five scholarships (tuition vouchers) to Advanced Technology for every fifty Advanced Technology enrollments. The program has been expanded to other Advanced Technology facilities in the Washington, D.C., area. It began its third year in fall 1986 with an expected enrollment of 150 students.

Figures 6, 7, and 8 illustrate how to write a contract with a business to offer a credit course, a noncredit course, and how to specify terms regarding use of facilities. Figure 7 may be used in conjunction with either Figure 6 or Figure 8.

Figure 6. Sample Contractual Agreement for a Credit Course.

name
title
organization
address

Dear *(name of contracting officer):*

The following letter of agreement sets forth the terms by which *(university)* will provide courses and utilize classroom space at *(organization)*.

PROGRAM

The *university* will offer courses leading to a *title of certificate or degree* which includes the following courses:

　　　　　　　　course number　　　　　　*title of course*

Students must complete all courses and fulfill the foundation requirements in *(subject)* in order to be eligible for the *(certificate or degree)*. Course scheduling and faculty selections will be at the discretion of the university through consultation with *(organization)*. It is anticipated that students will move through the program from *(month, year through month, year)*.

REGISTRATION AND ADVISEMENT

The *(university)* will hold on-site registration for two hours at *(organization)* in a room identified by *(organization)* each semester. An academic advisor will be available during registration.

The *(university's)* course operations at *(organization)* will commence prior to *(date)*.

SCHEDULE

All courses will be offered in *(number)* week sessions. Classes meet for *(number)* hours one night a week as follows:

　　　　　　　　begin/end　　　　　　　　*meeting times*

Sincerely,

(name)
(title)
(university)

Figure 7. Sample Contractual Agreement for Use of Facilities.

All classrooms will be provided by *(organization)*. Students and faculty will use designated classrooms only.

Audiovisual equipment will be provided by *(organization)*, as required by instructors.

FEES

(organization) guarantees the fixed price per course is *(dollars)* for up to *(number)* students. There is no minimum enrollment. Students will be accepted in the class up to a course maximum of *(number)*.

BOOKS

Students will be responsible for purchasing their own books. The university will make every effort to have books available for purchase prior to or at the first class meeting at *(organization)*.

CANCELLATION

Courses must be canceled by *(organization)*, sixty days prior to the first class meeting to avoid incurring a fee. *(organization)* guarantees *(dollars)* for any course canceled after this time. There is no cancellation fee for the first course.

PARTICIPANTS

Courses are open to employees of *(organization)* and others designated by *(organization)* who satisfy university requirements for nondegree status and meet the necessary course prerequisites.

LIABILITY

(organization) agrees to indemnify and save the university harmless from all damages and liability arising out of or in connection with the presence of the university on *(organization)* premises, provided, however, that such damage and liability shall not have been caused by the negligence of employees of the university.

BILLING

The university will bill *(organization)* as soon as the enrollment for each course is finalized. *(organization)* will promptly pay the invoice upon receipt. Should *(organization)* payment not be paid within 30 days, the university may, at its sole discretion, assess a 1.5 percent interest charge to the overdue balance.

Upon your approval of the foregoing, please sign the enclosed copy of this letter and return it to me. The university looks forward to offering this program designed to meet the needs of *(organization)* employees.

Sincerely,
(name)
(title)
(organization)

Figure 8. Sample Contractual Agreement for a Noncredit Course.

(date)
(title)
(organization)
(address)

Dear *(name of contracting officer):*

The following letter of agreement sets forth the terms by which *(university)* will provide *(number)* session(s) of *(course number)*, a noncredit Professional Development Seminar for *(organization)*.

The seminar, *("course title, ")* taught by *(name of instructor)*, will be held on [*date(s)*]. Hours will be [*time(s)*]. Dates and times may be changed by mutual agreement of *(university)* and the *(organization)*.

The price of this seminar is [*(dollars)/(dollars per day)*], payable upon completion of the seminar. A maximum of twenty participants may attend each day.

We look forward to presenting the *(subject matter)* seminar in conjunction with the *(organization)*. Contract seminars demonstrate the *(university's)* ongoing commitment to providing training opportunities to area corporations and federal agencies.

Upon request, we provide certificates of completion to clients. The *(organization)* is responsible for filling in participants' names and workshop titles, with the assistance of the instructors. Certificates can then be distributed in class at the end of training.

Please return one signed copy of this letter. Payment should be sent to

(name)
(title)
(address)

within 30 days of receipt of an invoice.

Thank you again for your interest in *(university)*.

Sincerely,

(name)
(title)
(university)

References

Aslanian, C. B. "Market Analysis Is the Key to Finding Adult Students." In *The Admissions Strategist: Recruiting in the 1980s.* New York: College Entrance Examination Board, 1985.

National Center for Education Statistics. *Participation in Adult Education: 1981.* Washington, D.C.: National Center for Education Statistics, 1982.

National Center for Education Statistics, 1985.

PART THREE

Partnerships for Research: Lessons from Experience

Frederick Betz

10

The Nature
of Cooperative Research:
Reaching Agreement
on Process, Uses, and Ownership

A central question concerning university-industry partnerships is, What kind of research—basic, applied, or developmental—may properly be undertaken through such projects? Inherent in the question is a challenge to the very mission of the modern university, dedicated to education, research, and service. Traditionally, university-based research has been undertaken to advance basic knowledge. In extending the university's service mission to encompass applied or even developmental research undertaken for businesses, will not differences in the research cultures involved inevitably have considerable effect on the broad range of related university traditions, including such fundamentals as academic freedom? This concern was on the minds of National Science Foundation officials who administered the Industry/University Cooperative Research (IUCR) Program.

Industry/University Cooperative Research Program

The Industry/University Cooperative Research Program of the National Science Foundation was founded in 1977 and was carried as a separate budget element in the National Science

Foundation's program structure through 1986. Afterward, the project was decentralized into discipline-oriented research programs. During its years of central administration, the IUCR program provided a rich opportunity to study the nature of research cooperation across a broad range of topics, disciplines, and industries.

The formal objective of the IUCR program was to advance scientific and engineering knowledge relevant to technological innovation. According to IUCR procedures, unsolicited research proposals were submitted jointly by university and industrial researchers to appropriate disciplinary departments of the foundation. The IUCR proposals were thus peer reviewed like other proposals submitted to the NSF. Only when a cooperative proposal received a very good or excellent rating was it accepted; the disciplinary program then funded 50 percent of the award, and the IUCR program funded the other 50 percent. The IUCR program encouraged the submission of cooperative proposals, administered NSF-wide policies on cooperative research, and provided a funding incentive for disciplinary programs to sponsor cooperative research. The program grew from an initial level of 50 projects in 1978 to 140 projects in 1986.

The IUCR program was viewed as a kind of experiment in basic research cooperation between universities and industry. Proposals were unsolicited and accepted in the broad categories of science and engineering supported by NSF. Companies participating came from a range of industries; universities participating were predominantly the research universities usually supported by NSF. The program experience confirmed some of the previous studies on research cooperation, such as studies of motivations for cooperation (Peters and Fusfeld, 1983, p. 34). In addition, other aspects of cooperation were revealed, such as the type of research undertaken, modes of cooperation used, how research results are used in industry, and policies that facilitate research cooperation.

The participants in NSF cooperative projects were research-intensive universities and industrial firms. This involvement reflected the broader pattern of research performance in the United States; that is, about 200 research universities exist in the United States, and the top 100 account for 85 percent of federally sponsored research at universities and colleges. Industrial research is similarly concentrated, with about seven major industries accounting for 80 percent of all company R&D.

For each cooperative project in the NSF program, research was justified both in terms of the fundamental scientific issues being addressed and the way in which technology would be advanced. Additional discussions with the industrial managers, to whom the industrial researchers reported, further emphasized the interest of these participating firms in research in fundamental but technologically relevant areas. One could thus generalize from the NSF sample that both research universities and research-intensive firms are primarily interested in cooperative research in fundamental areas.

Targeted basic research performed cooperatively is efficient for companies. Although such research is important to companies over the long term, companies usually give priority to research that meets short-term needs. Accordingly, basic research receives lowest priority for company funding. Industry spends an average of only about 3 percent of its research budget on basic research. Thus, leveraging their fundamental research effort by cooperating with a university makes sense to companies. In the IUCR program, NSF funded university costs, and industry then had access to the skills and facilities necessary to research tasks for which they did not bear the costs. Cooperative research was also effective for companies, because the ideas and directions generated from collaboration between university and industrial researchers usually would not have been arrived at by either participant alone. The university researchers, in defining the research structure, tended to emphasize fundamental questions, and the industrial researchers tended to emphasize applications. Thus, cooperative projects sponsored by the NSF involved both basic and technological questions, an exciting combination because technological advances often emerge from such research.

Policy Implications of the NSF Experience

Several policy implications emerged from the NSF experience. First, if universities want close research cooperation with research-intensive industries, they should focus on basic research that is targeted toward technological opportunities relevant to these industries. Second, if applied research is to be performed by universities in a cooperative mode, it should be limited in order to avoid distorting the scientific mission of the university, and it should be closely tied to an educational program, perhaps at the master's level.

The fields of research in which NSF cooperative proposals were most often received were the science disciplines of chemistry, physics, mathematics, computer sciences, biology, and materials research; and the engineering disciplines of chemical, electrical, mechanical, and civil engineering. These disciplines reflect the mutual interests of the academic and industrial researchers in advancing basic knowledge while simultaneously expanding the knowledge base applicable to current and future technology. Such disciplines lend themselves to fundamental questions that have technological relevance. In fact, the effect of the technological focus is to cause certain phenomena to be probed in more detail than academic science would normally consider. For example, because of their utility to semiconductor electronics, the elements of silicon and gallium have received a great deal of attention in the disciplines of solid state physics and chemistry. However, in technological areas relevant predominantly to governmental rather than industrial functions, cooperative research proposals were rare—for example, in the environmental sciences.

An Example of Cooperative Materials Research. An example of an NSF-sponsored cooperative research project intended to improve understanding of the scientific phenomena underlying a technology is a project on conducting polymers performed by D. B. Tanner at the University of Florida and A. J. Epstein at Xerox Webster Research Center. Although plastics do not ordinarily conduct electricity, in the 1970s a university chemist, Alan MacDermiod, invented a way of making them conductive by "doping" (adding metallic atoms to them). Applications for conducting plastics were quickly conceived: batteries, non-electrostatic carpets, and conductive plastic casings. However, the exact way in which electrons were conducted in doped plastics was not understood.

Tanner, a physicist, was skilled in performing spectroscopic studies, and Epstein, a chemist, was skilled in creating conducting polymers. Together they began a series of studies, formulating plastics at different levels of doping and spectroscopically observing the modes of electronic conduction. In the course of six years of research sponsored by NSF, they found different mechanisms of conduction at different levels of dopants. Knowledge gained proved useful in moving toward the technological goal of designing plastics with desired levels of conductivity. At the same time, science was advanced through this exploration of how electrons move in organic materials.

Promoting Cooperation Among University and Industrial Researchers. Industrial and academic researchers collaborate most effectively when the parties bring complementary skills and resources to a project. In the example just discussed, the two researchers were engaged in complementary disciplines. Tanner possessed the skills and instrumentation required to observe the phenomenon being examined, and Epstein possessed the skills and instrumentation required to create samples of the phenomenon.

In the cooperative projects sponsored by NSF, about three quarters of the theoretical tasks were performed by academic researchers, and almost all sample preparation tasks involving sophisticated technology were performed by industrial researchers. Experimental tasks were about equally divided between university and industrial laboratories. This reflected a general pattern apparent in academic and industrial research: academic research tends to emphasize theory, industrial research tends to emphasize technology, and academic and industrial research tend to emphasize experimentation equally.

Relationship of Cooperative Research to Industrial Technology

Firms most often involved in NSF cooperative proposals were research-intensive companies in the chemical, petrochemical, electronics, computer, telecommunication, pharmaceutical, aerospace, and defense industries. In addition, NSF received a few proposals from firms in the automotive and food processing industries. Because NSF predominantly funded basic research, in general only firms with corporate research laboratories participated in the program. Chemical and petrochemical firms were usually involved in chemical, chemical engineering, materials, or biological research. Electronics, computer, and communications firms were usually involved in physics, electrical engineering, materials, computer science, or mathematical research. Pharmaceutical firms were involved in chemical or biological research. The aerospace and defense firms were involved in the broadest range of research: in physics, electrical engineering, mechanical engineering, chemistry, chemical engineering, materials, computer sciences, and mathematics.

This distribution of research involvement reflects the science and engineering bases underlying the technologies utilized in the businesses. Since industry is principally interested in technology, the disciplines in which industrial researchers perform research are those that provide the knowledge base for the technologies. Accordingly, university and industrial researchers can cooperate in the disciplines providing the knowledge base for industrial technologies. Furthermore, since all technologies utilize more than one discipline, integration of research from several disciplines usually is required to advance the knowledge base of a technology; this was the responsibility of industrial researchers in the NSF cooperative projects. However, university researchers can play a more active role in integrating disciplinary knowledge for technological advance.

A Cooperative Project in Chemical Engineering. A project researching the formation of semipermeable membranes was proposed by two professors, W. Krantz and R. Sani, at the University of Colorado at Boulder and H. Lonsdale and R. Rife, both Ph.D.'s, of Bend Research Corporation. Semipermeable membranes are plastic films with relatively large (on the molecular scale) holes on one side and small holes on the other. A semipermeable membrane in a water desalting device, for example, allows water molecules to be forced through the membrane but not the larger salt molecules. Semipermeable membranes had found a number of applications in chemical processing, but making them remained an art.

Lonsdale was an expert in producing semipermeable membranes, and Krantz and Sani were experts in modeling fluid phenomena. When Rife, a former student of Krantz and Sani, went to work for Lonsdale, the group developed an idea for a cooperative project involving modeling the process through which semipermeable membranes are formed. Experiments were performed at Bend Research and at the University of Colorado at Boulder, and modeling studies were conducted at Boulder. The group did succeed in modeling the complex vortex phenomena created by the heat transfer of the precipitating membrane on the surface of the solvent. The new models provided an important breakthrough in the design of semipermeable membranes and also made fundamental advances in research into vortex creation.

In this example, polymer chemistry and chemical engineering were disciplines underlying Bend Research Corporation's technologies. Both Lonsdale and Rife were trained in chemical engineering, and Krantz and Sani added the physics and mathematics sophistication required for the modeling effort. Thus the industrial researchers brought experimental and technological capabilities to the project, and the academic researchers brought theoretical and complementary experimental skills to the project. Again, the key to productive industry-university cooperative research lay in the correct combination of research skills required to probe the scientific underpinnings of technology.

Industry Interest in Performing Basic Research Cooperatively with Universities

Examination of the industrial relevance of the cooperative projects in the NSF/IUCR program reveals the following goals:

1. Improved understanding of basic scientific phenomena underlying technological processes, devices, and materials.
2. Improved design or operation of technological processes, devices, and materials.
3. Creation of new technological devices, processes, or materials.

4.   Creation of new research instrumentation or techniques.

NSF-sponsored cooperative research in science disciplines tended to focus on the first goal. Cooperative research in engineering disciplines tended to focus on the second goal. The conductive plastics project had the first goal, and the semipermeable membranes project had the second goal.

The third and fourth goals were pursued less frequently, but they were not uncommon. One example of a technological device created in a cooperative project was a very large scale integrated chip specialized for matrix inversion mathematics developed to solve robot-control problems. An example of scientific instrumentation created in a cooperative project was an ion probe for examining microstructures and etching semiconductor structures. Occasionally, a new device or instrument was revolutionary. For example, in a cooperative project between the University of Arizona and Bell Laboratories, the world's first fast, room-temperature optical switching device—the photonic equivalent of a transistor—was created by Hyatt Gibbs, Art Gossard, and Sam McCall.

How Cooperative Research Is Used in Industry. Cooperative research has been used by industrial researchers to deepen their understanding of phenomena underlying technologies utilized by their corporations and to improve design tools upon which their engineering staffs depend.

In addition, applied projects within companies have often paralleled cooperative basic research projects, thus applying the knowledge created in the basic research. For example, insights and data obtained by Epstein in working with Tanner were useful to Epstein's principal applied work at Xerox. He conducted a parallel applied project to develop a conductive plastic to use in a new generation of Xerox laser printers. That is, his participation in nonproprietary, fundamental cooperative research helped him design properties of materials in his proprietary, applied industrial research.

Werle of United Technologies. Additional understanding of how industry uses cooperative research can be gained by examining how one's industrial R&D manager expanded his group's industrial research capability by creating several cooperative research projects with universities. From 1980 to 1986, an NSF cooperative engineering research project was jointly performed by Michael Werle of United Technologies' corporate laboratory and by J. D. Walker and C. R. Smith of Lehigh University. The project involved modeling the flow of turbulent air across turbine blades, with Werle performing experimental tasks, and Walker and Smith performing theoretical and complementary experimental tasks.

The project was initiated by Werle, as manager of the gas dynamics and thermophysics section of the United Technologies Research Center at Hartford, Connecticut. In the early 1980s, United Technologies consisted of four groups of companies, classified as power, helicopters, building systems, and electronics. Werle's principal concern was for the turbine technologies of the subsidiary Pratt & Whitney Aircraft.

The design of turbine blades is critical to the efficiency and safety of jet engines. Turbine blades compress air with aviation fuel prior to engine ignition, and the smooth flow of air over the blades is necessary not only for fuel economy, but for safety. In the early days of jet aircraft, flameout killed many pilots. Flameout occurs when air flowing over turbine blades breaks into turbulence, stopping air flow into the jet combustion chamber and stopping combustion. Planes thus affected suddenly lose power and often crash. Flameout and stalling of an airplane are comparable problems because stalling is also caused by loss of smooth flow of air, in this case across the wings. The smoothness of air flow over turbine blades dramatically affects blade life and fuel economy.

Pratt & Whitney engineers had accumulated—partly from theory and partly from experience—a simplified analysis of gas turbine operation. This simplified analysis provided a knowledge base for Pratt & Whitney's design system. After designs were produced and evaluated, hardware was constructed to test the designs. The evaluation and hardware-testing operations were the most expensive steps in new engine development. By improving design methodology to reduce the need for evaluation and testing, costs could be significantly reduced. Thus, Werle's goals were to improve design methodology using information obtained through experimentation and improved analysis techniques.

From an engineering point of view, modeling gas and liquid flows over surfaces poses fundamental problems involving such techniques as finite-element analysis and differential equations of flow. Werle suggested to Walker and Smith that a joint project would utilize their complementary skills. From such a project, basic engineering knowledge could be advanced, and Werle could use the advances to improve Pratt & Whitney's design system. Publications from the joint project appeared in scientific and engineering journals, coauthored by Werle, Walker, and Smith (in appropriate combinations). At Lehigh, Walker and Smith used the research in graduate education, which resulted in several doctoral dissertations.

At the time of this cooperative project, Werle was also involved in nine other cooperative projects with faculty members at other universities. He had almost doubled the technical capability of his research group by matching his staff with university collaborators.

Intellectual Property in Cooperative Agreements

Intellectual property traditionally falls into four categories: patents, copyrights, trade secrets, and trademarks. The latter two, trade secrets and trademarks, seldom affect cooperative agreements, as companies generally perform such research internally. Since in the course of cooperative research, however, faculty members and graduate students may be exposed to proprietary information, companies may request them to sign agreements not to divulge such information. At the same time, a university cannot and should not undertake any cooperative agreement to guard proprietary information for a company. However, a sponsoring or cooperating company should be informed of any past or present consulting arrangements between university researchers and company competitors that may be viewed as liabilities toward confidentiality.

Cooperative agreements should address disposition of rights on patents and copyrights. A wide variety of policies currently exist in American universities concerning intellectual property rights in industrial cooperative research. In a 1981 National Science Foundation workshop on intellectual property rights in university-industry cooperation, some useful principles were discussed (National Science Board, 1982, pp. 255–265).

As a first principle, participants emphasized that the intention of fundamental research is to advance knowledge rather than to invent. If a project is intended to create invention or development of an invention, the project should be treated as a joint commercial venture between the company and the university (instead of as cooperative research). However, even in cooperative research, inventions often serendipitously occur, so that an agreement upon patent rights should be included in every cooperative research agreement.

Basic rights secured by a patent include

1. The right to practice (make use of or sell the invention).
2. The right to exclude others from practicing the invention.
3. The right to license others to practice the invention.
4. The right to receive royalties from licenses.
5. The right to license the right to exclude others from practicing the invention.

Factors to be considered in negotiating rights in cooperative agreements include

1. Who may decide whether to file for a patent.
2. Who holds title to the patent.
3. If the university holds title, whether the cooperating company has a right to an exclusive or nonexclusive license.
4. The conditions under which royalties may be collected.
5. Due diligence in the utilization of a patent by licensees.

Holding title to a patent involves two important considerations. First, the title holder is legally entitled to enforce the patent by suing for patent infringement. Therefore a university involved in a research partnership should develop necessary policies on pursuing patent infringement. Second, if federal funds were involved in supporting the research leading to an invention, then by current federal law the universities or small businesses that produced the invention may hold patent rights (some federal restrictions applying). It may accordingly be simpler when federal funds are involved in the research to have the university hold the title.

Another important consideration is exclusivity of the license. In some instances, individual patents are very valuable, whereas in other instances, only clusters of patents are valuable. For example, in the pharmaceutical and chemical industries, individual patents have been valuable. In comparison, in electronics and computers, cross licensing had been widely practiced. Thus, dependent upon the industries, in some cases companies may wish exclusive licenses, and in others nonexclusive licenses from the university may be more advantageous. Accordingly, royalties to universities may be maximized by either exclusive or nonexclusive licensing, as is appropriate. Occasionally, a patent may be so basic that it is in the best public interest not to provide an exclusive license, as was the case, for example, at Stanford in its work on recombinant DNA techniques for genetic engineering.

To deal with all these issues, a set of guidelines should be formulated to assist the university in negotiating patent rights. General practice has been if the university and industrial researchers jointly invent, then the university and company should jointly own the patents; and if either singly invents, then the patent is owned by the inventing institution. When the university invents in a cooperative project, then the participating company will usually request a right to an exclusive or nonexclusive license. Under all licenses that the university as title holder to a patent may issue, there should be reasonable royalties and conditions for expeditious use of the patent by the licensee.

Normally, exclusive licenses offer the most economic incentive to a company to develop the invention to a commercial stage. However, if the research has been sponsored by a consortium of companies, then nonexclusive licenses to the consortium will be the usual arrangement.

Proprietary Research Agreements. Proprietary research should normally be handled through private faculty consulting or by a separate contract research unit of the university. The reason for this is that proprietary research that cannot be published conflicts with the educational missions of the university to advance and communicate public knowledge. However, some proprietary research is justified as providing (1) access to industrial problems that can lead to generic research opportunities; (2) aid to master's level thesis problems, wherein the focus is developing problem-solving skills and not publishable advances in basic knowledge; or (3) special assistance in problem solving for industrial firms that are substantial supporters of fundamental university cooperative research.

Proprietary research agreements should be written as research and development contracts, with a clearly defined problem, deliverable outcome, and milestone schedule to reach the outcome. In addition to the direct and indirect costs of the research, the university should charge a fee that is used to seed basic, nonproprietary research.

Productivity-Applied Research at Rensselaer Polytechnic Institute. An example of a proprietary, contract research center at a university that was integrated into educational programs was the Productivity Research Center at Rensselaer Polytechnic Institute (RPI). It was established to provide problem-solving opportunities for master's level engineering students in manufacturing. The center focused on problems in production and quality control. Projects originated when a company, in consultation with the center's director, identified a manufacturing problem and contracted for its solution in a six-month to one-year period. The center director, in consultation with engineering faculty, identified master's students for whom a project would make an excellent master's thesis. Each project was supervised in the center by a technical project manager, who held a full-time, nonfaculty appointment. Project managers generally were young engineers with at least a master's degree and two years' industrial experience. They were employed under contract for two years with a single extension possible, and as a result, turnover occurred every two or four years.

The reason for using a professional project staff and not faculty was the time-constrained, proprietary nature of the project. Faculty generally were not accustomed to producing research results at the pace of a short-term schedule, and faculty supervision of the projects had frequently proven unsuccessful in meeting time deadlines. Moreover, because of the proprietary, nonpublishable nature of the research, faculty had also had little motivation to supervise work to ensure a successful problem solution. When projects did not result in successful solutions on schedule, the center lost industrial clients. However, since the projects did solve real industrial problems and were very valuable as master's-level engineering education, it was in the university's interest to see that the projects were well managed, and the hiring of the project management staff proved an effective way to do so. Faculty members were involved in the projects as thesis supervisors.

Contracts were charged at commercial rates. Graduate students were paid reasonable salaries for their work, and center profits were contributed to the engineering school. Proprietary rights to information, designs, software, or inventions were owned by the contracting industrial firms. Information generally was not published. The center work did provide access to industrial firms, which, if faculty followed up on the opportunities, could lead to cooperative research of a fundamental, nonproprietary nature.

Copyrights. Copyrights can be a problem in cooperative research, since copyrightable material can often have direct commercial value without further research and development. It is the further research and development that distances fundamental research or even patentable research from the nonproprietary interests of the university and the proprietary interests of industry. Material that can be copyrighted differs from patentable inventions in that the legal rights on copyrighted materials are limited to expression and reproduction of expression (and not to the ideas inherent therein, as in patents). In cooperative research, rights to software are negotiable between the university and the company. The share negotiated depends upon the proportion of research support the company is providing and the contribution by company employees in the research that creates the software.

Traditionally, in the university, copyrightable materials

such as books, articles, music, and so on have been the property of the creating faculty members. Computer software has yielded new problems, however, since a copyrightable piece of software can be so valuable as to even be the basis of a company to maintain and develop the commercial value of the software. Because of the importance of software in new industries, there has not yet emerged a consensus on the distribution of rights between universities and faculty or students involved in software production. Because of the present lack of accepted practices in dealing with software, there have been instances of bitter conflict between university administrators and faculty about software.

Conflict over Copyrighted Software at California Institute of Technology. As an example of the possibility of such conflict, Kolata (1983, p. 932) described a bitter dispute that took place at Caltech: "For the past two years, a bitter argument has been raging at the California Institute of Technology over who owns a potentially valuable computer program and what constitutes a conflict of interest. The argument has involved persons at every level of the Caltech administration as well as members of its physics department. And the lasting effects of this dispute have left everyone unhappy. A brilliant young physicist has resigned from Caltech, the computer program's development has been abandoned, and rifts have grown between administrators and faculty."

Wolfram was an assistant professor in the physics department of Caltech, calculating particle interactions in quantum field theory. The algebra of the calculations was too complicated to do by hand or with existing computational programs, and Wolfram wrote a better calculational program, which he had working by June 1980. Wolfram recognized a wider use of his program and thought about commercializing it. He asked his department chairman for advice, who sent him to the patent lawyer at Caltech. A year of meetings followed, during which Wolfram thought he had reached an agreement with the university, in which he could use the software to form a company, to be called Computer Mathematics Corporation. The licensing agreement next required the signature of Caltech's provost. Throughout this negotiation, Wolfram had assumed that Caltech owned or shared in the ownership of the program, since it had been written as a part of Wolfram's official duties in performing research.

The provost, however, refused to sign the agreement, for two reasons: "First, he wanted to be sure the interests of the Department of Energy (which sponsored the research) were looked after . . . [and, second] he wondered whether it was proper for the university to enter into an agreement with a company in which Caltech faculty members had substantial stakes" (Kolata, 1983, p. 933).

At this point, tempers flared. Wolfram now began to argue that in fact the copyright did not belong to Caltech. Two years of contention followed, at which time Wolfram was given an ultimatum to resign from the company or from the university. Wolfram resigned from Caltech, accepting an appointment at the Institute for Advanced Study in Princeton. In his new position, Wolfram requested and received a letter from the institute waiving all rights to any inventions he might produce.

Meanwhile, back at Caltech, new policies were instituted. Bylaws were changed asserting the university's rights to copyrightable material if the institute or a funding agency financed the project in which it was developed. The university would obtain all royalties, unless other arrangements were made in advance. In addition, Caltech issued a statement on conflict of interest asserting that the "Institute should not make licensing agreements that pose a real or potential conflict of interest with respect to the obligations of any Faculty member of the Institute" (Kolata, 1983, p. 937).

Policies about copyrights still vary from university to university. At Stanford in 1984, for example, computer software copyrights belonged to the university. Massachusetts Institute of Technology also claimed all copyrights on software but shared royalties with the creators. Carnegie-Mellon University also shared royalties with the creators and, in addition, encouraged faculty to start outside companies.

Universities and Technology Transfer. The issues involved in setting policies about software and faculty-started companies are several. The first is whether or not all the parties contributing to the creation of valuable software are appropriately rewarded. The second is whether the transfer of the software technology from the university to the commercial sector is effectively achieved. The third is under what conditions it is appropriate for faculty to be engaged in commercial ventures.

With regard to the first issue, the principles involved in assigning rights to copyrighted software should be similar to those of assigning rights in patents. Since the university has contributed employment and facilities, the university should have some rights. Since the faculty (or students) have contributed creative ideas, they should also have some rights, as this encourages faculty to consider technology transfer from the university to commercial spheres. Effective transfer of technology occurs through people. Accordingly, faculty interest in seeing that their basic research not only results in publications but also in technology transfer is in the best interests of society.

Faculty involvement in starting companies, the third issue, is useful for society so long as it facilitates technology transfer. However, when faculty begin running companies, then conflicts arise. The principle should be that faculty may not participate as operating officers in companies, except for the first few years to get a new company started. After that they should choose to be faculty or businesspersons. Universities allow faculty to consult in order to improve professional competence. Therefore, consulting for a firm in which a faculty member is a stockholder can be allowed under the usual rules that consulting involves no more than a day a week. Care must also be taken that faculty do not use students to perform work for their own companies. In summary, the guiding principle should be that faculty predominantly serve their university roles of teaching and research, but may involve themselves in companies primarily for technology transfer and professional development. While doing so, they should avoid conflicts of interest in using university facilities and students in performing proprietary work for companies in which they have an interest.

Conclusions

Universities and industries can find areas of mutual research interest in the fields of science and engineering that underpin current or future technologies. As the NSF experience shows, university and industrial researchers can cooperate in research most effectively by providing complementary skills and facilities for the conception and performance of research that neither group could realistically perform independently.

The value to industry of cooperative research with universities lies in advancing knowledge of phenomena undergirding technology, improving principles for technological design, creating new research instrumentation, and creating new technologies. Industry is interested in performing fundamental research cooperatively with universities as a means of extending its basic research capability in parallel with its primary applied and developmental research capabilities that are focused upon future technologies. Industrial managers rely on cooperative fundamental research to produce theories, data, instrumentation, and ideas to improve their proprietary research and design programs.

Overall, the objectives in developing linkages between universities and industrial firms should be to improve the universities' contributions to national and regional economic development

1. By facilitating transfer of problems and knowledge between the scientific and technological sectors of the nation.
2. By improving university training of industrial personnel for technological innovation.
3. By effectively focusing national research resources upon technological advance and facilitating technology transfer from university research.

References

Kolata, G. "Caltech Torn by Dispute over Software." *Science,* 1983, *220,* 932–937.

National Science Board, 1982.

Peters, L. S., and Fusfeld, H. I. "Current U.S. University-Industry Research Connections." In National Science Foundation, *University-Industry Research Relationships: Selected Studies.* Washington, D.C.: National Science Foundation, 1983.

11

Organizing and Managing
a Cooperative Research Center

The organization of research operations differs according to the missions of the institutions performing the research. Because the traditional missions of higher education and industry are different, university and industrial research operations are organized differently.

University research operations have traditionally been organized into departments and schools. This departmental organization corresponds to the educational mission of the university to train future generations of professionals in research, medicine, law, engineering, business, and so on. Disciplinary research focuses upon the central concerns of the particular field. In contrast, industrial research is usually organized according to the technology or business focus of the firm. Industry's mission is to provide goods and services at a profit, using technology as a means of creating and producing products. Because of the technological focus of industrial research, industrial research operations tend to be multidisciplinary. The reason for this is that most technologies rely on bases in several disciplines. For example, semiconductor chip technology derives information and techniques from the disciplines of physics, chemistry, mathematics, electrical engineering, computer sciences, and engineering.

299

Lessons from Industry/University
Cooperative Research Centers

The National Science Foundation's Industry/University Cooperative Research (IUCR) Program has been described in Chapter Ten as a systematic attempt to discover the most effective ways to organize university research to stimulate industrial participation and support. Success of a center was judged by asking whether it could become self-supporting on industrial funds, as well as significantly contribute to the graduate programs of the university. By 1986, the NSF IUCR program had helped create thirty-nine cooperative centers at major universities. In that year, NSF provided $3 million to the centers, industry provided $15 million, and state governments provided $15 million. In helping create these centers, much was learned about how to make university-industry partnerships succeed.

The program began with an experiment in 1973 when three centers were initially funded: one at the Massachusetts Institute of Technology, one at the University of North Carolina, and one operated under a consulting firm named MITRE. The three centers were selected for comparison because they were different in form. The MIT center specialized in a high-technology research area (polymer engineering) and interacted with high-technology firms. The North Carolina center specialized in a low-technology area (furniture manufacturing) for a fragmented, low-technology industry. The third center, operated through the consulting firm, was formed to learn whether an intermediary between universities and industries would facilitate cooperation. Of the three centers, only one attained its goals. The MIT center was still operating in 1986, with an average annual budget of about $850,000.

From this experiment, several lessons were learned. First, an intermediary organization is not needed. Having universities deal directly with industries to learn how to organize cooperative research projects proved to be the most effective approach. Thenceforth, all grants to found cooperative centers were awarded by the National Science Foundation directly to universities.

The experiment also demonstrated the need for strong leadership by the center director and the need for the industry involved to be capable of utilizing the research for innovation. In North Carolina, the original director left the university and the center. Further, the furniture manufacturing industry then was fragmented in size and market: it was a low-technology industry composed of many mom-and-pop businesses that were incapable of using and transforming research into innovation. In contrast, the MIT center director provided continuity and strong intellectual and administrative leadership in working with high-technology firms.

The thirty-nine centers that were in the NSF cooperative program in 1986 are listed in Table 11. These centers have provided an effective means for focusing fundamental, university-based research on technological problems. In addition, they have provided critical levels of activities and facilities required for science to stimulate significant technological change. Certain features of a cooperative center were found to be essential to its success. These include a focus that was on a frontier of basic research, a well-defined technological orientation, adequate experimental facilities, integration of research with graduate education, and industry support and participation in setting the research agenda. The last factor is particularly important, since the best cooperative research program can fail if businesses cannot or will not take advantage of its research advances.

Since industry has its own research capability for designing and developing products and processes, need for the cooperative centers lay in focusing on research more generic than the specific product orientation of most industrial research and more fundamental than industry ordinarily is interested in performing.

For example, the three cooperative centers that specialized in polymers research (located at MIT, the University of Massachusetts, and Case Western Reserve) all performed generic, fundamental research, yet with different emphases. The MIT Polymer Processing Center focused on the mechanical aspects of polymer processing, such as impact formation of polymers, mixing of reacting liquids, injection molding, and composites strengths. The University of Massachusetts Center for Industry Research on Polymers focused on the chemical aspects of molecular networks in polymers, polymer surfaces and interfaces, and polymeric foams. The Case Western Reserve University Applied

Table 11. National Science Foundation Industry-University Cooperative Research Centers.

LOCATION	RESEARCH AREA	YEAR INITIATED	P.I. NAME
MASSACHUSETTS INST. OF TECH	POLYMER PROCESSING	1973	DR. T. GUTOWSKI
RENSSELAER POLYTECHNIC INST.	COMPUTER GRAPHICS	1979	DR. M. SHEPARD
UNIVERSITY OF MASSACHUSETTS	POLYMERS (PROPERTIES)	1980	DR. S. KANTOR
OHIO STATE UNIVERSITY	WELDING	1980	DR. D. DICKINSON
CASE WESTERN RESERVE UNIV.	POLYMERS (APPLIED)	1981	DR. ANNE HILTNER
NORTH CAROLINA STATE UNIV.	TELECOMMUNICATIONS	1982	DR. J. GAULT
RUTGERS UNIVERSITY	CERAMICS	1982	DR. J. WACHTMAN
GEORGIA INST. OF TECHNOLOGY	MATERIALS HANDLING	1983	DR. I. PENCE
TEXAS A&M UNIVERSITY	HYDROGEN TECHNOLOGY	1983	DR. J. BOCKRIS
PENNSYLVANIA STATE UNIV.	DIELECTRICS	1983	DR. J. BIGGERS
COLORADO SCHOOL OF MINES	STEEL PROCESSING	1983	DR. G. KRAUSS
UNIVERSITY OF WASHINGTON	PROCESS ANALYTICAL CHEM.	1984	DR. B. KOWALSKI
NEW JERSEY INST. OF TECH	HAZARDOUS WASTE MGMT.	1984	DR. J. LISKOWITZ
UNIVERSITY OF ARIZONA	OPTICAL CIRCUITRY	1984	DR. H. GIBBS
NORTHWESTERN UNIVERSITY	TRIBOLOGY	1984	DR. H. CHENG
U. OF NORTH CAROLINA/DUKE U.	MONOCLONAL LYMPHOCYTE TECH.	1984	DR. H. REISNER
UNIVERSITY OF ARIZONA	MICROCONTAMINATION CONTROL	1984	DR. J. O'HANLON
U.TX HLTH.SCI.CTR., SAN ANTONIO	CELL REGULATION	1985	DR. B. BOYAN
DARTMOUTH COLLEGE	ICE RESEARCH	1985	DR. E. SCHULSON

University	Research Area	Name	Year
CARNEGIE-MELLON UNIVERSITY	STEELMAKING	DR. R. FRUEHAN	1985
NORTHEASTERN UNIVERSITY	ELECTROMAGNETICS	DR. M. SILEVITCH	1985
LEHIGH UNIVERSITY	INNOVATION & RES. MGMT.	DR. A. BEAN	1985
IOWA STATE UNIVERSITY	NONDESTRUCTIVE EVALUATION	DR. D. THOMPSON	1985
OKLAHOMA STATE UNIVERSITY	WEB HANDLING	DR. K. REID	1985
LEHIGH UNIVERSITY	CHEM. MODELING & CONTROL	DR. C. GEORGAKIS	1985
UNIVERSITY OF MINNESOTA	BIOCATALYTIC PROCESSING	DR. M. FLICKINGER	1986
ALFRED UNIVERSITY	GLASS RESEARCH	DR. D. PYE	1986
UNIVERSITY OF TX, ARLINGTON	ADVANCED ELECTRON DEVICES	DR. R. CARTER	1986
UNIVERSITY OF TENNESSEE	MEASUREMENT & CONTROL ENG.	DR. E. MULY	1986
RUTGERS UNIVERSITY	PLASTICS RECYCLING	DR. M. McLAREN	1986
UNIVERSITY OF WYOMING	MATHEMATICAL MODELING	DR. R. EWING	1986
NM INST. ON MINING & TECH.	ENERGETIC MATERIALS	DR. P. PERSSON	1986
UNIV. OF FLORIDA/PURDUE UNIV.	SOFTWARE ENGINEERING	DR. R. ELLIOTT	1986
UNIV. OF CALIFORNIA, BERKELEY	INTEGRATED SENSORS	DR. R. MULLER	1986
ILLINOIS INSTITUTE OF TECH.	INTEGRATED INFO. & TELE SYS.	DR. A. VACROUX	1986
UNIVERSITY OF PUERTO RICO	PHARMACEUTICAL	DR. G. PYTLINSKI	1986
UNIV. OF SOUTHERN CALIF.	MANUFACTURING AUTOMATION	DR. G. BEKEY	1987
THE UNIVERSITY OF IOWA	SIMULATION OF MECH. SYSTEMS	DR. E. HAUG	1987
NORTH CAROLINA STATE UNIV.	ASEPTIC PROCESSING	DR. K. SWARTZEL	1987

Source: National Science Foundation, 1987.

Polymer Research Center also focused on the chemical aspects of polymers, but specifically on the relationships among structure, properties, and processing variables aimed at applications (examples of the subjects of past projects include surface modification of contact lens materials, liquid-crystalline polyester plastics, short-fiber reinforced polyvinylchlorides, and conducting polymers).

As other examples, the Rutgers University Center for Ceramics Research focused upon creation and processing of ceramics, particularly in the areas of powder processing; corrosion; surfaces; and the relationships among microstructure, strength, and toughness. The University of Rhode Island Center for Robotics focused on robotics software and applications of robot manipulation to flexible manufacturing assembly. The Center for Welding Research at Ohio State University focused on welding techniques and automation (such as laser arc welding and sensing and control for arc welding) and on welding strength and continuity processes. The Center for Communications and Signal Processing at North Carolina State focused on data communication, speech processing, image processing, and computing and communication architecture. At the Materials Handling Research Center of Georgia Institute of Technology, research focused on warehouse automation, quality control, containerization and delivery logistics, utilization of robotics, advanced sensors, and computerized scheduling.

These examples show that in every successful center, research was technologically based (for example, on polymers, robotics, and so on) and focused on either a generic technology (such as communications or computers) or a generic industrial function (such as materials handling). The research could be described as ''frontier'' because it generated knowledge bases of future technologies, or because it improved basic understanding of current technologies.

Origin of the University of Arizona Cooperative Center for Optical Circuitry

To see an example of research at the interface between science and technology, consider the origin of the Arizona center.

In 1981, Hyatt Gibbs, a new professor at the University of Arizona, submitted a cooperative project proposal to the National Science Foundation. Gibbs held a doctorate in solid state physics from the University of California at Berkeley and, after graduation, had been employed at the Bell Laboratories of American Telephone and Telegraph. There he learned about an optical switch, invented by a colleague, that operated so that a single laser beam shining into the device produced no light output, but two laser beams did produce an output. Such a switch is an example of a classic "AND" gate, where inputs A AND B produce output C, although neither A nor B alone produces C. Gibbs realized that, if such an optical switch could be perfected, it would have immediate applications in fiberoptic communications systems and be of immense technological and economic importance. Gibbs further realized that to perfect the idea a different phenomenal base than in the original invention had to be sought. His idea was to use new materials called *super lattices*, which are thin films of alternating kinds of materials (as thin as only a few atomic layers, created by a technique called *molecular beam epitaxy*). One of Gibbs's former colleagues at Bell, Art Gossard, was one of the world's experts in this new technique. In addition, Sam McCall, another former colleague at Bell and a theoretical solid state physicist, also was interested in Gibbs's idea for an optical switching device made of a super lattice.

    Gibbs submitted a cooperative project proposal to NSF, which provided funding. Within a year, the industrial-academic team of Gibbs, Gossard, and McCall invented the world's first bistable optical device to operate quickly at room temperatures. (The original device switched slowly at low temperatures.)

    Thereafter, Gibbs performed research to develop this class of devices into something technologically useful. Eventually, an NSF program officer, Alex Schwarzkopf of the Industry/University Cooperative Research Center Program, was introduced to Gibbs with the idea that a cooperative center might be created with Gibbs as the director.

    Such a center was thought to be desirable for several reasons. First, the new devices were potentially very important technologically, and large research efforts were required to hasten their perfection. Second, Gibbs had the potential for becoming a successful cooperative center director. He was the world's leading researcher in the new switching devices. He understood and had experience in and respect for industrial research. He had experience in and desire for collaborative research with peers. He was working on a research problem broader than he could manage with his particular skills alone. In addition, other outstanding researchers already were present at the University of Arizona who could form a center with him. Finally, a cooperative center to study the new devices would extend Gibbs's contacts to industrial firms and researchers beyond his acquaintances of Bell Labs, offering him a broader base of research support and, equally important, a broader range of input for research ideas. Because all factors seemed promising, a cooperative center was funded by NSF in 1985.

The research objectives of the Optical Circuitry Cooperative, directed by Gibbs, were focused on the underlying principles of optical circuitry, principles that are the basis of a major electronics revolution. The missions of the center were to accelerate advances in the new technology and to decrease the time lapse between discoveries and applications in the field. Industrial members of the center included AMP, Celanese, Du-Pont, GTE, IBM, Lockheed, Motorola, Sperry, 3M Company, and TRW. In 1986, fourteen firms were expected to be members, with annual membership fees of $50,000 each. The Optical Circuitry Cooperative was administratively located in the Optical Sciences Center of the University of Arizona.

Organizing a Cooperative Center

It has been the experience of the National Science Foundation that approximately one year is required to organize a successful cooperative research center. Preliminary discussions among faculty and visits by the director to potential industrial sponsors take about four months. An additional four months is required to conduct planning activities among faculty, devise a preliminary research agenda, plan the center organization, and obtain preliminary support within the university administration. Then a formal organizing meeting must be held with potential industrial sponsors. After this meeting, another four months generally elapse while industrial sponsors obtain permission to commit to membership.

Thus, the NSF cooperative program provided planning grants of one year's duration for the planning period, plus a follow-on grant for the first five years of center operation. The amount of each planning grant varied from $50,000 to $100,000. The amount of the five-year operating grants has averaged $500,000 in recent years.

In the experience of the NSF program officers, the planning period for the center turned out to be critical. In fact, during the four months following the formal organizing meeting, program officers could reasonably well judge whether a center would succeed; the key criterion was whether a minimum of six industrial researchers formally joined the center during that period.

Structure of a Cooperative Center. Organizationally, all cooperative centers had a director and a minimum of two other faculty participants, an industrial advisory board, a faculty advisory board, and an administrative assistant. The center director reported to a dean of a school or to the provost or vice-president of research but never to a department chairperson, as this would be antithetical to the cross-disciplinary nature of centers. A minimum of three faculty members was required to be associated with the center to provide the group research activity for which the center had been organized. The industrial advisory board set the research directions of the center, drafted policies, selected research projects, and finalized budgets. The board was the critical organizational feature that distinguished cooperative research centers from other university research centers or institutes. In cooperative centers, the industrial advisory board actively participated in the management of a center. It functioned like a board of directors in a corporate organization or like a board of trustees in an academic organization. Its locus of power lay in the funding it represented (for example, the industrial memberships), plus the research expertise its members brought to the center. When faculty members proposed research projects, the industrial advisory board advised the director on which projects to fund and at what level. Later, the board advised on when to terminate support of a project. The power balance within a cooperative center was about evenly divided between industrial members and faculty participants. Without industrial members, industrial funding would disappear, but without faculty members, research would not be performed.

Under this agreement, the fear most often expressed was that the industrial members would force center research to become applied and proprietary. In fact, this fear was unfounded because sponsorship came from a consortium of industrial firms, and firms are reluctant to jointly sponsor proprietary research with competitors. Industrial members agreed that research should be fundamental and nonproprietary while at the same time technologically focused. Proprietary information describes a firm's products and production processes, whereas generic information constitutes the shared technological and scientific knowledge base of an industry. Industrial members of a consortium look to university researchers to perform the generic research and to train graduate students in generic techniques.

Designing a center's research agenda and selecting research projects in which all (or most) industrial members had an interest turned out to be the secret to successful creation of a cooperative center.

Florida/Purdue Center for Software Engineering. The organizing meeting of one successful center reveals how a community of researchers with common research interests can be created between academic and industrial researchers. The Cooperative Research Center for Software Engineering was jointly conceived by the University of Florida and Purdue University and begun in 1986 under two codirectors, Roger Elliott and Samuel Conte. Elliott was a professor of computer and information science and electrical engineering at the University of Florida, and Conte was a professor of computer science at Purdue. Joining them as a center team was the chairman of computer science at Purdue, John Rice, and several junior and senior faculty members at Purdue and Florida. Objectives of the center were to perform basic and applied research in software engineering and development. The two universities formed the center jointly because they possessed complementary strengths; for example, in software metrics at Purdue and in database technology at Florida.

The organizing meeting of the center was held near Orlando, Florida, in January 1986. The Florida and Purdue faculties had prepared a research focus for the center, an organizational structure, a policy statement, and a potential research agenda. This meeting followed six months of planning, during which many discussions between faculty members and administrators had taken place and many visits to potential industrial sponsors had been made. In the morning of the first day of the meeting, Elliott and Conte presented the concept, organization, and policies of the proposed center to invited industrial researchers. Discussions between academic and industrial participants then focused on conditions of membership, publication policy, and patent policy. After differences were discussed and a group consensus formulated, the principal investigators affirmed that new center policies would follow the group consensus.

Then the afternoon meeting began with presentation by faculty members of proposed research projects for the center. Each professor made a fifteen-minute presentation describing the goals, methodology, problems, status, and budget of the proposed research. After each presentation, each industrial researcher filled out a form grading interest in the proposed projects as (1) interested, (2) interested with changes, (3) not interested, or (4) no comment. Comments also were written on the form, explaining the interest or lack of it. These ratings were tabulated, and comments were abstracted for each project. Then a large poster summarizing the ratings and written comments was made for each project and hung on the wall for all to see.

It was uncomfortable for the faculty to so expose their ideas and be graded on them. To create a successful center, however, faculty members must learn to submit their research plans to a peer group of industrial colleagues, just as they submit their proposals for peer evaluation at federal granting agencies. The purpose of this rating procedure was to establish the climate and mechanism for obtaining feedback from industrial researchers about how to bring research directions more in line with industrial interests.

At this point in the meeting, the attitudes of industrial participants were perceived as highly critical. This critical attitude usually occurs when peers evaluate research proposals and focus upon shortcomings in a colleague's ideas. By the time the last proposed faculty research project had been described, the mood of the entire industrial group could be felt by the academics as being negative and critical. The new center's existence seemed to be in jeopardy.

What happened next, then, was to have the industrial participants meet alone, apart from the academics, to address the task of formulating an ideal research agenda for the center. After listening for an afternoon to other people's ideas and judging their strengths and weaknesses, the industrial researchers were primed to participate. As soon as their meeting began, they were transformed from critical to creative participants. Enthusiasm pervaded the industrial group, and an insightful research agenda was produced. This change in attitude by the industrial researchers carried over to the next morning, when the entire group reconvened. Then a new atmosphere pervaded; an interactive research community had been formed. As the industrial group presented its research agenda, it was seen by all to be a modification of the agenda originally proposed by the academics. Both groups agreed that proposed software engineering projects should span the range of the software creation system (from program specification through program writing and testing to program maintenance) as originally proposed by academics. However, the input from the industrial researchers focused the emphasis on initial program specification. The reason for this is that the industrial researchers thought this part of the research spectrum was the least known and most risky.

Next, the research projects of the previous day were again discussed by the group, so that industrial researchers could explain their earlier criticisms. Now, however, harshness in the industrial criticism moderated, and the tone of the discussion became supportive. The industrial researchers made positive suggestions for modifying the projects to make them more useful. In this interaction, faculty participants were learning how to modify and refocus project ideas to increase industrial interest.

Finally, the academics were asked to leave the room, and the industrial participants were cloistered with the NSF program officer, Alex Schwarzkopf. He asked for frank discussion of any weaknesses or problems that remained unresolved. After this discussion, he then asked for a show of hands as to how many intended to join the center. Two-thirds of the companies present indicated their intention to join, which in numbers (twelve) was large enough to start a center. After the meeting, the principal investigators modified the policies and research agenda in accordance with the feedback of the organizing meeting. Then a revised center proposal was sent to each industrial participant, with an invitation to join. After six acceptances were received, the principal investigators submitted a proposal to NSF for funding. After a peer review of the operating proposal, an award was made in July 1986, and a new Industry/University Cooperative Research Center had been created.

Planning a Cooperative Center. The general lessons illustrated in this example are

1. The planning process is critical to creating centers because research goals must be the result of a compromise between academic perceptions of research opportunities and industrial perceptions of research needs.
2. Appropriate compromises on research may not occur unless careful preparations are made for the organizing meeting and it is led by someone sensitive to the agenda of both types of participation.
3. A specific procedure should be followed that promotes compromise on project goals. Stages in the procedure are
    a. Industrial rating of academic project proposals.
    b. Industrial formulation of a research agenda.
    c. Group consensus on research agenda and constructive discussion of how to modify proposed projects to improve their industrial relevance.

In other words, in a successful organizing meeting, future participants learn how to identify areas of mutual research interest and how to review project proposals together in a constructive manner. Once this group learning has occurred, industrial participants are more likely to join, and the center is given a fair chance of succeeding—having been launched with a program of focused research and policies and procedures that have resulted from consensus among participants.

Operating a Cooperative Center. Operating a cooperative center involves developing an administration, selecting and evaluating projects, integrating center activities with educational programs, encouraging technological transfer to industry, and maintaining industrial membership. The director is responsible for overall administration of the center. Since academic leadership is essential in organizing cooperative research centers, the director of a center must be

1. Prominent as a researcher.
2. Capable of engaging in collegial research with academic peers.
3. Capable of respecting and communicating with industrial researchers.
4. Interested in research problems of industrial relevance.
5. Competent as an administrator.

Research prominence is necessary both for credibility within the university and in industry. Faculty and graduate students are attracted to outstanding research programs. Industrial sponsors seek out quality research centers that are willing to focus research around industrial problems. The director also must be capable of assembling research teams in the university environment. This can require considerable effort, since the university disciplinary orientation and departmental structure place value on independence and autonomy in researchers. These factors, if taken to extremes, however, discriminate against collegial research. It is important that academic participants in a cooperative center value the nature of industrial contributions and respect the professional competence and motivations of industrial researchers. When academics approach industry for advice and support, any lack of honest respect and appreciation of the industrial perspective is immediately apparent and is resented by industrial personnel. Finally, if the center director is not interested in research problems that are relevant to industrial problems, then research of mutual interest to academics and industrial researchers will not be identified. This "relevancy" lies precisely in the interface between technology (industry's interest) and science (academics' interest).

In addition to a director, a deputy director is essential as an internal technician who can pay close attention to the intellectual performance of the center on a project-by-project basis. The deputy director should be entirely familiar with the progress of every project as well as with every detail of faculty and student involvement. The director must simultaneously monitor program development within the center and seek to satisfy industrial sponsors. The deputy director must also help the director monitor the center's internal research to ensure that integration and synergism are occurring among projects. Otherwise, a center may become a mere collection of projects that lack the creative interaction that sparks major advancements in the knowledge base for new technologies. An administrative assistant for the director is also essential to administer the budgets, logistics, and coordination involved in managing a team of academic researchers.

Without a competent deputy director and administrative assistant, a center director may rapidly burn out, becoming disgusted with the apparently insurmountable administrative burdens and yearning for the peace and calm of scholarly, individual research. As various NSF centers have matured, other reasons for turnover in directors have emerged, including career moves, conflicts between directors and deans, and substantial changes in the strategic vision of a center. Such turnover requires establishment of a strong administrative structure that can provide quality management not only during but between tenures of directors. However, it has been difficult to replace good directors: the intellectual stature, collegial research ability, and ability to communicate with industrial researchers that are the hallmarks of a good director are rare qualities among faculty.

Establishing center procedures to select and evaluate projects is also essential to ensure internal peer review of project quality and to avoid autocratic definition of research direction by the director. In addition to establishment of procedures, appointment of a research panel to advise the director can be beneficial. Such a panel usually is composed of faculty members internal and external to the center, industrial researchers, and members of other university faculties.

Annually, each faculty member participating in the center has the opportunity to submit to the director a proposal describing research projects, their objectives, and their integration with other center research projects, and the staffing and budget of proposed projects. A project review panel recommends to the director projects to be funded, with recommended budgets. From this list, the director recommends to the industrial advisory committee those projects that seem particularly promising. The industrial advisory committee then advises on and approves the director's budget.

To facilitate integration of the research activities of a cooperative center with the educational programs of the parent university's departments, a cooperative center usually also organizes an academic advisory committee, consisting of faculty members both internal and external to the center. This committee advises the director on center policies to integrate the center with the educational objectives of the university. In addition, proposed research projects are reviewed by the academic advisory committee to assess their impact on graduate and undergraduate education. Chairpersons of departments relevant to the research of the center are usually included in this committee.

A cooperative center must be interested not only in presenting research results to the larger scientific and technological communities, but in facilitating transfer of knowledge to the member companies who are paying for center research projects. Accordingly, technology transfer is an important function of cooperative centers. Such transfer usually is accomplished through publications, industrial research symposia, continuing education, and data and software services. Cooperative centers hold annual research symposia for their industrial members to report on research progress made during the previous year. In addition, research plans for the coming year are reviewed and approved by the industrial advisory council. Industrial sponsors often are especially interested in graduates of the center as candidates for possible future employment. To facilitate industrial members' meeting graduate students, poster sessions are also held at the annual industrial center meetings. In these poster sessions, graduate students summarize their research projects and are available for conversations with industrial researchers who inspect the posters. Industrial sponsors and additional technical personnel from their companies attend the symposia. Industrial sponsors also attend advisory council meetings.

A center also offers continuing education in the form of short courses and workshops, either at the center or at industrial sites. In addition, centers increasingly are embedding their research results in software and databases. Industrial members of the centers not only receive copies of any research publication issuing from the center but also any software created by center researchers.

Research focus and results, publications and software, continuing education, and training of graduate students are products of a cooperative center that justify industrial sponsorship. To maintain sponsorship, a center must create returns that industrial sponsors perceive to be of sufficient value to justify the cost of company membership and the time commitments involved. Annual membership fees for a cooperative center have ranged from $25,000 to $50,000, which represents from one-fourth to one-half the cost of employing a professional in industry. Thus, industrial participants must be willing to expend a fraction of the salary of a professional from their research budget.

In the mid 1980s most centers required ten memberships ($500,000) as minimum funding. Dealing with a large number of companies becomes difficult for a director, so that about thirty memberships ($1,500,000) approaches the maximum for a center.

Administrative Assumptions
to Promote Effective Research Cooperation

Administration policies capable of promoting effective industry-university research cooperation require a broad vision of the role of science in society. Active leadership to strengthen the interaction between science and technology also is required. In practical terms, this means that effective administrators of centers promote cross-disciplinary research among faculty members and establish research centers as structures complementary to departments.

Envisioning the role of science in society requires a center director to understand that the directions of scientific research evolve from both intrinsic and extrinsic criteria (Weinberg, 1967). Intrinsic criteria depict the interests of disciplinary groups— such as physicists, chemists, or mathematicians—which focus on the generality and ubiquity of phenomena in the defined ranges of their disciplines. In other words, scientists are interested in discovering what phenomena exist in their fields and how frequently such phenomena occur, under what conditions, and according to what laws. Moreover, when paradigms are established in a discipline, research is guided by problems in the paradigms (Kuhn, 1970).

By contrast, extrinsic criteria arise from users of knowledge who are external to the discipline that organizes the knowledge. For example, chemical engineers use a chemistry knowledge base, and electrical, mechanical, and civil engineers use both physics and chemistry knowledge bases. In general, extrinsic criteria arise from the problems and technologies that define professional areas of practice, and such areas use knowledge from scientific disciplines. For example, the technologies of semiconductor electronics have scientific knowledge bases in physics, chemistry, materials, and electrical engineering. Likewise, the profession of medicine has scientific knowledge bases in biology, chemistry, physics, and psychology. Therefore, research directions in physics, chemistry, materials, and electrical engineering are influenced by questions that arise in semiconductor electronics technologies; and research directions in biology, chemistry, physics, and psychology are influenced by questions that arise in medicine.

Central to this broad vision are three terms: *science, engineering,* and *technological innovation.* A useful, modern comparison of these terms was nicely made by Erich Bloch (1986, p. 28): "Science is the process of investigating phenomena. This process leads to a body of knowledge consisting of theory, concepts, methods, and a set of results. Engineering is the process of investigating how to solve problems. This process leads to a body of engineering knowledge consisting of concepts, methods, data bases, and frequently physical expressions of results such as inventions, products, and designs.

"Technological innovation is the process that leads to more effective production and delivery of new or significantly modified goods or services. This process also creates a body of concepts, techniques, and data." One can always argue over definitions, but what is important to the administration of cooperative research is a broad view of both the generation and use of knowledge and the interaction between generation and use in defining research opportunities. This broad view underlies the concept of university-industry research cooperation. An administrator who is successful in promoting effective industry-university cooperative research projects must have the breadth of view to create policies that facilitate the interaction of knowledge creation and use. In the past, many in university administration have assumed that creation and utilization of knowledge were totally independent and separable—the first being the job of the university and the second the job of industry. This was the traditional view of the university as an ivory tower, existing apart from society. That separatist view missed, however, the subtle interconnections between fundamental research questions and larger societal problems that refine the directions and depths of the fundamental questions; and in missing that, it also missed many opportunities for making the university more useful to society, while at the same time strengthening the research capability of the university. Organizing for cooperative research is an implementation in practical terms of the improvement of connecting knowledge creation to knowledge use.

A center administrator must be able to perceive these interconnections in order to define research problems precisely, to design experiments to shed light on such problems, to construct theories to represent such problems, and to promote use of research results. This means that industry-university research cooperation should be seen as a means of the university increasing its societal responsibility by strengthening the interface between university science and engineering and industrial technology.

National Science Foundation
Engineering Research Centers

In the summer of 1983, both the National Academy of Engineering and the National Science Board of the National Science Foundation issued statements calling for the NSF director to chart a new and more vigorous course for NSF engineering research and education programs. Concern for the state of U.S. engineering had been growing because strong engineering was perceived to be one of the reasons for Japanese success in international economic competition (as well as a traditional foundation of U.S. economic competitiveness). While recognizing U.S leadership in basic research, the problem perceived by NSF, the president's science adviser, and the National Academy of Science was that U.S. scientific advance was not being translated into technological innovation effectively or in a timely manner. Moreover, they believed that the link between science and technology was engineering research, and this was precisely what had to be strengthened in the United States.

Roland Schmitt (1986, p. 20), chairman of the National Science Board, expressed the views of the administration then by stating: "An understanding of the link between research and international competitiveness leads instead to a third conclusion. We must build on, rather than abandon, one of our greatest strengths—our fundamental research capability. But we also must ensure that it is our nation, not another, that receives most of the benefit from the strength. How can we do this? First and foremost, we must put our own fundamental advances to use more quickly than others do. We have to increase our effort in the kind of research that bridges the gap between fundamental scientific research and application. That kind of research is engineering research."

Earlier in 1983, Edward Knapp (then NSF director) and

George Keyworth (then the president's science adviser) had acted upon their shared concern for engineering education by asking Robert White (then incoming president of the National Academy of Engineering) to "provide NSF with the Academy's views on the Foundation's Engineering Program" (McNinch, 1986, p. 2). White convened an ad hoc advisory committee, which in July 1983 issued a paper citing problems with NSF's engineering programs. In the academy's opinion, the programs had become increasingly analytical, decreasingly experimental, and too narrowly disciplinary in scope. The NAE recommended that NSF provide support for larger-scale facilities emphasizing experimental and cross-disciplinary research. Subsequently, in discussions among the foundation, the academy, and the Office of Science and Technology Policy, the idea of establishing engineering research centers emerged.

In December 1983, Knapp again asked White for NAE's help in "developing these engineering centers"; and in February 1984, NAE issued a report entitled *Guidelines for Engineering Research Centers*. These guidelines suggested that the engineering research centers should focus on important industrial technologies, perform systemwide breadth research, involve industrial participation and support, and improve engineering education at both graduate and undergraduate levels. Meanwhile, NSF had submitted a budget to Congress to establish such centers the following year.

As a result, in 1985 six new engineering research centers were established:

1. Center for Composites Manufacturing Science and Engineering at the University of Delaware.
2. Center for Intelligent Manufacturing Systems at Purdue University.
3. Center for Robotic Systems in Microelectronics at the University of California at Santa Barbara.
4. Center for Telecommunications Research at Columbia University.
5. Systems Research Center at the University of Maryland.
6. Biotechnology Process Engineering Center at the Massachusetts Institute of Technology.

Underlying this concern for U.S. engineering research and education was a historical pattern of change in science and technology production in the world. In the late nineteenth and early twentieth centuries, the university had become the principal producer of science, and industry the principal producer of new technology. Moreover, as this production was, and continues to be, performed separately, time has often been lost in translating science into technology, and opportunities also have been lost in defining scientific questions focused upon technological interest. The hope embodied in NSF's move toward university-based engineering research centers was to find out if, in the future, universities might play a larger role in technology creation (while maintaining their traditional role in science creation). Accordingly, the organizational model for the new ERC's followed the IUCR centers model with two important differences. First, the ERC was to have systemwide breadth of research scope, and second, significant federal funding was to be maintained in the ERC along with industrial funding. The practice for the IUCR centers had been to withdraw federal funding after five years, aiming to have the IUCR center wholly supported by industrial funds.

Every technology is a kind of system that involves a number of stages or components that are related to each other in a way that can accomplish some functional transformation. For example, an automobile consists of components that include an engine, chassis, body, drive train, fuel supply, and controls. The relation of these components produces a vehicle capable of providing the function of transportation, of moving from one place to another. Computers are another example of a technological system, components of which in this case are a central processing unit, memory, internal bus, input-output interface, and peripheral devices, all related by systems software and applications software. This system enables the functional applications of calculations, word processing, and modeling, among many others.

When a university research center is wholly dependent on industrial funding, the center is forced to concentrate on certain aspects of a technological system, specifically those that currently are most puzzling to industrial users of the technology. For example, in the Florida/Purdue Software Engineering Center, consensus between academic and industrial participants focused research on the specification of a software engineering system. In spite of the natural desire of industrial sponsors to focus research on pressing issues, engineering education and university engineering research should have systemwide breadth. The engineering community, as represented by the National Academy of Engineering, thus recommended that the NSF Engineering Research Centers provide host universities with research capabilities across the entire breadth of the technological systems under study. Otherwise, new engineers would lack systemwide perspective. To obtain this breadth, it thus was necessary for federal funding to complement the industrial funding in an ERC.

University of Delaware Cooperative Research Center

The Center for Composites Manufacturing Science and Engineering at the University of Delaware provides an example of systemwide breadth in engineering research centers. It was one of the first cooperative centers, established in the mid 1970s by Byron Pipes. Although it did not receive any NSF support, it (along with the MIT Polymer Engineering Cooperative Center) provided a model for the National Science Foundation in developing programs, policies, and procedures for the cooperative centers. The Composites Center was successful in creating an effective technological transfer program, first by compiling a composite materials handbook and later by developing design software for its industrial participants. In 1985, the center was supported by both federal and industry funds. In 1986, when Pipes was promoted to dean of engineering at the University of Delaware, Richard Wilkins was named center director. Wilkins came from McDonnell Douglas, which had been an industrial sponsor of the center.

By 1985, the center had broad objectives:

1. Multidisciplinary research on composite materials and manufacturing.

2. Training engineers and scientists in composite materials and manufacturing knowledge.
3. Providing a national repository on composite materials and manufacturing database and design software.
4. Effectively transferring knowledge about composite materials, design, and manufacturing between university and industry.

A multidisciplinary research approach was necessary since composite materials form technologies that involve knowledge from many disciplines. Research areas of the center focused on understanding

1. How processing composite materials affected the microstructure of the resulting materials.
2. How microstructure created macro properties of materials.
3. How macro properties behaved mechanically under stress deformation and load.
4. How stress deformation affected performance of materials in applications.
5. How knowledge of the interrelations among processing, microstructure, property, stress, and performance could be used in engineering design to optimize performance of composite materials in applications.

Center personnel called this breadth of research focus a *system view* of composites technology. This broad, systemwide perspective on technology, requiring multidisciplinary research, distinguished the Composites Center from the disciplinary departments.

To manage cross-disciplinary, systems-oriented, technology-focused research effectively, the center was organized into four programs that focused on important aspects of the system: manufacturing and processing science, materials design science, materials durability, and mechanics and design science. These four respectively emphasized the intellectual aspects of the composite materials technology system; namely, processing affecting microstructure, microstructure affecting properties, properties affecting stress deformation, and design procedures to optimize performance (once processing-microstructure-property-stress relationships are understood).

In addition, a fifth center program—for computation, software, and information transfer—translated this knowledge base into useful tools for industry. The program structure of the center reflected the technological system perspective and produced not only research papers but useful software programs for industrial participants.

Organizationally, the academic managers of the research programs reported to the center's director. Assisting the director were an associate and a deputy director. The large number of administrators was due to the large size of the center caused by its systemwide breadth and to the need to distribute administrative burdens among faculty (who also were teaching and conducting research). The deputy director of the center was primarily responsible for budgetary, clerical, and administrative matters, and the associate director focused on research affairs. To provide industrial input for the center's research agenda, the associate director worked with an industrial advisory board that consisted of representatives of the eighteen industrial sponsors of the center. To ensure that center operations met university policies, an additional board had been organized, consisting of faculty members and science advisors from other institutions. These two boards were structured to provide industrial perspectives on center research from the technological side and academic perspectives on the research from the scientific side. Departments participating in the research center included chemistry, chemical engineering, electrical engineering, mechanical and aerospace engineering, materials, and metallurgy.

In 1985, the center's budget totaled $4.1 million, of which industry contributed $1.7 million, a federal agency (NSF) contributed $1.1 million, and the state and university contributed $1.3 million. A total of seventy-four research projects had been undertaken. Ten faculty members, plus ten research postdoctoral fellows and visiting scholars, were at work on center projects. Thirty graduate students were being trained, and twenty undergraduates were involved in the projects. Twice a year, the center offered continuing education short courses and evening courses. Two textbooks were being completed, and two were in progress.

The undergraduates involved in center projects were employed for ten hours per week during their sophomore, junior, and senior years and full time during the summers. They worked at the center laboratory one summer and at a participating industry the next summer. In their senior year, undergraduates produced senior research theses.

In addition to providing major funding support, industrial participants played an essential role in maintaining the center's research focus on scientific research essential to technological progress. The industrial advisory board was organized into committees on research, long-range planning, policy, facilities, technology transfer and computer software, and honors.

The Research Committee reviewed and advised on the center's research programs and projects. The Long-Range Planning Committee pondered major changes that might occur in the center in the future. The Policy Committee set policies regarding intellectual property, such as patent rights and royalties. The Facilities Committee advised on the design of a new laboratory for the center. The Technology Transfer and Computer Software Committee advised on translation of research results into useful design tools for industry. The Honors Committee encouraged academic excellence with an industrial flavor. The point is that duties of these committees were those usually assigned to the committees associated with a university center. The difference in this case was that membership of the committees consisted of industrial representatives who were able thereby to play unusually direct and significant roles in university training and research programs serving these industries.

Innovation Centers

Until now, this chapter has discussed the organization of research to provide the knowledge base for new technologies. However, knowledge for industrial innovation includes not only technical knowledge but management knowledge. Another kind of university center has been formed to facilitate innovative management practices and technology transfer. In fact, several such innovation centers were established by the NSF in the 1970s to improve education for entrepreneurial managers. These centers were associated either with business schools or with business schools linked with engineering schools. Other purposes of the innovation centers were to study the innovation process and to assist in the creation and development of small businesses by providing management and marketing consulting services. A total of ten innovation centers were funded by NSF before the program was terminated in 1981. By 1986, five had survived independently, with one at the University of Utah becoming independently incorporated (Scheirer and others, 1985).

Conclusions

In the 1980s, research interactions of increasing numbers, depth, scope, and duration between universities and industrial firms became the most significant trend in the science and technology policy of the United States. Although there has been a history of relationships between universities and industrial firms, the significance of research cooperation in planning the long-term technical future of industries has become more important than in the past. Many contemporary observers noted this trend. For example, in 1986 Erich Bloch, the director of the National Science Foundation, wrote: "One of the most exciting and interesting developments in the world of R&D in the U.S. is the rapid growth of research relationships between industrial corporations and the nation's universities" (Bloch and Kruytbosch, 1986).

Both intellectual and organizational leadership are essential to the success of a cooperative center and must be provided by the director. Intellectual leadership should provide a strong grasp of technological problems and the various scientific approaches that may illuminate these problems. Organizational leadership is needed to create academic research teams, to communicate with industrial advisers and sponsors, and to keep projects focused. Participation in the management of a cooperative center by industry sponsors is vitally important, particularly when definition of research areas and selection and review of research projects are involved. In addition, researchers employed by industrial sponsors should be encouraged to participate in performance of some of the projects. Certain cultural differences are apparent between academic and industrial researchers; for example, academics tend to emphasize advancement of fundamental knowledge and tend not to work in teams, whereas industrial researchers tend to emphasize advancement of technology and tend to work in teams. Industrial participation in management of the center brings into the academic culture two important elements: a technological focus for integrating multidisciplinary research and encouragement of the teamwork necessary for academia to conduct multidisciplinary research.

Recapitulating, university research that is cooperatively conducted should be organized so that it is basic but relevant to technology and supportable by industry:

1. Research should be basic in science, generic in technology, multidisciplinary in breadth, and have an industrial focus.
2. The director of a center should provide both intellectual and organizational leadership.
3. Industrial participants should be involved both in supporting and in managing the center.
4. The university's administration should be supportive of multidisciplinary activity.
5. Federal support of basic research in the center should be structured to encourage university-industry interaction.

References

Bloch, E. "Science and Engineering: A Continuum." In *The New Engineering Research Centers*. Washington, D.C.: National Academy Press, 1986.

Bloch, E., and Kruytbosch, C. "The NSF Role in Fostering University-Industry Research Relationships." *IEEE Transactions on Education,* 1986, *E-29* (2), 51-57.

Kuhn, T. S. *The Structure of Scientific Revolutions.* Chicago: University of Chicago Press, 1970.

McNinch, S. *Background of the NSF Engineering Research Centers Program.* Washington, D.C.: National Science Foundation, 1986.

National Academy of Engineering. *Guidelines for Engineering Research Centers.* Washington, D.C.: National Academy of Engineering, 1984.

National Science Foundation, 1987.

Scheirer, M. A., and others. *Innovation and Enterprise: A Study of NSF's Innovation Centers Program.* (Pamphlet.) Washington, D.C.: National Science Foundation, Dec. 1985.

Schmitt, R. "Engineering Research and International Competitiveness." In *The New Engineering Research Centers.* Washington, D.C.: National Academy Press, 1986.

Weinberg, A. M. *Reflections on Big Science.* Cambridge, Mass.: MIT Press, 1967.

Higher Education–Industry Partnerships: Procedural Rules and Guidelines

Principal author: David R. Powers

These procedural rules and guidelines may be used as an example of a document designed to guide implementation of legislation promoting university-industry partnerships. The document has been approved by the West Virginia Board of Regents, with funding sought during the 1988 legislative session.

West Virginia Procedural Rules: Higher Education–Industry Partnerships, Governor's Office of Community and Industrial Development, Chapter 5B, Article 2A, Series I

Section 1. General

1.1 Scope—These procedural rules describe the Higher Education–Industry Partnerships (HEIP), the process for estab-

Source: David R. Powers, principal author, unpublished document developed for the West Virginia Board of Regents, Charleston, West Virginia, 1986. Some of the language in Section Seven is drawn from "1986-87 Program Year Guidelines for Project Applicants," unpublished document issued by the Ben Franklin Partnership Fund Board, Challenge Grant Program for Technological Innovation (Harrisburg, Pennsylvania: Department of Commerce, Commonwealth of Pennsylvania), January 1986.

lishing a university-industry research and development center, the process of applying for grants for higher education–industry collaboration and technical assistance, the procedures for allocating funds through the Vandalia Partnership Fund, and general policy governing HEIP operations.

1.2 Authority—*West Virginia Code* §5B-2A-1 et seq., as enacted in Enrolled Committee Substitute for Senate Bill No. 403, 1986, regular session of the Legislature.

1.3 Filing Date—July 1, 1986

1.4 Effective Date—September 1, 1986

Section 2. Higher Education–Industry
Collaboration and Technical Assistance

2.1 Any institution of higher education and any corporation may engage in collaborative projects designed to assist companies to adapt or develop new technology; such cooperation does not require approval of the Board of Trustees or the Board of Regents. There is no need to establish a center or other structure for this purpose.

2.2 Each such project may be eligible to apply for financial support through the matching grant programs defined in this article.

2.3 Each institution and each approved UIRD center (see Section 3 below) is authorized and empowered to solicit and accept financial support from sources other than the State, subject to customary State and Board of Regents' policies.

2.4 A special revenue account in the State treasury shall be established for each institution receiving these funds, and for each UIRD center. Each shall deposit all funds received from grants provided through sections 5 and 6 herein and any required matching funds, if in monetary form, which are not otherwise restricted by the donor or Board of Trustees.

Section 3. Establishing University-
Industry Research and Development Centers

3.1 University-industry research and development (UIRD) centers shall be established as not-for-profit centers located near or on selected college and university campuses. Each shall have a board of directors (see 3.8 below).

3.2 Designation of an organization proposed to function as a UIRD center for the purposes of these regulations requires approval of both the Board of Trustees, described below, and the Board of Regents.

3.3 Application to create a UIRD center must be submitted by a college or university, public or private, with not-for-profit status, which is regionally accredited and authorized to grant graduate level degrees in the State of West Virginia. Such an application is submitted initially to the West Virginia Board of Regents.

3.4 Initial review shall be made by the Board of Regents and it shall make its judgments based on the merits of proposals, as judged against the purpose of the partnerships, as specified in the *West Virginia Code*, §5B-2A-1 through §5B-2A-9. After. approval by the Board of Regents, independent approval by the Board of Trustees described below is required, using the same criteria. Not more than one center shall be established in each metropolitan area, but each center may have several satellite centers at different locations or formal focused sub-centers to explore particular subjects or offer particular services at the same or different locations. Each center should specify research and development programs and fields. Establishment of each satellite must be approved by the Board of Regents and the Board of Trustees. Each research activity will not be submitted for approval.

3.5 Proposals to establish centers need not have for-profit corporate participants at the time of application, but letters of commitment to work in partnership with the center from for-profit corporations should justify special consideration in the determinations of both Boards.

3.6 Proposals to establish centers need not involve other colleges or universities in or outside any geographic region, but letters of commitment by other institutions agreeing to work with such a center should justify special consideration in the determinations of both Boards. (See 6.2.7 below.)

3.7 Applications to establish centers should affirm that institutions will match funds made available by the State for projects, that faculty effort will be assigned as required, that institutional policy regarding reassignment of instructional obligations and payment for services rendered is appropriate, that the number of faculty members involved and competency of the teams made available could draw upon much of the talent available in higher education in the region, and that significant strengthening of the permanent research and development base of the institutions is likely to occur.

3.8 The board of directors that is responsible for a center will seek means to foster effective communications and consultation on planning, program evaluation, and related matters. To that end, each board is encouraged to appoint one or more liaison committee(s) composed at least of one person representing each college or university that has agreed to participate in programs of the center, one representative from the Governor's Office of Community and Industrial Development, the Board of Regents, organized labor, and businesses or industries.

3.9 For each funded formal research program or field, the board of directors of a center shall appoint a "program advisory committee," no less than one third of which shall consist of faculty members expert in the field, and no less than one third of which shall consist of persons from private sector companies that are participating in the research program. The remaining appointees may represent state or local government or other organizations considered relevant to the program. . . .

*Section 4. Vandalia Partnership Program
for Research and Technical Assistance*

4.1 The Board of Trustees shall have the authority to review all applications and approve all grants, according to the *West Virginia Code,* Chapter 5B, Article 2A, and these regulations.

4.2 Under policies established by the Board of Trustees, the Director of HEIP shall have the authority to allocate any funds available to higher education–industry projects operating under the provisions of article 2A of Chapter 5.

4.3 Applications for grants may be submitted by a college or university, public or private, with not-for-profit status, which is regionally accredited and authorized to grant degrees in the State of West Virginia. There is no need to establish a separate structure or center unless application for funds is for a UIRD Center. Such an application is submitted initially to the Director of HEIP. Each year the Board of Trustees shall establish minimum matching fund requirements for grants.

4.4 The Vandalia Partnership program is intended to bring together, through challenge or matching grants, partners from the business, industry, public and educational sectors to develop and apply technologies which will strengthen existing business and stimulate the formation of new firms and products. Projects will include:

4.4.1 Joint research and development projects, which shall require a joint effort of a company or companies operating in West Virginia and a higher educational institution or institutions located in this State with the potential for preserving or creating jobs in this State.

4.4.2 Education and training projects, which shall include employment training, retraining or upgrading, labor market and occupational analysis, new courses, sharing of costly equipment, educational or technical assistance with the small business innovation centers.

4.4.3 Entrepreneurial development projects, which shall include technical assistance, development of business plans, management counseling, technology transfer, venture capital assistance and other services, with emphasis on establishing new projects, processes or services.

4.5 Since needs of companies exist all over the State, it is expected that education and training service and technical assistance and entrepreneurial development will be replicated throughout the State, as dictated by the needs of the private sector.

4.6 Education and training services will generally be offered by institutions (or consortia or centers) within pre-specified geographic service regions to avoid duplication of efforts. Service regions approved by the Board of Regents should apply to these efforts, and exceptions and waivers to provide instruction outside approved service regions should be approved by the chancellor of the Board of Regents, according to specified Board of Regents' mechanisms.

4.7 Technical assistance and entrepreneurial development services will generally be offered within geographic service regions, and exceptions and waivers should be approved as described above. The Board of Regents may also authorize State-wide activity for certain programs. Needed expertise may reside, however, in the faculty of any institution in the State. Through the Center for Education and Research with Industry (CERI), faculty members with expertise needed on a project may be identified within or outside a service region or outside the State. Institutions are encouraged to release faculty members to engage in projects undertaken by institutions (or consortia or centers) in any service region, without prior approval by the Board of Regents or the Board of Trustees. When some services associated with a project must be provided by faculty members from institutions outside a service region, and the institutions involved cooperate in making the necessary arrangements, the resulting cooperative proposal will be given special consideration in application for matching Vandalia Funds.

4.8 The Board of Trustees will not censor selection of specific research topics nor intervene in the academic freedom of individual researchers in pursuing research topics and issues of their choice.

4.9 Each UIRD center should define specific research and development fields or programs. Support from the Vandalia Fund for each research proposal requires approval by the Board of Trustees. Any other funding for research efforts at the centers does not require approval by the Board of Trustees. Institutions and centers are encouraged to develop cooperative programs, to share research efforts and equipment, even if complementary activity on related topics is undertaken at several centers.

Section 5. Vandalia Partnership Fund

5.1 The Vandalia Partnership Fund shall receive State appropriations, gifts, grants or other moneys as may be available to the fund. The State shall invest and reinvest the fund and the income thereof, pending use for properly designated purposes.

5.2 The fund operates as a revolving fund whereby all ap-

propriations and payments may be applied and reapplied by
the State for properly designated purposes.

Section 6. Application for Grants; Eligibility and Criteria

6.1 Applicants for grants shall submit a proposal in a form
approved by the Board of Trustees which shall set forth the
nature of the project, the commitment from the partners either
in money, equipment or in-kind services and the request for
funding. Private, public and educational financial support shall
be required as part of each application. Proposals for funding
will be reviewed on a competitive basis by a panel of experts
appointed by the Board of Trustees and such sub-panels and
boards of reviewers as the Board of Trustees or Director of HEIP
may appoint to provide the technical expertise to appropriately
review each proposal fairly and competently on its merits only.

6.2 Among the criteria used to evaluate each proposal
will be:

6.2.1 Probability of advancing the success of a company
operating in the State

6.2.2 Likelihood of creating jobs, conserving jobs, or
leading to a new or expanded industry or venture in the State

6.2.3 Promise of transferring the research and development findings to marketable products

6.2.4 Level of financial contribution from corporate or
other sources

6.2.5 Technical or scientific feasibility of the effort, and
competency of the team to produce useful results

6.2.6 Probability of strengthening the permanent research
and development base of both the institutions of higher education in West Virginia and industry or sustaining partnerships

6.2.7 Involvement of more than one institution of higher
education in the project, when such involvement broadens the
base of expertise available or provides other benefits

6.2.8 Focus of project identified by the Board of Trustees
as targeted to overcome deficiencies in West Virginia that tend
to constrain its economic growth

6.2.9 Promise that any new technology created or patented

through or funded under this program could result in production or operation in West Virginia

6.2.10 Other such criteria as may be approved by the Board of Trustees. . . .

Section 7. Matching Requirements

7.1 Each year, the Board of Trustees shall establish minimum matching grant requirements. Non-State government sources of matching funds may include private businesses, corporations and other entrepreneurs, foundations, public or private not-for-profit corporations and federal resources.

7.2 Private businesses, corporations and entrepreneurs, in total, must account for some portion of the specified minimum of non-State government funds provided to a project or effort. The Board of Trustees may allow substitution of federal funds for part of this match. Such requirements may vary among and within each category of grants specified in 4.4 above.

7.3 Private sector contributions normally should be monetary in nature but centers also may consider private sector contributions in the form of state-of-the-art equipment, donated space for incubators, or other in-kind services, where such services are an integral part of the proposed project. Equipment must be an integral part of the proposed project to be considered as match. Monetary contributions will be favored over "in-kind" contributions, except for capital items such as donated equipment. Each proposal shall contain a letter from each private sector firm, signed by an authorized representative of the firm, which declares the intent of the firm to contribute a specified matching amount, identified in the letter as being monetary or in-kind. Only funds directly contributed to a college or university for a joint project can be counted as private sector monetary matching.

7.4 Unless targeted as Economic Development funds, or support for University-Industry Partnerships or federal training programs, including those from the U.S. Department of Commerce, U.S. Department of Labor, or similar programs, federal funds already received by an academic institution prior to January 1, 1986, cannot be used to provide any of the non-State government share. Normally, only new federal funds that directly relate to the objectives integral to the program plan of the institution (or consortia or centers) may be used as match, but such funds may be devoted to these projects and activities.

7.5 State project grants obtained from agencies of the State government are not eligible to meet the non-State government share, but may be devoted to these projects and activities.

7.6 State funds may not be directly used to cover any matching requirement associated with a center's program. Indirect costs can be considered in evaluation of proposals, but only as it exceeds the minimum non-State government matching share amount.

7.7 In cases of projects with firms not located in West Virginia, evidence should be provided that such firms will establish facilities within the State, expand existing facilities in the State, or enter into specific joint ventures with West Virginia based firms.

7.8 Capital contributions to a university building campaign are a normal fund-raising function of a college or university and will not be counted as match, unless targeted for an UIRD center.

7.9 Standard educational discounts for computer and other equipment from manufacturers of the computers or other items may not be counted as match. Discounts beyond the standard discount may be counted as equipment match provided satisfactory documentation is available.

7.10 Private sector funds are treated only as a monetary match if funds are transferred to a college or university. If these funds are thereafter contracted back to the firm for work on the project by the firm's employees, the funds are considered only as in-kind. Likewise, supplies and materials provided to university or college researchers by a firm are considered in-kind, or non-monetary. Equipment, salaries and other direct work done on a project by a firm are in-kind. Equipment donated for use by a college or university for a limited time can only be valued at its annual equivalent rental cost and counted as private sector equipment. Contributions of buildings can be counted as private sector in-kind, either on an annual depreciation basis or according to equivalent annual rental value, but not both.

7.11 In terms of classifying matching funds, private sector monetary matching includes gifts and direct funds received by the UIRD center or a college or university affiliate. In-kind private sector match includes donated space, salaries, materials and other services contributed. Equipment includes donated equipment and contracts or other contributions, including monetary, which are limited or restricted to purchase of equipment. Equipment may be counted as equivalent to monetary at the discretion of the Board of Trustees.

7.12 Foundations, including corporate-sponsored research institutes and foundations, should be considered as not-for-profit/foundation contributors, rather than private sector contributors.

7.13 University contributions will be considered as monetary only when they involve an allocation of new discretionary funds to a project to undertake additional activity. Release time of faculty or similar practices are considered in-kind university match.

7.14 In order to encourage small technology-oriented firms and entrepreneurs to participate, the research and development and product development work of such firms may be considered as in-kind match. If equity funds are provided by a third party to start-up firms, the amount of such funds to be used during the project year for research and product development work can be considered as private sector monetary matching.

Section 8. Charges for Instructional Programs

8.1 Tuition and other appropriate fees should be charged for courses offered for credit, unless exempted by Board of Regents policy for full-cost contracts.

8.2 Charges for off-campus, credit courses offered on site for a company must be in accordance with Board of Regents policy. If fees above on-campus rates are charged, such funds may be deposited through either center or college accounts and are available for appropriate expenditure.

8.3 Total charges for non-credit instruction should be sufficient to meet all direct costs, plus a reasonable indirect cost recovery.

8.4 Income received for a non-credit instruction may be deposited through either center or college accounts and is available for appropriate expenditure.

Section 9. Competition with the Private Sector

9.1 Each center shall require that any testing and instrumentation work required under the program shall be referred to and be performed by appropriate private commercial research and development laboratories in any instance where an institution of higher education cannot routinely perform these services. As further guidance in this matter, each center will utilize National Science Foundation Important Notice 91 as the basis for determining the applicability in each situation. Centers also are encouraged to undertake joint research and development projects with laboratories under this program.

Section 10. Acceptance of Grants and External Funds

10.1 Acceptance of grants and funds from sources external to State appropriations to the Board of Regents is subject to the conditions and review process specified in Board of Regents' Policy Bulletin No. 28 or the HEIP Board of Trustees.

Section 11. Management of Funds

11.1 Grant or contract funds to a center are not subject to the usual Board of Regents' or Governor's Office of Community and Industrial Development expending and reporting procedures. However, expenditure of State funds from the Vandalia Fund or appropriations must be handled as required by State regulations.

11.2 Expenditures of private funds given to the Centers shall be audited in accordance with commonly accepted standards, and all funds that are not from State sources shall be managed responsibly. Records should be available for State auditor review on proper and reasonable request.

11.3 The policies and regulations which apply to personnel employment by the centers should be those set forth in State regulations. Appointment procedures, employment conditions, and related matters fall under the normal policies, rules, and regulations by which State institutions operate, and in the case of faculty status, comply with Board of Regents' policies.

11.4 As a State agency, the Board of Regents and the institutions in its system of higher education shall comply with all State and Federal laws and regulations. As State employees, faculty and staff shall not enter into arrangements which violate State laws or regulations. Centers funded through support from the Vandalia Fund are expected to maintain similar standards.

Section 12. Conflict of Interest

12.1 It will be deemed a conflict of interest for any full-time employee of public institutions (or for a corporation or association of which such an employee, or his or her spouse, or child under twenty-one years of age, or any combination thereof, who owns or own a majority of the stock or interest) to furnish to the institution any goods, services, or any other thing, and to receive therefore any remuneration other than the employees' contracted salary or wages, except as may be approved by the president of the institution. In that same spirit, it is expected that the centers will conduct their business under the same policy. (Nothing in this policy is to be construed to apply to (1) any work written, or thing invented independently by such employee; (2) services performed for external sponsors by such an employee within the institution's consulting time policy where the funds to pay for such services are not provided to the institution through a grant form, or a contract or other arrangement with some outside agency.) When accepting funding for research, consulting or other activities, information of any equity holdings, administrative position, patents or other rights, or favored position must be disclosed. With regard to government-sponsored research, the joint statement of the Council of the American Association of University Professors and the American Council on Education, "On Preventing Conflicts of Interest in Government-Sponsored Research at Universities," should be used as guidance.

Section 13. Responsibility for Results

13.1 Individual faculty members or employees hold ultimate responsibility for the results of their research. Use of the institution's or center's name should be for identification purposes only. The findings or recommendations of research should not be identified as the position of the institution, or of the center, or of the Board of Regents, or of the State of West Virginia, but solely of the author or investigator.

Section 14. Consulting Through Personal Services Agreements

14.1 Individuals are not precluded from entering directly into individual consulting agreements, which were independently arranged, subject to conditions specified by institutional policy and Policy Bulletin No. 36, Section 3.

14.2 One working day per week (within a 5 day week) may normally be used for consulting for organizations other than the institution of higher education, unless such activities interfere with the adequate performance of academic duties. The administrators of each institution shall establish a program of periodic review of outside services of appointees to guide faculty members. Use of institutional equipment or other resources requires prior approval by the institution and reimbursement for associated direct costs. Faculty are encouraged to perform such work under institutional auspices.

14.3 Faculty may request overload (6th day) payment from external sources consistent with existing policy on a term-by-term basis, subject to approval of the funding agency and president. The overload payment should represent at least 20 percent of weekly salary of the faculty member for a full sixth day of work.

Section 15. Patent Policy for State Projects

15.1 Patent Policy will be governed by practices established at each institution, or for inter-institutional efforts, according to the policy of one of the partners, or, alternatively, by mutual agreement, according to policy parallel to the approved policy of West Virginia University. All patents derived from inventions conceived or reduced to practice by personnel at the institutions or at the centers shall belong to the respective institution or center and not the Board of Regents or the Board of Trustees. The State of West Virginia and its agencies shall have available for their own internal use, on a nonexclusive, royalty-free basis all patents and copyrighted or non-copyrighted material generated through Vandalia funded projects. Corporate sponsors may be given nonexclusive royalty-free rights to patents developed from research if substantial financial support is provided by them. In each case, a patent agreement must be negotiated with each sponsor which does not conflict with State and Federal law, and recognizes the relative proportion of investment by each sponsor in a discovery. Requests for an exclusive license or shared ownership of patents must be approved by the Board of Regents. If one or more corporate sponsor(s) request that a patent be secured, the sponsor must pay all associated costs to secure and protect the patent, and may then be provided an exclusive license and pay fair royalties to the institution.

15.2 Although the individual faculty or staff member has an equity in any patentable discovery or invention, regardless of the source of funds supporting the experimental work, those activities undertaken through externally-sponsored grants and contracts may be constrained by the terms and conditions of the agreement with the sponsor. Any invention or patentable discovery made by a faculty or staff member with all or a portion of the time, facilities, and/or other resources provided by the institution or center from any source, gives the institution or center equity in the invention or discovery. Certain awards from the Vandalia Fund may, on an exceptional basis, provide for some royalty rights back to the fund in exchange for financial support. In all cases, the invention or discovery should be used and controlled in ways to produce the greatest benefit to the institution and the public.

15.3 A faculty or staff member who makes a discovery or invention outside his or her regular duties, on his or her own time, at his or her own expense, and without the use of institutional facilities, is entitled to full ownership of it. Regardless of the question of equity, the institutions will assist any staff member, so far as possible, in evaluating inventions and discoveries and, if advisable, in patenting them.

Section 16. Use of Human Subjects

16.1 There is an obligation to protect human subjects as part of all research activities, funded or nonfunded. The obligation applies to every member of an institution's faculty, staff, and student body conducting studies which involve human subjects. In case of students (including interns and residents), the supervising faculty or staff member is responsible for seeing that a study is approved or exempted by the appropriate institutional review board for the protection of human subjects before the use of any human subjects in the study, and for supervising the conduct of the research.

16.2 The institutional review board for the protection of human subjects provides direction in assuring the rights of individuals serving as research subjects by establishing and maintaining a set of guiding principles designed to elicit the highest professional standards in dealings with subjects, and by independently reviewing projects which involve human subjects in order to ensure that proper standards are met and that procedures do not infringe upon the safety, health, and welfare of the subjects.

*Section 17. Protection of Proprietary
Information and Publication Rights*

17.1 Information provided by a for-profit corporation may be protected by development of a written agreement in each case. However, it is important to publish results of research to advance knowledge consistent with the best practices of higher education. Publication of results may be withheld for a maximum period of six months, if required for the filing of a patent application, provided that a sponsoring company makes a written request for such a delay within thirty (30) days of mailing to the company. Researchers are responsible for determining in advance whether any patent or commercial product mentioned in a publication requires prior consent by the sponsoring corporation. In addition, the right of prior review and comment by the sponsor may be required in a written contract. Protection of proprietary information is the primary responsibility of the faculty, staff, and students involved, and they must be party to, and sign concurrence with, any such agreement.

Section 18. Contractual Training and Development Programs

18.1 *Faculty*. Participation of faculty members and staff as teachers in externally-funded programs on or off campus may be arranged as part of their regular full-time workload. Where faculty members do not have available time, assignments may be on an overload basis, and are made first to regularly employed faculty members of the host or other higher education institutions, and then to other qualified personnel.

18.2 *Credits*. Every provision shall be made to ensure that the quality of off-campus classes offered for credit is commensurate with the quality of those offered on campus. Furthermore, the policies for such credit work are to be compatible with standards and policies of the North Central Association of Colleges and the accrediting agencies for the professions.

18.3 *Television Teaching*. Board of Regents' Policy Bulletin No. 48, adopted January 4, 1977, summarizes the rights and responsibilities of those involved in television instruction.

Section 19. Compensation of Full-Time Faculty
from Non-State Sponsors if Arranged by Center

19.1 Policies of each college or university regarding release time for research, consulting, public service, and other related matters are set by the president of the institution within guidelines established by the Board of Regents. If outside employment or service interferes with the performance of the regular institutional duties of the appointee (faculty member, administrator, or staff), the institution has the right to make such adjustments in the compensation paid to such appointee as are warranted by the services lost to the institution.

19.2 When Federal sponsorship is involved, compliance with various Federal regulations, such as OMB A-21 and other related guidelines, is reaffirmed.

19.3 Faculty may request release from a course on a term-by-term basis to devote additional effort to research, consulting, or public service. As a minimum, the replacement cost of part-time faculty (or overload to others) must be met by external sources. Approval by the president is required.

19.4 Faculty may request overload (6th day) payment from external sources consistent with existing policy on a term-by-term basis, subject to approval of the funding agency and president. The overload payment should represent at least 20 percent of weekly salary of the faculty member for a full sixth day of work.

19.5 At times the development of an externally-funded course (on- or off-campus) requires new and unusual efforts in its preparation, and it is clear that these efforts will not bear a direct or long-term relationship to the regular instructional program of the college involved. With approval by the president concerning the relationship and rates, the faculty involved in the development may be compensated accordingly from contract funds for course development work.

19.6 Academic year salary rates for faculty may be influenced by success in research and public service and by a continuing pattern of external support as provided by institutional policy, and when feasible, an appropriate portion of salary should be supported by external sources, not solely by the institution.

19.7 Faculty may be compensated at no less than their calendar daily rate for short-term consulting work funded from external sources at rates approved by the president of his or her institution.

19.8 Any special compensation to the faculty may not be less than the daily rate charged to a Federal agency. It may, however, be more, if approved by the president of the institution.

19.9 Faculty may be compensated through their institution for summer research or public service efforts at a weekly rate of at least 1/36 of the base academic year salary, not to exceed two and a half months of full-time income for the summer.

19.10 Ordinarily, faculty who accept leaves yet remain on campus for research or public service purposes are encouraged to teach one course to sustain the quality of the university's instructional programs.

19.11 Faculty will be expected to seek means to involve students in research efforts, both to contribute to the education and experience of the student, and to provide financial support for students. The integrity of the academic process and protection of the interests of the students must be assured.

19.12 Recipients of research support who are on nine-month contracts may be compensated from external sources during the summer months. Recipients on twelve-month contracts, and, during a regular semester, recipients on nine-month contracts, are permitted to undertake such research by an appropriate adjustment of their contractual duties to the institution. Salary increments from grant or contract funds are not permitted without approval by the president.

Section 20. Other Conditions

20.1 In arranging consulting agreements with business and industry, institutions and centers are encouraged to charge rates that are comparable with those charged by private organizations that provide similar services.

20.2 Institutions, centers and the Board of Regents expressly disclaim any warranties, express or implied, as to the conduct of the research project or its findings, or as to the accuracy of the results or their utility, merchantability, or fitness for any purpose.

20.3 In the case of any inventions licensed to the sponsor as a result of the research, the burden is placed on the sponsor to indemnify and hold harmless the institution, or the Board of Regents, and officers, agents, and employees from any liability arising out of the manufacture, use, or sale of products covered by the license(s) and suffered by the sponsor or by users or purchasers of such products.

20.4 There will be a clear contractual understanding concerning any limitations on use of the name, trademark, logo, or other identifying marks of the institution, the centers, the Board of Trustees, the Board of Regents, or the State of West Virginia, and of the names of researchers, students, or staff, for advertising or promotional purposes.

Index

364 Index

This page constitutes a continuation of the copyright page, vi